D1681675

The Federal Capital

Government Institutions

**Studies of the
Royal Commission on
Bilingualism and
Biculturalism**

| 1 | Kenneth D. McRae
Editor | *The Federal Capital: Government Institutions* |

To be published

| 2 | John C. Johnstone | *Young People's Images of Canadian Society: An Opinion Survey of Canadian Youth 13 to 20 Years of Age* |
| 3 | Gilles Lalande | *The Department of External Affairs and Biculturalism: Diplomatic Personnel and Language Use* |

In preparation

| Ramsay Cook | *Provincial Autonomy, Minority Rights, and the Compact Theory, 1867-1921* |
| Frederick W. Gibson
Editor | *Cabinet Formation and Bicultural Relations: Seven Case Studies* |
| Claude-Armand Sheppard | *The Law of Languages in Canada* |
| Ronald L. Watts | *Multi-Cultural Societies and Federalism* |

Studies of the
Royal Commission on
Bilingualism and
Biculturalism

1 | The Federal Capital

Government Institutions

Edited by
Kenneth D. McRae

This study has been prepared for the Royal Commission on Bilingualism and Biculturalism. Although published under the auspices of the Commission, it does not necessarily express the Commission's views.

© Crown Copyrights reserved

Available by mail from the
Queen's Printer, Ottawa,
and at the following
Canadian Government bookshops:

HALIFAX
1735 Barrington Street

MONTREAL
Æterna-Vie Building, 1182 St. Catherine Street West

OTTAWA
Daly Building, Corner Mackenzie and Rideau

TORONTO
221 Yonge Street

WINNIPEG
Mall Center Building, 499 Portage Avenue

VANCOUVER
657 Granville Street

or through your bookseller

Price $3.00 (subject to change without notice)

Catalogue No. Z1-1963/1-1/1

ROGER DUHAMEL, F.R.S.C.
THE QUEEN'S PRINTER,
Controller of Stationery
Ottawa, 1969

Contents

List of Tables   vii

List of Maps and Diagrams   xii

Preface   xv

Chapter I   The Capital Area: Land and People   1

        A. Geographical and Political Framework   1
        B. Language Patterns   5
        C. Socio-economic Structure   14
        D. Residential Patterns   25
        E. Bilingualism   33

Chapter II   The Provincial Framework   41

        A. Introduction   41
        B. Provincial Government and the Citizen   42
            1. Ontario   43
            2. Quebec   52
            3. Ontario and Quebec: Comparison and Evaluation   60
        C. Provincial Government and the Municipalities   62
        D. Summary   67

Chapter III   Municipal Administration: Ottawa   69

        A. Introduction   69
        B. Language of Service to the Public   73
        C. Attitudes towards the Provision of Bilingual Service   78
        D. Composition and Language Skills of Administration   81
        E. Summary   90

Chapter IV   Municipal Administration: Other Municipalities   93

        A. Introduction   93
        B. The City of Hull   94
        C. The City of Eastview   99
        D. The Other Administrations   105
        E. Summary   112

Chapter V   The Impact of the Federal Government   115

        A. The Federal Presence   115
        B. The National Capital Commission   118
        C. Other Federal Agencies   127
        D. Language Usage of Federal Agencies   132
        E. The Geographical Context of Federal Activity   137
        F. Summary   143

Contents   vi

Chapter VI   The Legal Systems   145
                A. Introduction   145
                B. The Legal System of the Ontario Sector   148
                C. The Legal System of the Quebec Sector   152
                D. The Legal Profession in the Ontario and Quebec Sectors   156
                E. Summary   159

Chapter VII   Political Representation   161
                A. Introduction   161
                B. Representation: The Cities of Ottawa, Hull and Eastview   162
                   1. Ottawa   163
                   2. Hull   175
                   3. Eastview   176
                C. Language Usage: Thirteen Municipal Councils   178
                   1. Ottawa   178
                   2. Hull   179
                   3. Eastview   180
                   4. The Other Municipalities   180
                D. Representation: Federal and Provincial   183
                   1. Federal   183
                   2. Ontario   187
                   3. Quebec   188
                   4. Representation and Language Usage   189
                E. Summary   190

Appendices   193
                A. Tables A to O   195

                B. The Influence of Certain Factors on Inequalities in Labour Income   212

                C. Bilingual Traffic Signs in Ottawa   221

                D. Correspondence between the Royal Commission on Bilingualism and Biculturalism and the Cities of Ottawa, Hull and Eastview   223

                E. Language Usage in Selected Municipal Agencies   248

                F. The Ottawa Police Department and Ottawa Transportation Commission   251

                G. Tables A to E   254

                H. National Capital Commission Expenditures, 1947-67   259

                I. Property Acquisitions by the National Capital Commission   261

Contents   vii

       J. Payments to the City of Ottawa   262

       K. Case Studies of Federal-Municipal Relations   263

       L. Comparative Federal Expenditures   268

       M. Registration of Documents in Carleton County   269

List of Tables

Tables in Chapter I

1.1 Population growth of the nine largest metropolitan areas in Canada, 1951-1966   4
1.2 Distribution of population, Ottawa metropolitan area, 1961 and 1966   5
1.3 Population density per square mile, municipalities of Ottawa metropolitan area, 1961 and 1966   6
1.4 Percentage distribution of population, Canada and principal metropolitan areas, by mother tongue, 1961   7
1.5 Percentage distribution of population, Canada and Ottawa metropolitan area, by mother tongue, 1961   8
1.6 Percentage distribution of population, Ottawa metropolitan area, by mother tongue, 1961   11
1.7 Percentage distribution of population, Ottawa metropolitan area, by ethnic origin and mother tongue, 1961   11
1.8 Population distribution, Ottawa metropolitan area, by ethnic origin, 1941, 1951, 1961   13
1.9 Percentage distribution of male labour force, Ottawa, Montreal, and Toronto metropolitan areas, by industry, 1961   14
1.10 Percentage distribution of the total labour force, aged 15 years and over, by industry, 1961   15
1.11 Percentage distribution of total population and labour force, Ottawa metropolitan area, by ethnic origin, 1961   16
1.12 Average income of labour force, Ottawa, Montreal, and Toronto, by ethnic origin, 1961   16
1.13 Percentage distribution of male labour force, Ottawa metropolitan area, by ethnic origin and industry, 1961   17
1.14 Average income of male labour force, Ottawa metropolitan area, by ethnic origin and industry, 1961   18
1.15 Percentage distribution of male labour force, Ottawa metropolitan area, by ethnic origin and educational level, 1961   19
1.16 Average income of male labour force, Ottawa metropolitan area, by ethnic origin and educational level, 1961   19
1.17 Percentage distribution of male labour force, Ottawa metropolitan area, by ethnic origin and occupation, 1961   20

1.18 Average income by male labour force, Ottawa metropolitan area, by ethnic origin and occupation, 1961   21
1.19 Percentage distribution of male labour force, Ottawa metropolitan area, by ethnic origin and age group, 1961   22
1.20 Average total income of male labour force, Ottawa metropolitan area, by ethnic origin and age group, 1961   22
1.21 Percentage of population in selected age categories attending school, Ottawa metropolitan area, by ethnic origin, 1961   24
1.22 Residential patterns: mother tongue by linguistic concentration and dispersion, 1961   26
1.23 Residential patterns: mother tongue by average income of sectors, 1961   27
1.24 Percentages of various populations living on the Ontario and Quebec sides of the Ottawa metropolitan area, by mother tongue, 1961   31
1.25 Percentage distribution of population, Canada and principal metropolitan areas, by official language, 1961   34
1.26 Percentage distribution of population, Ottawa metropolitan area, by official language, 1961   35
1.27 Percentage distribution of population, Ottawa metropolitan area, by official language, 1951 and 1961   36
1.28 Percentage of population officially bilingual by ethnic origin, Ottawa metropolitan area, total population and labour force, 1961   37
1.29 Bilingual members of the labour force expressed as a percentage of the total in each category by ethnic origin and level of schooling, Ottawa metropolitan area, 1961   37
1.30 Bilingual members of the labour force expressed as a percentage of the total in each category by ethnic origin and occupation group, Ottawa metropolitan area, 1961   38
1.31 Differences in average income between bilingual members of the labour force for each level of schooling, by ethnic origin, Ottawa metropolitan area, 1961   39
1.32 Differences in average income between bilingual members of the labour force and total labour force for each occupation group, by ethnic origin, Ottawa metropolitan area, 1961   40

Tables in Chapter II

2.1 Percentage distribution of Ontario population, 1961, and provincial public servants, 1961 and 1966, by mother tongue   48
2.2 Ontario public servants, mother tongue by official language, 1961   48
2.3 Language capabilities of Ontario public servants in the Ottawa area, 1966   50
2.4 Language usage of Quebec public servants, 1965   55
2.5 Percentage distribution of Quebec population and provincial public servants by mother tongue, 1961   57
2.6 Quebec public servants, mother tongue by official language, 1961   59

Contents   ix

Tables in Chapter III

3.1 Availability of Ottawa municipal services in French, 1966   75
3.2 List of positions identified as preferably bilingual, Ottawa municipal administration   80
3.3 Ottawa, mother tongue of city population and administration, 1961   82
3.4 Ottawa municipal employees by ethnic origin, percentages, 1961 and 1965   82
3.5 City of Ottawa municipal employees, ethnic origin by income category, 1965   83
3.6 Municipal employees in Ottawa, by ethnic origin and employment income, percentages, 1961   83
3.7 City of Ottawa municipal employees appearing on the organization chart and earning $6500 or over, by ethnic origin, 1965   84
3.8 Municipal employees in Ottawa, ethnic origin by occupation group, percentages, 1961   84
3.9 Municipal employees in Ottawa, mother tongue by official language, percentages, 1961   85
3.10 Municipal employees in Ottawa, occupation group by official language, 1961   86
3.11 Municipal employees in Ottawa, total number and percentage of the total who are bilingual for each ethnic origin and occupation category, 1961   87
3.12 City of Ottawa salaried employees, mother tongue by French-language facility, 1965   87
3.13 City of Ottawa salaried employees, French-language facility by department, 1965   88
3.14 City of Ottawa salaried employees, French-language facility by degree of public contact, 1965   89
3.15 City of Ottawa salaried employees, French-language facility by job classification, 1965   89

Tables in Chapter IV

4.1 Hull, city population and administration by mother tongue   97
4.2 Hull municipal employees, language knowledge   97
4.3 Hull municipal employees, second-language knowledge   97
4.4 Hull municipal employees, job classification by second-language knowledge   98
4.5 Hull municipal employees, degree of public contact by second-language knowledge   99
4.6 Eastview, city population and administration by mother tongue   102
4.7 Eastview municipal employees, language knowledge   103
4.8 Eastview municipal employees, second-language knowledge   103
4.9 Eastview wage-earning and technical employees, public contact by second-language knowledge   104

4.10 Eastview municipal employees, degree of public contact by second-language knowledge   104
4.11 Seven Quebec municipalities, demand for service in English as a percentage of total demand for service   106
4.12 Municipalities and their administrations in the Ottawa metropolitan area, 1966   108
4.13 Eight municipalities, proportion of municipal servants capable of giving service in English or French   109
4.14 Eight municipalities, bilingual municipal servants by mother tongue   110
4.15 Eight municipalities, bilingual municipal servants as percentage of total in each job classification   111
4.16 Eight municipalities, bilingual municipal servants as percentage of total for each level of public contact   111

Tables in Chapter V

5.1 Payments of grants in lieu of taxes to selected municipalities, 1957-1966   130
5.2 Percentage distribution of Ottawa civil servants in contact with the public by ability to perform their duties in one or both of the official languages, selected agencies, 1965   134
5.3 Percentage distribution of commissionaires in Ottawa federal buildings by language knowledge, 1965   136
5.4 Buildings and floor-space owned or leased by the federal government in Ottawa, Hull and Eastview, March 31, 1967   139
5.5 Taxes and grants in lieu of taxes paid by the federal government and Crown corporations to municipalities in the National Capital Region, 1963 tax year   140
5.6 Total of taxes and grants in lieu of taxes paid by the federal government and Crown corporations to the cities of Ottawa and Hull, 1963-1966   141

Tables in Chapter VI

6.1 Carleton county legal profession, ethnic origin and firm structure, 1964   158
6.2 Legal profession in Hull, Pontiac and Labelle districts, ethnic origin and firm structure, 1964   159

Tables in Chapter VII

7.1 City of Ottawa, controllers by origin in ten-year periods, 1908-1967   164
7.2 City of Ottawa, aldermen by origin in five-year periods, 1869-1967   165
7.3 City of Ottawa, origin of aldermanic candidates in five elections, 1958-1966   167
7.4 City of Ottawa, aldermanic candidates by origin, 1958-1966 summary   167
7.5 City of Ottawa, percentage of vote received by selected candidates for board of control, 1962-1966   169

7.6 City of Ottawa, percentage distribution of vote for board of control by wards, civic election, 1966   171
7.7 City of Ottawa, percentage turnout by ward in voting for mayor, 1958-1966   173
7.8 City of Hull, municipal councillors by origin in five-year periods, 1875-1967   176
7.9 City of Eastview, municipal councillors by origin in five-year periods, 1927-1966   177
7.10 National Capital Region, population by mother tongue and ethnic origin of federal constituencies, percentages, 1961   183
7.11 National Capital Region, candidates at federal elections by origin, 1953, 1957, 1958, 1962, 1963 and 1965   184
7.12 National Capital Region, Ontario sector, candidates at provincial elections by origin, 1955, 1959 and 1963   187
7.13 National Capital Region, Quebec sector, candidates at provincial elections by origin, 1952, 1956, 1960, 1962, and 1966   189

Tables in Appendix A

A Numerical distribution of population, Ontario and Quebec sides of Ottawa metropolitan area, by mother tongue, 1961   195
B Percentage distribution of population, Ottawa metropolitan area, by mother tongue, 1961   196
C Percentage distribution of population, Ottawa metropolitan area, by ethnic origin and official language, 1961   197
D Percentage distribution of population, Ottawa metropolitan area and cities of Ottawa and Hull, by ethnic origin and mother tongue, 1961   197
E Distribution of population, city of Ottawa, by ethnic origin, 1871-1961   198
F Distribution of population, city of Hull, by ethnic origin, 1881-1961   199
G Percentage distribution of population, Ottawa metropolitan area, by ethnic origin and mother tongue, 1961   200
H Percentage distribution of male labour force, Ottawa metropolitan area, by occupation, level of education, and ethnic origin, 1961   201
I Percentage distribution of population by mother tongue, Ottawa metropolitan area census tracts, in order of average wage and salary income per tract, 1961   202
J Distribution of federal public servants within the Ottawa metropolitan area, 1961   204
K Distribution of federal public servants earning over $10,000, within the Ottawa metropolitan area, by mother tongue, 1961   205
L Incidence of official bilingualism in selected Canadian municipalities (20,000 and over), 1961   206
M Percentage distribution of population, Ottawa metropolitan area census tracts, by official language spoken, 1961   207

Contents

N   Total labour force, Ottawa metropolitan area, by ethnic origin, official language, educational level, and average annual employment income, 1961   209

O   Total labour force, Ottawa metropolitan area, by ethnic origin, official language, occupational category, and average annual employment income, 1961   210

Tables in Appendix B

A   Level of schooling and difference in labour income between males of British and French origins, Ottawa metropolitan area, 1961   215

B   Influence of certain factors on the inequality of incomes between males of British and French origins, Ottawa, 1961   219

C   Influence of selected factors on income differences between males of British and French origins, Ottawa, Montreal and Toronto metropolitan areas   220

Table in Appendix F

A   Ottawa Transportation Commission, mother tongue of wage and salaried employees, 1965   252

Tables in Appendix G

A   Municipalities in the Ottawa metropolitan area, population and municipal administration, by mother tongue, percentages   254

B   Municipalities in the Ottawa metropolitan area, municipal servants able to give service in English or French, percentages   255

C   Municipalities in the Ottawa metropolitan area, municipal servants by second-language knowledge, percentages   256

D   Municipalities in the Ottawa metropolitan area, municipal servants by job classification and bilingualism   257

E   Municipalities in the Ottawa metropolitan area, municipal servants by degree of public contact and bilingualism   258

List of Maps and Diagrams

Maps

1.1   The National Capital Region   at 30
1.2   Ottawa metropolitan area, 1961   at 30
1.3   Census tracts, Ottawa metropolitan area, 1961   at 30
1.4   Linguistic concentrations, Ottawa metropolitan area, 1961   at 30
1.5   Richest and poorest sectors, Ottawa metropolitan area, 1961   at 30
1.6   Degree of bilingualism, Ottawa metropolitan area, 1961   at 30
7.1   Ottawa ward boundaries and linguistic concentrations, 1966   at 174
7.2   Voting turnout and average income, Ottawa civic elections, 1958-1966   at 174

Contents xiii

7.3 Linguistic concentrations and federal electoral boundaries, Ottawa metropolitan area, 1953-1965   at 174
7.4 Linguistic concentrations and revised federal electoral boundaries, Ottawa metropolitan area, 1966   at 174
7.5 Federal electoral boundaries, National Capital Region, 1953-1965   at 174
7.6 Revised federal electoral boundaries, National Capital Region, 1966   at 174
7.7 Provincial electoral boundaries, National Capital Region, 1952-1966   at 174
7.8 Revised provincial electoral boundaries, National Capital Region, 1966   at 174
7.9 Linguistic concentrations and provincial electoral boundaries, Ottawa metropolitan area, 1952-1966   at 174
7.10 Linguistic concentrations and revised provincial electoral boundaries, Ottawa metropolitan area, 1966   at 174

Diagrams

1.1 Population distribution by mother tongue, Quebec and Ontario sectors, Ottawa metropolitan area, 1961   9
1.2 Linguistic concentrations and average income of census sectors, Ottawa metropolitan area, 1961   30
6.1 Civil and criminal courts, Carleton county, Ontario, at January 1966   147
6.2 Courts of the judicial district of Hull, Quebec, at January 1966   154
7.1 Percentage turnout (vote for mayor) by selected wards, Ottawa civic elections, 1958-1966   174

Preface

From its earliest meetings in the autumn of 1963, the Royal Commission on Bilingualism and Biculturalism has felt the capital of Canada to be one of its prime areas of concern. As the seat of the federal government itself, the city of Ottawa and its vicinity must play a very special role—indeed a symbolic and pathfinding role—in the development of the "equal partnership" concept enunciated in the Commission's terms of reference.

The Commission's interest in the capital was expressed at its preliminary public hearing in Ottawa on November 7, 1963. When the research programme was begun systematically in May 1964, one of the first projects to be undertaken was a thorough study of the federal capital area from the standpoint of the Commission's terms of reference. In time this study was expanded to include both the governmental and non-governmental sectors. Special attention was devoted to education and to the cultural facilities of the area. Some aspects, such as municipal government, proved to be more complex than was at first expected. The end result was a study of considerable proportions.

In the meantime, while the study progressed, governmental relations in the area were in a state of flux. In 1964 the government of Ontario initiated a special commission of inquiry into municipal government and intermunicipal relations in Carleton county. The Jones Commission, as it was known, brought in its final report and recommendations in June 1965. While the recommendations were not accepted in detail, planning for a new regional government continued. On February 1, 1967, the Ontario Minister for Municipal Affairs, the Honourable J.W. Spooner, presented an official proposal for a new metropolitan form of government for the whole of the Ontario portion of the Ottawa area, suggesting that it be studied by municipal representatives and revised with a view to enactment by the Ontario legislature in 1968.

During the same period another body, the Ontario Advisory Committee on Confederation, commissioned Professor D. C. Rowat to prepare an essay on the arguments for and against the establishment of a federal district around the capital. The existence of this study was made known in December 1966, and its publication in April 1967 served to increase public interest in the prospects for a change of governmental structures in the area.

In the meanwhile, the Quebec side of the capital area was not inactive. Some form of closer association among the several municipalities had been discussed intermittently for some time. The public debate occasioned by the Rowat Report concerning a federal district aroused interest in the Quebec portion of the capital area as well. In a brief to the government of Quebec, Le conseil économique régional de l'Ouest du Québec advocated the creation of a Quebec agency to assume for the Quebec portion of the National Capital Region functions exercised by the federal government through the National Capital Commission. In August 1967 the Dorion Commission on the Territorial Integrity of Quebec held a series of hearings in Hull to study the problems of western Quebec.

The end result of these developments in both provinces is difficult to foresee, but major changes in the status of the federal capital area may well be in the offing.

The discussion to date, while thorough in some directions, has left certain other major issues virtually untouched. Perhaps because of the provincial boundary, there has been little thought given to the metropolitan area on both sides of the Ottawa River as a single urban complex, even from the standpoint of regional planning and development. Little attention has been directed towards the interests of the federal government in the area. The Jones and Spooner plans in particular have failed to consider the special linguistic and cultural complexion of the capital area. The Commission's research on the federal capital, on the other hand, has concentrated specifically on its linguistic and cultural dimensions.

In the light of these rather special circumstances, the Commission decided to publish its research findings on the capital area as a contribution to the evolving public debate. This volume deals broadly with governmental and judicial aspects. The widespread discussion in recent months as to the future governmental status of the capital area has led the Commission to believe that the data in this volume may be a useful contribution to the public understanding of a complex question.

This volume does not contain formal recommendations. The Commission has already published general recommendations as to the appropriate language régime for the capital in Book I of its *Report* (§ 380). At the same time it noted that more than a linguistic régime would be required to bring about an effectively bilingual and bicultural capital; its detailed recommendations as to what reforms are needed and how they might be brought about will be dealt with in a later Book of the *Report*.

Research on this project was under the supervision of Kenneth D. McRae, who also acted as project director. The following were at one stage or another members of the research staff:

Lyse Beaulieu	Robert Campbell	N.F.W. Gates
Régine N. Bergeron	Mireille D. Desjarlais	Guy Robitaille
Brian B. Buckley	Judy M. Dibben	Reginald Whitaker
David R. Cameron	Jean T. Fournier	

In addition to the full-time research staff, several academics gave specialized assistance, including Richard D. Abbott (legal questions), John Johnstone (survey research methods), Roman R. March (data analysis), Gilles Paquet and André Raynauld (economic questions), Guenther F. Schaefer and A. M. Willms (interviews). Mrs. Claire M. ApSimon, Mrs. Eileen L. Cameron, and Mrs. M. C. Janine Pellerin assisted with telephone inquiries, and Mrs. Simone Chaussé with the typing of the manuscript.

Maps were prepared by the Department of Geography of McGill University, under the supervision of Professors Frank C. Innes and Jan Lundgren.

Boxing Day, 1967.

Chapter I
The Capital Area: Land and People

A. Geographical and Political Framework

The National Capital Region is situated on both sides of the Ottawa River some 75 miles west of its juncture with the St. Lawrence at Montreal. As may be seen from Map 1.1,* the Region is in the shape of an irregular rectangle, bisected in an east-west direction by the Ottawa River and in a north-south direction by the Gatineau and Rideau Rivers. These three rivers together form a cross, and the point of their intersection is more or less the centre of urban development—the Ottawa-Hull metropolitan area.

North of the Ottawa River is the province of Quebec; to its south, Ontario. The Region as a whole is approximately 1,800 square miles in size, of which 1,050 are on the Ontario side and 750 on the Quebec side. At the census of 1961 the population of the Region was just under half a million, or more specifically 492,000.

Topographically, the Gatineau hills are the most prominent landmark. Pre-Cambrian mountains worn down by glaciers, they form part of the Canadian Shield. The retreat of the glaciers about 10,000 years ago left only a thin layer of soil so that agriculture in the uplands is difficult; the mineral and forestry resources of the Gatineau, however, played a major role in the early economic development of the capital region. Today the uplands are increasingly used for recreational purposes.

The glaciers which wore down the uplands also depressed the level of the land so that after their retreat the sea covered much of the area up to the Gatineau. When the land rose and the seas retreated, a deep layer of silt, sand and clay was deposited over a bed of sedimentary rocks. Thus, in contrast to the rugged and picturesque Gatineau hills, the land to the south and west is gently sloping and suited to agriculture—particularly dairy farming, meat and seed production, and market gardening for local sales. Another economic resource of the lowland area is the building material found in the underlying sedimentary rocks. Industry in the capital region tends to be of the type servicing the natural resources of forestry and agriculture—pulp and paper, cement, dairy plants, meat packing, among others. However, industry is of secondary importance to government in the economic life of the Region.

---
* Maps for Chapter I are collected together at 30.

In the central urban area, variations in altitude are far less pronounced. Rising from the Ottawa River, which is some 135 feet above sea level at Ottawa, the land is gently rolling. Most of the urban area, in fact, is below the 300-foot level.

The only major topographical obstacles within the urban centre of the Region are the waterways: the Ottawa River and its two tributaries, the Gatineau and Rideau Rivers, along with the Rideau Canal. The Ottawa River widens considerably west of the city to form Lake Deschênes, which is two miles wide in some places; to the east it passes through a series of rapids before flowing over the Chaudière Falls. The Gatineau River descends from the wooded areas to the north on the Quebec side, while the Rideau River rises in flat, rural country to the south. The Rideau Canal, constructed for military purposes between 1827 and 1832, links the Ottawa River at Ottawa with Lake Ontario at Kingston. Formerly important from a commercial point of view, these waterways are now used almost exclusively for pleasure boating during the summer. However, there is still some logging on the Ottawa and Gatineau Rivers.

The Ottawa River is clearly a geographical element of major importance to the Region as a whole and to its urban core. The land on either side slopes down toward the river, forming a valley which has been a natural funnel of human settlement. Moreover, it was the importance of the Ottawa as a communication and transportation line, its confluence with the Gatineau and Rideau Rivers, and the existence of the Chaudière Falls and the various rapids, which provided the original stimulus for urban growth.

Yet, paradoxically, if the Ottawa River has been the foundation and focus of development, it also divides the area, both politically and physically. The Ottawa forms the border between the provinces of Ontario and Quebec, and thus the boundary between two political jurisdictions with differing linguistic, cultural, and legal orientations. This perspective is somewhat blurred by the mixture of French- and English-speaking population on both sides of the river, but the legal and political systems are separate, and the river's role as a physical barrier is matched by the part it plays as a provincial border.

To consider the geographical side more closely, it is apparent that the Ottawa, together with the Rideau and Gatineau Rivers, forms the only natural obstacle to transportation and communication in the built-up area which, as we have noticed, is relatively flat and regular in topography. If, for instance, one were to construct an imaginary model of the capital region, and then remove the Ottawa River from the model, there would seem to be few significant economic and geographical reasons why the presently asymmetrical pattern of urban development should not have proceeded in a more "rounded" fashion, that is to say, why the Quebec side should not have developed apace with the Ontario side.

However, the double role of the Ottawa as both a physical and political division seems to have had a certain negative impact on attempts to reduce its divisive effects on transportation and communication. In other words, man's attempt to superimpose his own environment on his natural surroundings has, in the case of overcoming the natural obstacle of the Ottawa River, been made more difficult by the river's role as a political boundary. The practical consequences of this may be measured in terms of bridging facilities.

In 1967 four bridges with 14 lanes of traffic crossed the Ottawa River. Before the opening of the Macdonald-Cartier Bridge on October 15, 1965 there were only eight lanes. The situation is quite different in respect to the Rideau River where there are at least 36 lanes distributed among 10 bridges over a distance of seven miles from Mooneys Bay to its confluence with the Ottawa River. Three bridges with a total of seven lanes span the Gatineau between Wakefield and the Ottawa River at Pointe-Gatineau. There is no bridge over the Ottawa River east of Ottawa before reaching Hawkesbury and none west of Ottawa before Chenaux—that is, for 55 and 50 miles respectively.

These traffic routes are not only necessary for urban expansion, but also for the social and economic development of the metropolitan area and for the integration of its different parts. While many factors have contributed to the unequal development of the two provincial components of the area, the paucity of bridge connections between Ontario and Quebec, in comparison with those over the Rideau, for instance, has undoubtedly played its part. While the Rideau has long since ceased to represent an obstacle to the flow of population, the Ottawa River, on the other hand, has remained both a political and a physical limitation on the normal growth pattern of the urban area.

Municipalities. The National Capital Region is a complex of interlocking governmental jurisdictions, ranging from the federal and provincial levels to some 70-odd jurisdictions on the level of local government.

The first settlement in the area was on the north shore of the Ottawa River. What is now the city of Hull began as a predominantly English-speaking, Protestant community, but by the time of Confederation the French-speaking Roman Catholic element was strong. In 1875 the settlement was incorporated as a city. Ottawa traces its origins to what began as two separate villages—Upper Town, along the Ottawa River west of the Rideau Canal, and Lower Town, east of the canal—the latter having a more Francophone[1] orientation than the former. The two villages grew together and in 1827 became known as Bytown, which was then incorporated as a town in 1850, and as the city of Ottawa in 1855.

The city of Ottawa now covers a territory of over 30,000 acres (larger than the area of the city of Toronto), bordered on the south, east, and west either directly by the federally-owned Greenbelt (a zone limited to non-urban land use) or by buffer zones of suburban development in Nepean and Gloucester townships, both of which are of mixed rural-urban character. In the north-east corner of Ottawa, within the city boundaries, are the autonomous municipalities of the city of Eastview and the village of Rockcliffe Park.

On the north shore of the Ottawa River, the city of Hull, whose trend of development has been northward, is flanked on the east by Pointe-Gatineau, Gatineau, and Templeton. To the west lie Lucerne (formerly Hull South), a large, mixed rural-urban area, the village of Deschênes, and the town of Aylmer, an older, independent community now merging with the growing suburban development to its east.

The concept of a metropolitan area was developed by the Dominion Bureau of Statistics to embrace all the parts of a contiguous urban area in close economic, geographical and social relationship with each other. According to the 1961 census the metropolitan area of Ottawa included some 13 separate municipalities, of which eight were on the Quebec side and five on the Ontario side (*see* Map 1.2). At that time the population of the census metropolitan area was 429,750, or about 87 per cent of the total population of the National Capital Region. By the 1966 census this figure had grown to 489,392.

---

[1] The terms "Francophone" and "Anglophone" are used from time to time throughout this study as synonyms for "French-speaking" and "English-speaking."

The Ottawa area, like other large centres, reflects the rapid urbanization of Canada in recent years. It not only ranks fifth highest in population among the major Canadian metropolitan areas but, as shown in Table 1.1, its growth rate over the past 15 years is the fourth highest. Between 1951 and 1966 its population increased by 67.5 per cent.

Table 1.1. Population growth of the nine largest metropolitan areas in Canada, 1951-1966

Metropolitan area	Population		Percentage increase
	1951	1966*	
Calgary	142,315	328,258	130.9
Edmonton	176,782	398,587	125.5
Toronto	1,210,353	2,145,637	77.3
Ottawa	292,476	489,392	67.5
Montreal	1,471,851	2,418,984	64.3
Hamilton	280,293	447,197	59.6
Vancouver	561,960	884,095	57.3
Quebec	276,242	407,731	47.5
Winnipeg	356,813	505,255	41.5

Source: Census of Canada, 1961; Catalogue 92-535. Interim Census, 1966, first compilations.
* 1966 figures are provisional.

The rapid growth of the population has not, however, proceeded in an even fashion throughout the capital area. As indicated by Table 1.2, the urban core (Ottawa, Hull, and Eastview) has accounted for a diminishing percentage of the total metropolitan area population. Relatively speaking, these municipalities are already highly developed (*see* Table 1.3), and thus their prospects for expansion are limited. Because of their restricted territory, Aylmer and Deschênes are faced with more or less the same situation. In contrast, the outlying, mixed urban-rural areas of Nepean and Gloucester townships in Ontario, and Lucerne and the area east of the Gatineau River on the Quebec side are expanding rapidly. Nepean, for instance, more than doubled its population between 1961 and 1966, and yet it still has a low density of population in comparison with most of the other 13 municipalities.

It seems likely that a high growth rate for the metropolitan area will continue in the future. Population projection figures provided by the National Capital Commission forecast that, by the year 2001, the city of Ottawa and those parts of Nepean and Gloucester townships inside the Greenbelt will have a population of over 540,000. The area west of the Greenbelt will house some 180,000 persons; south of the Greenbelt 120,000; and east of the Greenbelt 65,000. The area on the north shore west of the Gatineau River will have a projected population of 160,000; the area east of the Gatineau River, 115,000. The projected total for the entire metropolitan area for the year 2001 is 1,180,000, of which some 275,000 or 23 per cent would live on the north shore of the Ottawa River.[2]

---

[2]*Statistical Review with Explanatory Notes: National Capital Region.* (Ottawa/Hull Area Transportation Study by the Study's Technical Co-ordinating Committee and Land Use Sub-Committee, Ottawa, 1964.)

Table 1.2. Distribution of population, Ottawa metropolitan area, 1961 and 1966

Municipality	Population 1961		Population 1966	
	N	%	N	%
Total M.A.	429,750	100*	489,392	100*
Ottawa	268,206	62.4	288,735	59.0
Eastview	24,555	5.7	24,047	4.9
Nepean	19,753	4.6	43,420	8.9
Gloucester	18,301	4.3	23,002	4.7
Rockcliffe Park	2,084	0.5	2,155	0.4
Total Ontario	332,899	77.5	381,359	77.9
Hull	56,929	13.2	58,902	12.0
Gatineau	13,022	3.0	17,434	3.6
Pointe-Gatineau	8,854	2.1	10,903	2.2
Aylmer	6,286	1.5	7,150	1.5
Lucerne	5,762	1.3	8,042	1.6
Templeton	2,965	0.7	3,219	0.7
Deschênes	2,090	0.5	1,772	0.4
West Templeton	943	0.2	611	0.1
Total Quebec	96,851	22.5	108,033	22.1

Sources: Census of Canada, 1961; Catalogue 95-528. Interim Census, 1966, first compilations.
* Percentages do not necessarily add up to 100 because of rounding in this and all other tables of the study.

B. Language Patterns

To investigate the linguistic and cultural orientation of the population of the federal capital area is to raise some rather subtle problems. A man may be fully bilingual in French and English for all practical purposes, yet he may lean strongly towards one or the other language in terms of his own personal cultural preferences. It is not our purpose here to probe the complex inter-relationships between language, culture, and ethnic affiliation. These questions are explored in other aspects of the Commission's work.[3] Our present aim is simply to sketch the broad linguistic and cultural pattern of the population in the federal capital area.

---

[3] For example, *Report of the Royal Commission on Bilingualism and Biculturalism*, I (Ottawa, 1967), General Introduction, xxxiv-xxxviii; Book I, 17-18.

Table 1.3. Population density per square mile, municipalities of Ottawa metropolitan area, 1961 and 1966

	1961		1966	
Municipality	Area in square miles	Population density per square mile	Area in square miles	Population density per square mile
Total M.A.	335.02	1,282	334.83	1,462
Ottawa	45.44	5,902	45.44	6,754
Eastview	1.15	21,352	1.15	20,910
Nepean	85.84	230	85.84	506
Gloucester	115.63	158	115.63	199
Rockcliffe Park	0.67	3,110	0.67	3,216
Total Ontario	248.73	1,338	248.73	1,533
Hull	6.81	8,359	8.67*	6,794
Gatineau	3.72	3,500	6.47*	2,697
Pointe-Gatineau	1.76	5,030	1.76	6,195
Aylmer	2.24	2,806	2.24	3,192
Lucerne	35.97	160	33.90*	237
Templeton	2.91	1,018	2.91	1,106
Deschênes	0.28	7,464	0.28	6,329
West Templeton	32.60	28	29.87*	21
Total Quebec	86.29	1,222	86.10	1,255

Source: Columns 1 and 3 prepared by the Dominion Bureau of Statistics, Census Division; columns 2 and 4 calculated from figures in Table 1.2.
* Indicates change in area in 1966.

For this purpose three indicators are offered by the Census of Canada: mother tongue, ethnic origin, and official language. In the census, mother tongue is defined as the language first learned in childhood and still understood. This factor offers the best guide we have as to the extent to which various languages are presently spoken, though actually it measures childhood behaviour rather than current usage. Ethnic origin is determined by the ethnic or cultural affiliation of the respondent or his paternal ancestor on first coming to North America. While this variable is less valuable than mother tongue in determining current practice, it does offer certain evidence as to language usage over a longer period of time and to language retention or transfer. The census classification of official language refers to the ability to speak one or both of the official languages of Canada. The significance of this variable for our purposes is that it indicates both the extent of official bilingualism (*see* 33 ff) and the tendencies towards use of one or the other official language in the public sector, especially among those whose mother tongue is neither French nor English.

Mother tongue. The main features of mother-tongue distribution in the larger cities and in Canada as a whole are indicated in Table 1.4. If we compare the Ottawa metropolitan area with the pattern for Canada as a whole, it will be noticed that the Ottawa area figures are relatively close to the national average. At 55.7 per cent of the population, those speaking English are just slightly under the Canadian average (58.4). The Francophone population of the metropolitan area accounts for 37.7 per cent of the total, rather higher than the national average of 28.1 per cent. Other languages are spoken in the Ottawa area by 6.6 per cent of the population, as compared with the average for Canada of 13.5 per cent. The over-representation of the Francophone population in the Ottawa metropolitan area should be noted. In terms of numerical proportions, the federal capital area comes considerably closer to a balance between the Francophone and Anglophone groups than does Canada as a whole.

Table 1.4. Percentage distribution of population, Canada and principal metropolitan areas (population of 200,000 or more), by mother tongue, 1961

Region	Total	Mother tongue		
		English	French	Others
Canada	100	58.4	28.1	13.5
Ottawa	100	55.7	37.7	6.6
Montreal	100	23.4	64.8	11.8
Toronto	100	76.6	1.4	22.0
Vancouver	100	82.0	1.7	16.3
Winnipeg	100	67.9	5.9	26.2
Hamilton	100	80.0	1.5	18.5
Quebec	100	3.8	95.4	0.8
Edmonton	100	71.9	3.3	24.8
Calgary	100	82.1	1.3	16.6

Source: Census of Canada, 1961; Catalogue 92-549.

If the Ottawa figures are compared with those for other major urban centres, as shown in Table 1.4, it will be seen that even a partial balance between the official-language groups is a rare thing. Only Montreal, among the cities of over 200,000 in population, even approximates the balance found in Ottawa, though in this case the Francophone population is the more numerous. The rest of Canada's major cities are either predominantly Anglophone or, in the case of Quebec City, overwhelmingly Francophone.

Even among the medium-sized and smaller cities in Canada, relatively few have a close balance of Francophone and Anglophone population. Thus, measured by mother tongue, Sudbury (population 80,120) was 49.7 per cent Anglophone and 30.7 per cent Francophone in 1961, the rest of the population having other mother tongues. Timmins (40,121) was 46.2 per cent Anglophone and 34.3 per cent Francophone; Cornwall (43,639) 54.8 per cent and 42.4 per cent respectively; and Moncton (55,768) 66.2 per cent and 32.5 per cent respectively. It will be noticed that all these examples are situated within the relatively bilingual area that constitutes a loosely defined linguistic boundary between the parts of Canada that are predominantly Anglophone or predominantly Francophone. Both Ottawa and Montreal fall within the same bilingual belt. Outside this bilingual area few major cities come close to a balance between the official language groups. Thus in Windsor only 10.3 per cent of the population is of French mother tongue, while in Sherbrooke only 10.5 per cent is of English mother tongue.

As noted above, a rather low proportion of the population of the Ottawa area has a mother tongue other than French or English. For individual languages the pattern is rather uneven. Table 1.5 shows the distribution of the 11 largest language groups by mother tongue in Canada in 1961 and their corresponding figures for the Ottawa metropolitan area. It will be seen that a language such as Italian, more frequently heard in urban than rural areas, is as strong in the Ottawa area as in the country at large. Other languages, such as Ukrainian, or the Indian and Eskimo languages, are spoken by relatively small numbers; several others, including German, the Scandinavian languages, and Magyar, are well below their proportions for Canada as a whole. As a result, Italian is the third-ranking language of the Ottawa area, both absolutely and in percentage terms, but for every person who has Italian as his mother tongue there are 24 who have French and 36 who have English.

Table 1.5. Percentage distribution of population, Canada and Ottawa metropolitan area, by mother tongue, 1961

Mother tongue	Canada	Ottawa M.A.
Total	100	100
English	58.5	55.7
French	28.1	37.7
German	3.1	1.4
Ukrainian	2.0	0.4
Italian	1.9	1.6
Dutch	0.9	0.6
Indian and Eskimo	0.9	0.02
Polish	0.9	0.5
Scandinavian	0.6	0.2
Magyar	0.5	0.2
Yiddish	0.4	0.3
Others	2.2	1.4

Source: Census of Canada, 1961; Catalogue 92-549.

When one passes from the Ottawa metropolitan area as a whole to an analysis of its two provincial components separately, the element of linguistic balance is sharply reduced. Diagram 1.1 illustrates the distribution of each language group on either side of the provincial boundary.

As indicated earlier, just over three quarters of the total metropolitan population live on the Ontario side. Of the Anglophone group, roughly one person in 20 lives on the Quebec side. The Francophone population, however, is divided almost exactly in equal proportions by the provincial boundary. When measured by mother tongue, some 50.6 per cent live

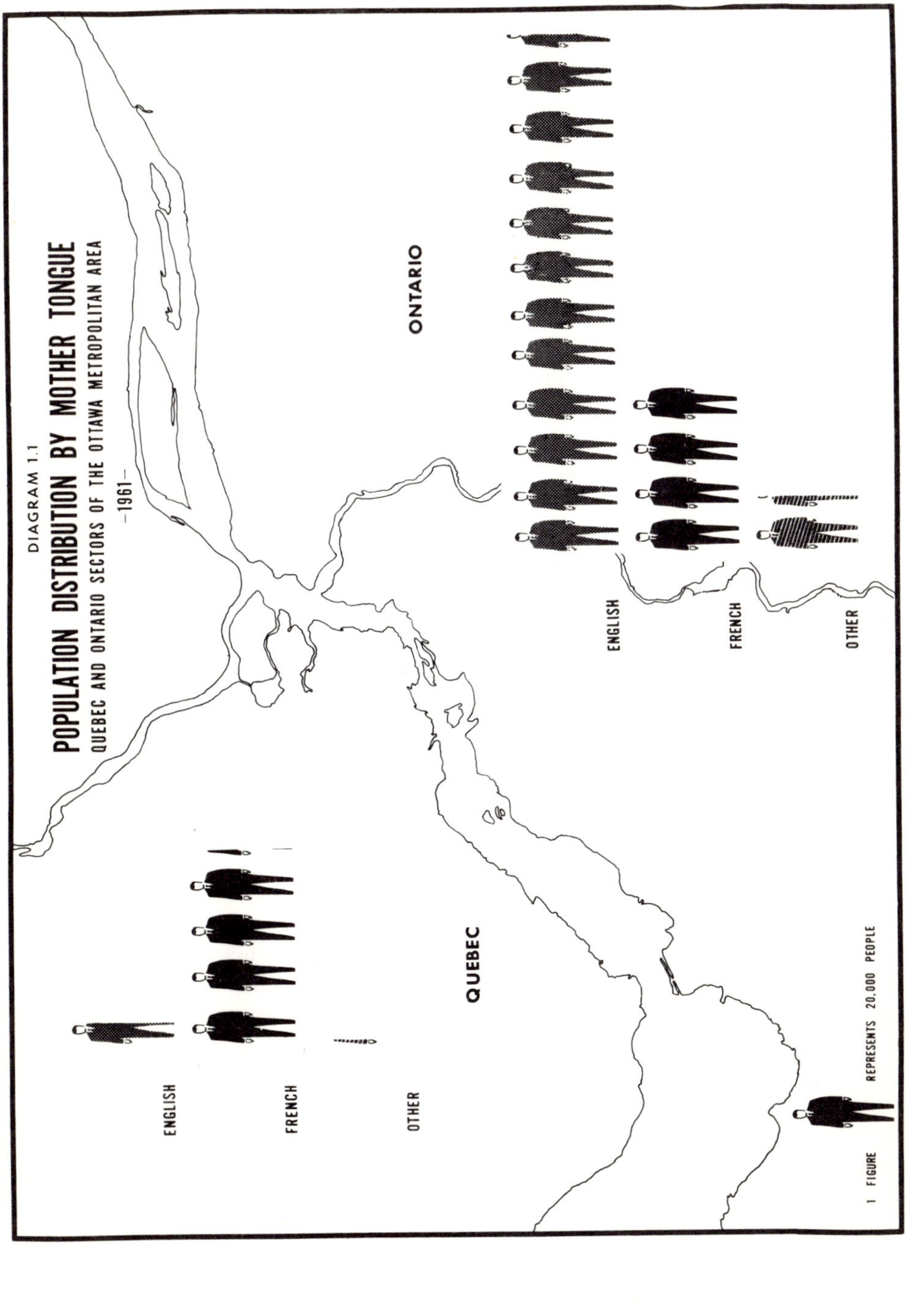

DIAGRAM 1.1
POPULATION DISTRIBUTION BY MOTHER TONGUE
QUEBEC AND ONTARIO SECTORS OF THE OTTAWA METROPOLITAN AREA
—1961—
ONTARIO
ENGLISH
FRENCH
OTHER
QUEBEC
ENGLISH
FRENCH
OTHER
1 FIGURE REPRESENTS 20,000 PEOPLE

on the Quebec side while 49.4 per cent live in Ontario. If, however, we measure by the alternate criterion of French ethnic origin, we find that the majority (53.2 per cent) live on the Ontario side. As a result, one half of the French-speaking community in the capital area is in certain respects oriented towards Quebec, while the other half is similarly oriented towards Ontario.

When viewed from the standpoint of each province separately, each sector of the federal capital area shows a fairly marked predominance of one language or the other. Thus, approximately five out of every six persons on the Quebec side are of French mother tongue, while approximately two out of every three persons on the Ontario side are of English mother tongue. In both sectors the numerical importance of the predominant language group is reinforced by the linguistic composition of the province as a whole.

However, when one looks at individual municipalities, the picture must be qualified still further. At the 1961 census, the city of Eastview in Ontario had a Francophone majority of 61.0 per cent, while Lucerne (formerly Hull South) on the Quebec side had an Anglophone majority of 52.2 per cent. These are the limiting cases, but some of the other metropolitan area municipalities also had quite a substantial representation of the other official language group. The township of Gloucester in Ontario, for example, was 39.6 per cent French by mother tongue; the town of Aylmer in Quebec was 41.3 per cent English by mother tongue. Nor should we forget the city of Ottawa itself, which was 21.2 per cent French by mother tongue. Ottawa is the largest of the area municipalities, and in absolute numbers its population of French mother tongue is the largest concentration of Francophones of any municipality in the area. (For a detailed description by municipalities, *see* Table B, Appendix A.)

If we pause to emphasize these variations from one part of the metropolitan area to another, it is to make clear the rather important implications of the territory we are considering as the capital area. As the figures in Table 1.6 indicate, the imbalance between the Francophone and Anglophone populations is smallest for the metropolitan area as a whole, including both the Quebec and Ontario sectors; it widens very considerably when the Ontario portion alone is considered, and becomes wider still within the city of Ottawa itself.[4] The population on the Quebec side therefore must be considered a significant demographic factor in the linguistic structure of the federal capital area. Its effect is to increase the relative population of French mother tongue from about one out of five in the city of Ottawa to three out of eight in the wider urban community.

Ethnic origin. While the data on mother tongue offer perhaps the most direct evidence that the census can provide as to current language usage, some further insight can be gained by the use of data on ethnic origin. From these we can make inferences about language usage in the past, and when these data are combined with the mother-tongue variable we can measure in approximate terms the degree of maintenance of an original language, presumably corresponding to ethnic origin, or, as the case may be, the degree of

---

[4]The recent proposal by the Ontario government for an Ottawa metropolitan government would include all of Carleton county (population 352,932) and the township of Cumberland (population 5,478) in Russell county. In 1961 the proportions by mother tongue within this area were 68.7 per cent English, 23.4 per cent French and 7.9 per cent other languages. Information supplied by the Dominion Bureau of Statistics.

transfer to another language. These also enable us to gauge the relative pull towards one language or another in areas where two or more languages are currently in use.

Table 1.6. Percentage distribution of population, Ottawa metropolitan area, by mother tongue, 1961

Area	Total		Mother tongue		
	N	%	English	French	Others
Ottawa M.A.	429,750	100	55.7	37.7	6.6
Ontario side (Ottawa, Eastview, Gloucester, Nepean, Rockcliffe Park)	332,899	100	67.8	24.1	8.1
City of Ottawa	268,206	100	70.1	21.2	8.7

Source: Census of Canada, 1961; Catalogue 92-549.

Table 1.7, then, presents an overall comparison of mother tongue and ethnic origin, in order to show the net gains and losses of French, English and all other languages in relation to population figures by ethnic origin. Such a measure can only be a rough approximation. It does show, however, that for the metropolitan area as a whole the population is 55.7 per cent of English mother tongue, but only 44.0 per cent British by origin. Conversely, 37.7 per cent of the population is French by mother tongue, but a larger number, 40.8 per cent, are of French origin. The highest rate of change is found among the other groups, who account for 15.2 per cent of the population by origin but only 6.6 per cent by mother tongue. As the table shows, the tendencies for the metropolitan area as a whole are reflected in both Ottawa and Eastview. Hull is slightly different in that both French and English show a net gain at the expense of other languages.

Table 1.7. Percentage distribution of population, Ottawa metropolitan area, by ethnic origin and mother tongue, 1961

Municipality	Total	British ethnic origin	English mother tongue	French ethnic origin	French mother tongue	Other ethnic origins	Other mother tongues
Total M.A.	100	44.0	55.7	40.8	37.7	15.2	6.6
Ottawa	100	55.2	70.1	25.5	21.2	19.2	8.7
Hull	100	7.8	8.2	89.4	90.2	2.8	1.6
Eastview	100	26.4	34.0	63.3	61.0	10.3	5.0

Source: Census of Canada, 1961; Catalogues 92-545 and 92-549.

Analysis of the data on mother tongue and ethnic origin points towards two broad trends in language behaviour. First, there is a fairly strong tendency for those of non-French, non-British origins to adopt one of the official languages—in this case usually English—as mother tongue. Second, as some further analysis will show, there is some tendency for those of one official language to have the other as mother tongue where the latter predominates in the community.

In the Ottawa area, residents of other origins have a strong tendency to adopt English rather than French in making a transfer to one of the official languages. The distribution of mother tongues for the groups of non-French, non-British origins is given in Table G, Appendix A. It shows that more than half those of German origin (57.4 per cent) now have English as their mother tongue, while only 3.5 per cent of this group have French as mother tongue. Almost all of the remainder (38.4 per cent) retain German as mother tongue. Perhaps a more interesting example is the group of Italian origin: 24.5 per cent of those of Italian origin in the Ottawa area now report English as their mother tongue, against only 3.6 per cent reporting French. In Montreal, by comparison, the relative pull of French is perceptibly stronger: 12.0 per cent of the Italians report French as their mother tongue as against 5.6 per cent who report English.

However, census data on official languages give us the clearest view of the linguistic orientation of the population of non-British, non-French origins. In Table C, Appendix A it will be seen that all those of other than French or British origins tend to have a knowledge of English only as their predominant official-language pattern. The proportions range from 63 per cent to over 90 per cent. For all origins, those knowing French only form 3 per cent of the group or less. It should perhaps be noted that 94.7 per cent of the people of non-French, non-British origins live on the Ontario side, a predominantly Anglophone sector.

If we examine more closely the mother-tongue data for those of French and British ethnic origins, a second question that emerges is the incidence of transfers from one official language to the other. Table D, Appendix A suggests that for the metropolitan area as a whole there is a net language transfer from French to English. Specifically, 11.9 per cent of those of French origin have English as mother tongue, while 2.3 per cent of those of British origin have French as mother tongue.

But the interesting phenomenon to be observed from Table D is that the pattern seems to differ between Ottawa and Hull. In the city of Ottawa 22.1 per cent of those of French origin reported English as mother tongue, while the proportion of British origin which has adopted French as mother tongue is almost insignificant (1.4 per cent). In the city of Hull, on the other hand, the proportions are almost exactly reversed: 25.2 per cent of the population of British origin recorded French as their mother tongue, while only 1.8 per cent of those of French origin recorded English as mother tongue. It may be concluded that the rate of transfer from the minority to the majority language in each city is very closely comparable. What accounts for the net transfer from French to English in the metropolitan area as a whole is the fact that the population of British origin in Hull is very small in absolute numbers in comparison with the population of French origin in the city of Ottawa.

The historical pattern of language usage in the Ottawa area should also be mentioned, as it must be remembered that both languages have long been spoken in the Ottawa valley. Because figures for mother tongue are available only since 1931, for earlier years it is necessary to rely upon data on ethnic origin. But is seems reasonable to assume a fairly close correlation between language and origin for the early period at least.

Tables E and F in Appendix A give the ethnic distribution of the population in the period since Confederation for Ottawa and Hull respectively. In Ottawa, the population of British origin fluctuated at or just above the 60 per cent mark from 1871 to 1951. During the same period those of French origin remained fairly close to 30 per cent of the population—a little higher during the 19th century, a little lower in the period after 1921.

The population of non-French, non-British origins in Ottawa has stayed around the 8 per cent level since 1911. However, this proportion changed considerably in the 1961 census. Doubtless due to the heavy influx of immigrants into the area since 1945, the proportion of the population of non-French, non-British origins rose from 8 per cent in 1941 to 19 per cent in 1961. As a result the groups of French and British origins were reduced proportionally.

There is a similar situation in the city of Hull with regard to the position held by the two main groups. Since 1881 people of British origin have formed between 6 and 13 per cent of the total population while those of French origin formed between 86 and 93 per cent. People of other origins have always made up a very low percentage of the population. This percentage rose from 1 in 1881 to 2.8 in 1961.

For the urban area as a whole, the changing proportions of the various language groups over the years are difficult to calculate. The concept of a census metropolitan area dates back to 1941 only. Its boundaries have been changed from census to census. Where in 1941 it encompassed seven municipalities, the metropolitan area is now composed, as we have seen, of 13 municipalities. Table 1.8 shows the general pattern for the metropolitan area since 1941. In this period the population of French origin has remained relatively stable. The population of non-French, non-British origins has more than doubled, while that of British origin has fallen in proportion.

Table 1.8. Population distribution, Ottawa metropolitan area, by ethnic origin, 1941, 1951, 1961

Year	Total	Ethnic origin		
		British	French	Others
1941	215,022	110,089	90,310	14,623
%	100	51.1	42.0	6.9
1951	281,908	135,243	121,680	24,985
%	100	48.0	43.1	8.9
1961	429,750	189,227	175,374	65,149
%	100	44.0	40.8	15.2

Sources: Censuses of Canada, 1941, II, Table 33; 1951, I, Table 36; 1961, Catalogue 92-545.

To sum up, the most significant characteristics of the metropolitan area are its linguistic proportions, the continuous presence of the two principal ethnic groups from the 19th century to the present day, the recent increase in the number of people of non-French, non-British origins and their strong tendency to adopt English rather than French as their official language.

Table 1.9. Percentage distribution of male labour force, Ottawa, Montreal, and Toronto metropolitan areas, by industry, 1961

Industry		Ottawa	Montreal	Toronto
Total	N	105,046	543,512	512,265
	%	100	100	100
Public administration		33.9	6.3	6.0
Manufacturing		14.0	33.2	32.8
Construction		10.3	10.0	9.4
Transport and communication		8.7	13.7	10.8
Commerce		14.9	17.1	18.6
Finance		3.7	4.5	5.2
Services		12.0	13.0	14.3
Not stated		2.0	0.6	.7
Primary industries		.6	1.8	2.3

Source: A. Raynauld, G. Marion, R. Béland, "La répartition des revenus selon les groupes ethniques au Canada" (study prepared for the Royal Commission on Bilingualism and Biculturalism, 1966), Statistical Appendix, Tables 46, 52, 64.

C. Socio-economic Structure

The labour force of the Ottawa metropolitan area possesses certain distinctive features, related at least partially to the area's special position as the federal capital. Most obviously, the public administration sector is by far the largest component of the work force, accounting for more than twice as many employees as any other sector.

Comparative figures for Ottawa, Montreal and Toronto, illustrating the predominance of public administration in the Ottawa metropolitan area, are given in Table 1.9.[5] It will be noted that public administration is of enormously greater significance in the capital, accounting for more than five times the proportion of male workers to be found in this sector in either Montreal or Toronto. But this is counterbalanced primarily by a far lower percentage within the manufacturing industry in Ottawa, and by a somewhat lesser emphasis on commerce, finance, transport and communication, and primary industry.

Table 1.10, using a slightly different information base, compares the economic structure in four municipalities of the Ottawa metropolitan area. The first point to be made is that within the public administration sector, it is the federal government that is predominant; in all four municipalities the municipal and provincial components are relatively small. Both in Ottawa and Eastview roughly one in every three members of the total labour force is a federal employee. In Hull this figure drops to about one out of five, and in Gatineau to one out of nine. Correspondingly the proportion of the work force employed in manufacturing

---

[5]Unless indication to the contrary is given, the statistics in this section have been calculated from a 20-per-cent sampling, i.e., the statistics taken from the study by Raynauld *et al.*, as well as the tapes (special compilations of 1961 census data) prepared for the Commission by the Dominion Bureau of Statistics. Note also that the category "primary industries" includes industries other than agriculture.

is lower in both Ottawa and Eastview than for the area as a whole. In Hull the proportion rises to 17.5 per cent, and in Gatineau it soars to 38.6 per cent.

Table 1.10. Percentage distribution of the total labour force, aged 15 years and over, by industry, 1961

Industry		Total M.A.	Ottawa*	Hull*	Eastview*	Gatineau*
Total	N	167,712	111,124	20,867	9,911	3,935
	%	100	100	100	100	100
Public admin.						
federal		30.7	33.2	21.0	32.9	11.0
provincial		0.3	0.3	0.7	0.3	0.1
municipal		2.0	2.3	2.0	1.1	2.2
diplomatic		0.3	0.4	0.1	0.3	–
Manufacturing		10.6	8.2	17.5	7.5	38.6
Construction		7.0	5.7	9.9	7.6	11.5
Trans. and comm.		6.8	6.8	6.9	7.9	4.4
Commerce		13.6	13.2	15.2	16.0	13.1
Finance		4.5	4.9	3.0	5.5	2.1
Services		20.6	21.8	20.6	17.3	14.6
Others**		3.6	3.2	3.2	3.6	2.5

Sources: Census of Canada, 1961; Catalogues 94-519 and 94-521.
 * Information available for these municipalities only.
** Includes agriculture, forestry, fishing, hunting and trapping, mining, and others.

By comparison with other major metropolitan areas, then, the federal capital is to a very considerable extent a civil service centre, in the sense that its economic structure is highly dependent on the federal government, although this applies to the Ontario municipalities of Ottawa and Eastview to a greater degree than to Hull and Gatineau. Since many employees in other sectors of the economy are engaged in supplying goods and services to federal employees, the degree of dependence on the federal government is actually far higher than the direct employment figures indicate.

Our basic aim in this section is to understand the position in the economic structure occupied by the Francophone and Anglophone groups, as well as by those speaking other languages. Most of the available economic and income data based on the census, however, are classified on a basis of ethnicity rather than mother tongue, and we shall have to use this measure for want of a more accurate indicator of language usage.

The labour force. The total labour force in the Ottawa metropolitan area, according to the 1961 census, comprised 155,643 persons, or approximately one out of three members of the total population. Of this number, some 67.5 per cent were males. Table 1.11 shows the breakdown by ethnic origin of this group. It will be seen from this table that in comparison with the population as a whole, those of French origin are under-represented in the labour force, and this under-representation is more pronounced in the female sector than in the male. Whether it is due to differences between groups as to age structure, levels of unemployment, or other reasons cannot be examined here. We should note, however, that the percentage of each group active in the labour force is the first factor that has some bearing on the economic status of the group.

Table 1.11. Percentage distribution of total population and labour force, Ottawa metropolitan area, by ethnic origin, 1961

	Total		Ethnic origin		
	N	%	British	French	Others
Total population	429,750	100	44.0	40.8	15.2
Total labour force	155,643*	100	45.0	38.5	16.5
Male labour force	105,046	100	43.8	39.2	17.1
Female labour force	50,597	100	47.7	37.1	15.2

Source: Tabulations based on the 1961 Census, prepared by Dominion Bureau of Statistics for the Royal Commission on Bilingualism and Biculturalism, Tape 3, Table 8, Part I, 34-36.
* A difference in the definition of the labour force accounts for the variation between this figure and that given in Table 1.10, which was based on Dominion Bureau of Statistics, Catalogue 94-519.

Table 1.12. Average income of labour force, Ottawa, Montreal, and Toronto, by ethnic origin, 1961

A. Males*

Metropolitan area	Total	Ethnic origin		
		British	French	Others
Ottawa	$4785	$5504	$4008	$4714
Montreal	4448	5896	3998	4502
Toronto	4812	5261	4168	4168

B. Females**

	Total	British	French	Others
Ottawa	$2447	$2731	$2155	$2253
Montreal	2255	2690	2158	2092
Toronto	2340	2488	2224	2079

Sources: * Raynauld et al., "La répartition des revenus," Statistical Appendix, Tables 42, 48, 60.
** Tape 3, Table 8, Part I, 35 (Ottawa), 17 (Montreal), 53 (Toronto).

The average wage and salary income for members of the labour force classified by ethnic origin for three metropolitan areas is given in Table 1.12. It will be seen at once from this table that the differences in average income received by males and females respectively are strikingly wider than those between ethnic groups. Hence a cause of differences in economic status could possibly be the different proportions of males to females active in the labour force from one group to another. In fact, the differences in this respect are very slight and such as they are point in the opposite direction. Thus, the group with the highest average income, the British, also has the highest percentage of females, 34.4 per cent, as against the comparable figures for the labour force of French and other origins of 31.4 and 30.0 per cent respectively (Tape 3, Table 8, Part I, 34-5). However, the analysis of incomes of the female work force raises certain special difficulties, and the remainder of this section will attempt to describe and analyze for the male labour market alone some of the further factors that contribute to income variations in the Ottawa metropolitan area. At least four further factors may be identified and their effects measured as revealed by the census data. We shall thus examine in turn industrial structure, educational level, occupational category, and age structure.

Industrial structure. We have already noted that the structure of the labour market in the capital area is substantially different from that of Montreal and Toronto in its emphasis on the public administration sector. Further analysis of the Ottawa data shows that those of British origin are considerably over-represented in this sector, while the proportions for those of French and other origins are somewhat lower.

Table 1.13 shows the relative representation of each group in each major industrial sector. When compared with the structure of the labour market as a whole, those of British origin are considerably over-represented in public administration and finance, and under-represented in manufacturing and construction. Those of French origin are correspondingly under-represented in public administration and finance, but over-represented in manufacturing and construction. Those of non-French, non-British origins are considerably over-represented in construction, service industries, and primary industry, but under-represented in transportation and communication, finance, and public administration.

Table 1.13. Percentage distribution of male labour force, Ottawa metropolitan area, by ethnic origin and industry, 1961

Industry		Total	Ethnic origin		
			British	French	Others
Total	N	105,046	45,988	41,111	17,947
	%	100	100	100	100
Public admin.		33.9	43.3	26.2	27.5
Manufacturing		14.0	10.9	18.1	12.7
Construction		10.3	5.7	13.2	15.7
Trans. and comm.		8.7	9.3	9.6	5.2
Commerce		14.9	12.7	16.4	16.9
Finance		3.7	4.7	2.9	2.8
Services		12.0	11.0	11.3	16.1
Not stated		2.0	2.0	1.8	2.3
Primary industries		0.6	0.4	0.6	0.9

Source: Raynauld et al., "La répartition des revenus," Statistical Appendix, Tables 51 and 52.

These variations in the representation of each group from one sector to another suggest a further possible cause of income differences: a group that is more concentrated in a well paid sector will tend to have a higher average income than one which is concentrated in a sector that pays less well. In Table 1.14 we have set out the average incomes received in each industrial sector for all males and for males of French, British, and other origins respectively. This table shows that the areas where we have noted over-representation of those of British origin (public administration and finance) yield incomes above the average for all sectors. The construction sector, on the other hand, where those of French and other origins are over-represented, pays average wages and salaries more than $1000 below the average level for all sectors.

Table 1.14. Average income of male labour force, Ottawa metropolitan area, by ethnic origin and industry, 1961

Industry	Total	Ethnic origin		
		British	French	Others
Total	$4785	$5504	$4008	$4714
Public administration	5335	5862	4290	5485
Manufacturing	4548	5360	4038	4432
Construction	3774	4360	3493	3776
Transport and communication	4479	5070	3825	4538
Commerce	4322	4731	3739	4821
Finance	6025	6425	5088	6489
Services	4947	5878	4335	4301
Primary industries	4069	5433	3145	3861
Not stated	3965	4450	3241	4061

Source: Raynauld et al., "La répartition des revenus," Statistical Appendix, Table 48.

Educational level. The position of individuals in the labour force is greatly influenced by the level of education attained. Here also the census data reveal considerable differences among those of French, British, and other origins; here also it is those of British origin who have, in the aggregate, a higher level of educational attainment. Table 1.15 gives a percentage breakdown by five levels of education for each of these three groups.

It will be noted that more than one in five of the males of both the British and the non-British, non-French groups have some university training, whereas only one in ten of the males of French origin is in this category. On the other hand, close to half of the male labour force of French origin have no more than elementary education, whereas only about one in six of the British males is in this category. Since educational attainment has a very direct bearing on occupational category and income, these differences are clearly of some significance to the economic position of members of each group.

In fact we find that the variations in educational level attained coincide with sharp differences in employment incomes. In all groups, for example, individuals with some university education average roughly three times the income of those who reported no education, and more than twice the average income of those with elementary education only. Table 1.16 gives the average income for those of French, British, and other origins for each of the five educational levels.

Table 1.15. Percentage distribution of male labour force, Ottawa metropolitan area, by ethnic origin and educational level, 1961

Educational level		Total	Ethnic origin		
			British	French	Others
Total	N	105,046	45,988	41,111	17,947
	%	100	100	100	100
None		0.4	0.1*	0.6	0.6
Elementary (1 year or more)		31.0	17.7	45.7	31.8
Secondary (1-2 years)		20.5	20.3	22.8	15.7
Secondary (3-5 years)		31.0	39.5	21.1	31.9
University (1 year or more)		17.1	22.5	9.8	20.1

Source: Raynauld et al., "La répartition des revenus," Statistical Appendix, Table 123.
* Statistically non-significant.

Table 1.16. Average income* of male labour force, Ottawa metropolitan area, by ethnic origin and educational level, 1961

Educational level	Total	Ethnic origin		
		British	French	Others
Total	$4785	$5504	$4008	$4714
None	2425	2688**	2481	2161
Elementary (1 year or more)	3535	3928	3385	3465
Secondary (1-2 years)	3978	4394	3615	3807
Secondary (3-5 years)	5049	5354	4462	4969
University (1 year or more)	7583	8023	6925	7059

Source: Raynauld et al., "La répartition des revenus," Statistical Appendix, Table 119.
* Calculated on the basis of those declaring an income.
** Statistically non-significant.

The steady progression in average incomes as the educational level rises is apparent for all groups but the difference is greatest in absolute terms for those with some university attendance. Clearly a group that is more concentrated at the upper end of the educational scale will derive considerable economic advantage from this favourable educational structure. However, it will also be noted that for each educational level those of British origin receive higher average wage and salary incomes than those of French or other origins, and that at the upper end of the educational scale this difference is of the order of $1000 per year. For an explanation of these differences we must look to other factors.

Occupational structure. Still another factor which can influence the position of all individuals in the labour force is their place in the occupational structure. The census data available to us classify the labour force into about a dozen broad occupational categories, ranging from managers to unskilled labourers, with income data for each. For the Ottawa metropolitan area we can accordingly compare the distribution by occupation for males of French, British and other origins, and then look at the average income distribution for each, in much the same way that we examined the educational structure and its influence on incomes. The distribution of the various occupational categories for members of the labour force of French, British and other origins is shown in Table 1.17.

Table 1.17. Percentage distribution of male labour force, Ottawa metropolitan area, by ethnic origin and occupation, 1961

Occupation		Total	Ethnic origin		
			British	French	Others
Total	N	105,046	45,988	41,111	17,947
	%	100	100	100	100
Managerial		13.2	16.3	8.8	15.6
Professional and technical		13.8	18.5	7.7	16.0
Clerical		13.6	14.5	14.6	8.9
Sales		6.1	6.5	6.1	5.3
Transport and communication		7.2	5.8	10.2	4.0
Service and recreation		14.6	16.8	11.8	15.2
Craftsmen		22.9	15.9	29.5	25.3
Labourers		5.4	2.5	8.5	5.7
Farmers		0.1	0.1	0.1	0.1
Other primary		1.0	0.9	0.9	1.5
Not stated		2.1	2.1	1.9	2.5

Source: Tape 3, Table 8, Parts I and II, 34.

In this table some wide variations come to light. Broadly speaking, those of British origin are represented twice as heavily as those of French origin in the managerial and professional sectors; on the other hand, those of French origin are represented almost twice as heavily as those of British origin in the trades sector, and more than three times as heavily as labourers. The groups of other origins are relatively close to those of British origin in the managerial and professional categories, but rather closer to those of French origin in the trades and labourer categories. They are under-represented in certain other sectors, notably clerical work, and transport and communication.

When we turn to the income pattern that the census shows for these occupational categories, once again sharp income differences occur between the highest and lowest categories. Table 1.18 shows the average income for those of French, British and other origins according to occupational category.

It will be noted that the average employment income of managers and professionals is of the order of three times the income of labourers, and this is broadly true both for the total labour force and for each group taken separately. Consequently the different occupational structures of the groups of French, British, and other origins will be a further factor in explaining the economic position of members of each group. As before, however, some further variations, according to origin within each of the occupational categories, remain after these structural differences are taken into account. These variations are more pronounced in some categories, such as managers, salesmen, and service workers, than in others, such as professionals or skilled tradesmen. In two sectors (labourers and other workers in primary industry) those of French origin have an income above the average for all three groups combined. Apart from these two cases, however, those of British origin have the highest average income in all the remaining categories.

Table 1.18. Average income of male labour force, Ottawa metropolitan area, by ethnic origin and occupation, 1961

Occupation	Total	Ethnic origin		
		British	French	Others
Total	$4785	$5504	$4008	$4714
Managerial	7760	8324	6902	7336
Professional and technical	6887	7119	6703	6405
Clerical	3733	3928	3528	3684
Sales	4494	4856	4000	4650
Transport and communication	3504	3886	3228	3710
Service and recreation	4429	5195	3360	4146
Craftsmen	3864	4175	3757	3648
Labourers	2402	2310	2443	2365
Farmers	4350	4739	3670	4338
Other primary	2667	2635	2827	2470
Not stated	3919	4406	3270	3858

Source: Tape 3, Table 8, Parts I and II, 34.

Age structure. One final factor which can be assessed with the aid of census data is the age structure of the labour force of French, British and other origins respectively. In general, any segment of the labour force will have higher earnings than others to the extent that its members are concentrated in the peak earning years. Conversely, a group more concentrated in the younger age groups might have lower than average earnings on account of its age structure. Proceeding as before, we can look first at the age structure of the Ottawa labour force according to ethnic origin (Table 1.19) and then at the pattern of average income for each group by age category (Table 1.20).

Table 1.19 shows that the labour force of French origin is, by and large, younger than that of British or other origins. In 1961, one in five of those of French origin was between 15 and 24 years of age, while the corresponding figure for the British and others was less than one in seven. One in three of those of British origin was in the 45-to-64 age group, against only one in four for those of French or other origins.

Table 1.19. Percentage distribution of male labour force, Ottawa metropolitan area, by ethnic origin and age group, 1961

Age group		Total	Ethnic origin		
			British	French	Others
Total	N	105,046	45,988	41,111	17,947
	%	100	100	100	100
15-24 years		15.9	13.2	19.9	13.9
25-44 years		52.7	50.8	51.8	59.6
45-64 years		28.4	32.2	25.9	24.6
65 years and over		3.0	3.8	2.4	1.9

Source: Tape 3, Table 4, 64-112.

Table 1.20 shows the effect of age upon average total income (including, in this case, unearned income). For all groups the 15-to-24 age category shows earnings far below all other age categories. The greater proportion of those of French origin in this group thus becomes significant. Nevertheless at certain age levels considerable income differences persist between those of French, British, and other origins. These are minimal for the 15-to-24 group, but they widen significantly for those between 25 and 44, and become wider still over the age of 45, where an amount of $2000 per year separates those of French origin from those of British origin.

Table 1.20. Average total income* of male labour force, Ottawa metropolitan area, by ethnic origin and age group, 1961

Age group	Total	Ethnic origin		
		British	French	Others
Total	$5103	$5862	$4281	$5035
15-24 years	2331	2325	2302	2444
25-44 years	5338	6011	4687	5164
45-64 years	6181	7019	4998	6221
65 years and over	5419	6328	4076	4584

Source: Tape 3, Table 4, 64-112.
* The figures given here are *total* income figures, including wages and salaries, earnings from business and professional practice, investment income, pensions and allowances; elsewhere in this section we deal with employment income only, i.e., wages, salaries, and earnings from business or professional practice.

Relative importance of factors. In the above paragraphs we have discussed the influence of industrial structure, educational level, occupation, and age upon the economic level of male members of the labour force of different origins in the Ottawa metropolitan area. It is interesting to make some estimate of the relative importance of each of these factors in explaining the income differences outlined in Table 1.12 above, and it is possible to make such an estimate by statistical means. One method for analyzing income differences between any two groups has been applied to the Canadian labour force by Professor André Raynauld and his associates in their research study.

The basic technique used in this study to assess the weight of any single factor is to calculate what the income differences would be if one group had the same structure as the other with respect to that factor. The weight of the factor concerned is then the difference between the actual disparity and the disparity that would remain if both groups were alike with respect to that factor. By doing this for each factor separately one can assess the relative weight of each as a proportion of the total income disparity between the groups. Certain problems arise, however. Among these, the influence of several factors in combination is not necessarily the aggregate of their influences individually. There is normally a degree of overlapping, and in discussing the overall relationship of all factors certain judgements must be made as to the degree of inter-relationship.

In Appendix B we present the results of a calculation of the type we have described that compares males of French and British origins in the Ottawa metropolitan area labour force. (Those of other origins have not been included because of the complexity of the further calculation and the considerable heterogeneity of those in this category.) Educational level and occupational structure have been taken as inter-related factors, and age and industrial structure independently. To these has been added an estimate of the influence of differential rates of unemployment for different educational levels based on data that are not available for Ottawa alone.

The calculation suggests that as much as 62 per cent of the total income disparity between those of French and British origins in the Ottawa area may be traced to differences in educational level and occupational structure combined. This compares with 45 per cent in Montreal and 44 per cent in Toronto. Differences attributable to dissimilarities in industrial structure, age, and employment rates are relatively low at about 8 per cent, 11 per cent, and 9 per cent respectively. Assuming no correlation among these remaining factors, the four factors of education-occupation combined, industry, age, and employment rate together account for about 90 per cent of the income differences between those of French and British origins, leaving a residue of about 10 per cent to be explained by factors other than those we have been able to examine statistically. It may be noted that by comparison the combined weight of these four factors calculated on the same basis is only 78 per cent for Toronto and under 70 per cent for Montreal; it is the far greater influence of the educational-occupational factor in Ottawa that primarily accounts for the difference.

It is clear, then, that by this method of calculation almost two thirds of the income disparity between males of French and British origins in the labour force may be traced to their differences in educational level and occupational category. Beyond this point, however, we must resort to hypotheses. On the one hand, the educational system may not be retaining proportionally as many students of French origin at the upper educational levels. Educational facilities for Francophone and Anglophone pupils in the capital area are to a substantial degree independent of each other, and this possibility must be seriously considered. Another hypothesis is that those of French origin may achieve high educational levels and yet not find satisfactory positions in the labour market. They may either enter lower-status, lower-income occupations or leave the area to work elsewhere. Since we have no statistics on migration to and from the area, this last possibility is hard to measure. We can, however, compare educational level with occupational category, and this is done for those of French, British and other origins in Table H, Appendix A.

Table 1.21 points to a noticeable variation in the proportion attending school in the age groups corresponding to higher secondary and post-secondary education. Of the age group from 15 to 19 years in 1961, more than seven out of 10 of those of British and other origins were attending school, but only five out of 10 of those of French origin. For the group from 20 to 24 years old, the percentage of those in attendance drops sharply for all origins, but the percentage for those of British origin is at this point more than twice that for those of French origin.

Table 1.21. Percentage of population in selected age categories attending school, Ottawa metropolitan area, by ethnic origin, 1961

	15-19 years			20-24 years		
	Br.	Fr.	Others	Br.	Fr.	Others
Total population	12,180	14,437	3,815	10,043	12,457	4,452
Total attending school	8,899	7,349	2,703	1,187	697	392
% of age group attending school	73.1	50.9	70.9	11.8	5.6	8.8

Source: Tape 3, Table 3, 16-30.

On the other hand, Table H, Appendix A suggests that even for those of the same educational level, those of British origin tend to be found more often in higher-status, higher-income occupations than those of French origin—though at certain levels those of other origins do proportionally better than both. In the administrative and professional categories, those of British origin are represented more heavily than those of French origin at all educational levels. For males with university training these two categories account for 74.2 per cent of those of British origin but only 60.1 per cent of those of French origin. On the other hand, some 15.7 per cent of the university-educated of French origin are in clerical occupations, as against only 5.6 and 5.4 per cent of those of British and other origins respectively.

On balance, both our original hypotheses appear to have some validity. Males of French origin do tend to leave school at an earlier age than their counterparts of British origin, but those who go on to the higher educational levels tend on balance to find somewhat lower-paid, lower-status positions in the occupational structure than males of British origin. It seems possible that the two tendencies reinforce each other: to the extent that further education is less certain to lead to a well-paid job, there will be that much less incentive to remain at school.

While we cannot analyze much further the causes of income disparities in the Ottawa area labour force, the existence of these disparities seems clear enough. Though the figures at our disposal relate to origin rather than to language, there is every indication that the Francophone and Anglophone communities in the federal capital live at substantially different economic levels, and that differences in incomes are reflected in broader differences in socio-economic status. When the weaker economic position of the Francophone population is set beside its minority position in demographic terms and its virtually equal split between the two provinces, it can more readily be appreciated why the Francophone presence in the federal capital has not been felt in the past as fully as might be expected.

D. Residential Patterns

Having looked at the linguistic and socio-economic composition of the Ottawa area, we turn now to see how these factors relate to residential patterns in the capital. Most of the study area is covered by 80 census tracts, of which 16 are on the Quebec side and 64 in Ontario (*see* Map 1.3). Within each the population may be broken down by mother tongue, and an idea of the economic status of the sector may be obtained by looking at the average wage and salary income of the male residents (*see* Table I, Appendix A). With this information two questions may be at least partially answered. First, do persons of the same mother tongue tend to cluster together, or are persons of English, French, and other mother tongues dispersed fairly widely throughout the capital area? Second, does the residential pattern vary according to the socio-economic status of the sector concerned, or is it more or less uniform?

When viewed from the standpoint of language alone, there is a general tendency in the capital for persons of the same mother tongue to cluster together. In 38 census sectors, those of English mother tongue form over 70 per cent of the population, while in a further 18, those of French mother tongue do so. Only 24 sectors fall between these levels. To put the matter another way, some 66.3 and 62.2 per cent of Anglophone and Francophone residents respectively live in sectors of high linguistic concentration (70 per cent or more). As those of other mother tongues make up less than 7 per cent of the Ottawa area population, it is not surprising that in no sector do they form a majority. However, some slight degree of concentration may be discerned in that 37.9 per cent of residents having other mother tongues live in 13 sectors in which they comprise 10 per cent or more of the population.

The location of these areas of concentration is interesting. In 11 of the 18 sectors of high French-speaking concentration, over 80 per cent of the population is of French mother tongue. These sectors are all on the Quebec side of the metropolitan area—that is, West Templeton, Gatineau, Pointe-Gatineau and eight of the nine Hull sectors. Of the remaining seven sectors, where from 70.0 to 79.9 per cent of the population is French-speaking, one is on the Quebec side (the remaining Hull sector), and six are in Ontario. Three of the five Eastview sectors fall into this latter category.

The areas of high English-speaking concentration are all on the Ontario side. As may be seen from Map 1.4, these sectors extend mainly to the west and south of central Ottawa, and are in fact largely suburban in character. The sectors in which those of other mother tongues show a slight tendency to concentrate are, with two exceptions, in the central part of Ottawa.

Although approximately the same proportion of French- and English-speaking people live in sectors of high linguistic concentration, the rest of the French-speaking population tend to differ from the rest of the English-speaking population in their residential pattern.

As may be seen in Table 1.22, 90 per cent of the English-speaking residents live in the 54 sectors where English is at least the language of the majority. The percentage of people living in sectors where their mother tongue is not spoken by the majority is almost three times as high for the French-speaking as for the English-speaking population.

Table 1.22. Residential patterns: mother tongue by linguistic concentration and dispersion, 1961

Kind of sector	No. of sectors	Population living in sectors	Mother tongue		
			English	French	Others
Total	80	415,740	100	100	100
High English concentration (70% +)	38	182,538	66.3	10.7	47.5
Mixed: English majority	16	91,940	23.8	17.0	38.4
Mixed: French majority	8	27,943	4.3	10.1	5.4
High French concentration (70% +)	18	113,319	5.6	62.2	8.7

Source: Tabulations based on Table I, Appendix A.

Those of other mother tongues tend, to a striking degree, to live in predominantly English-speaking sectors. Indeed, their residential pattern, in its very marked leaning towards these sectors, strongly corroborates the evidence given above—on the bases of mother-tongue transfers and knowledge of official languages—that those of other origins in the capital area tend towards linguistic and cultural identification with the population of English mother tongue (see 12). These tendencies are sufficiently pronounced in the overall picture that it may be helpful for certain purposes, as we shall see later, to view the residents of English and other mother tongues as a single community.

The possible reasons underlying these patterns of residence are many, and they will vary in importance according to the individual. To the person of low income, the choice of residence will be limited to those sectors containing housing that he can afford; to the person of higher income, social and prestige factors may enter into consideration. The locally born population will probably have a greater sensitivity than has the migrant population to such traditional patterns as the concentration of Francophone persons in the Ottawa Lower Town area. To some, the proximity of the appropriate schools, churches, and a whole range of other facilities will be of importance. The desire to be near the place of work, to live in an apartment rather than a house, to live in a suburban area rather than the centre of town, to be located on one or the other side of the provincial boundary, are all further elements that may affect the decision of where to live.

Residential pattern and economic level. Most of these factors that influence the pattern of residence cannot be studied in detail here, but the economic factor is worth further analysis, because the residential pattern for the higher-income census sectors seems to differ from that for the lower-income sectors. On Map 1.5 are marked the 20 richest and 20

The Capital Area

poorest census sectors in terms of average employment income per sector.6 Eight out of the 20 poorest sectors are on the Quebec side of the metropolitan area—West Templeton, Templeton, Pointe-Gatineau, Deschênes and four of Hull's nine sectors. This is to say that half of the Quebec sectors fall within that quarter of the metropolitan area's 80 sectors having the lowest income. The remaining 12 sectors within this quarter are on the Ontario side and are to be found in the older areas of central Ottawa. The 20 richest sectors, all in Ontario suburban areas, include Rockcliffe Park, 14 of Ottawa's 40 sectors, and five of Nepean's six sectors. Neither Gloucester nor Eastview contains any such high-income areas.

Because of the limited data available, we cannot say for each mother tongue where persons of high and low income live. However, by taking the average income of the sector as an indicator of the economic status of the neighbourhood, we can say in what kinds of areas persons of different mother tongues live. For example, Rockcliffe Park has an average income of $8326 and 217 persons of French mother tongue live there. Thus, while it cannot be said that 217 Francophones with high incomes live in the sector, it can be said that 217 Francophones do live in this high-income area.

If the population is broken down by mother tongue for the sectors of different economic status (Table 1.23), it appears that a very substantial majority of the French-speaking population live in the 40 sectors of lower income. For the English-speaking residents, a less pronounced majority live in the sectors of higher income. Given the general pattern of socio-economic disparities in the capital area, as described in section C (14 ff), this was more or less to be expected. Those of other mother tongues reside in roughly equal proportions at all four economic levels.

Table 1.23. Residential patterns: mother tongue by average income of sectors, 1961

Average income	Mother tongue		
	English	French	Others
Total	100	100	100
$2843 – $3450 (poorest 20 sectors)	12.3	40.5	29.7
$3457 – $4096 (next 20 sectors)	18.1	39.2	21.5
$4180 – $5226 (next 20 sectors)	32.3	15.6	28.7
$5253 – $8326 (richest 20 sectors)	37.3	4.6	20.1

Source: Tabulations based on Table I, Appendix A.

To clarify the pattern further we may combine the degree of linguistic concentration in each census sector with its average income level. One way of presenting these data is to make

---

6The 80 census sectors were arranged in order of their average income and then divided into four quarters. The population is fairly evenly distributed among them as follows:

Poorest 20 sectors	24.2%
Next 20 sectors	26.3%
Next 20 sectors	25.8%
Richest 20 sectors	23.8%
Total	100 %

a four-way division of the population according to the kind of census tracts in which they live. The four categories are arranged so as to show the percentage of the population that live in:
1) a *low* income sector in which over 70 per cent of the population has the same mother tongue;
2) a *low* income sector *without* such a linguistic concentration;
3) a *high* income sector *with* such a linguistic concentration; and
4) a *high* income sector *without* such a linguistic concentration.

The four resulting percentages, which add up to 100, enable us to produce the quartile diagrams shown below.

Population of French mother tongue

	Lower income (40 sectors)	Higher income (40 sectors)
In sectors of French concentration of 70% +	60.4%	1.8%
In non-concentrated sectors	19.4%	18.4%

When this technique is applied to the French-speaking population, it can be seen that of those living in the low-income sectors, more than three out of four live in areas of high French-speaking concentration. Of those who live in high-income areas, more than nine out of 10 live in non-concentrated areas. Table I in Appendix A shows that of the top 40 sectors only one, number 107 at the north end of Hull, has a majority of French-speaking residents, the other 39 having an English-speaking majority.

The English-speaking population, on the other hand, is distributed residentially in quite a different fashion. From the diagram, we can say that of the English-speaking population in higher-income areas, a large majority live in areas of high English-speaking linguistic concentration. Of those in the lower-income areas, a little less than one third live in areas of relatively high English-speaking concentration.

Population of English mother tongue

	Lower income (40 sectors)	Higher income (40 sectors)
In sectors of English concentration of 70% +	9.1%	57.2%
In non-concentrated sectors	21.3%	12.4%

For those whose mother tongue is other than French or English a different pattern again emerges, although here, as earlier, because of their smaller numbers we must use a lower criterion for defining linguistic concentration (in this instance 10 per cent). It can be said that where there is a slight tendency for the population of other mother tongues to cluster, this is done in the low-income sectors. There is a very pronounced tendency in the opposite direction in high-income sectors.

Population of other mother tongues

	Lower income (40 sectors)	Higher income (40 sectors)
In sectors of other-language concentration of 10% +	35.7%	2.2%
In non-concentrated sectors	15.5%	46.6%

The hypothesis was raised earlier that those of other mother tongues in the capital area tend to identify with the Anglophone population. If this is the case, one can also look at the distribution of the population having as their mother tongue *either* English *or* other languages. If this is done the result is to increase the number of sectors where there is high, non-French linguistic concentration from 38 to 45 and also to increase the proportion of persons living in low- rather than high-income areas. The quartile distribution of the population of English plus other mother tongues—in other words, the non-French-speaking sector—is as follows:

Total population of mother tongues other than French

	Lower income (40 sectors)	Higher income (40 sectors)
In sectors of English and other concentration of 70% +	19.9%	58.0%
In non-concentrated sectors	12.7%	9.4%

From this quartile distribution, it can be seen that a large majority of this population in high-income sectors live in linguistically concentrated areas. This same pattern, although less pronounced, is also visible in the lower-income sectors. In other words, to the extent that our hypothesis is correct, both the Francophone and the non-Francophone populations tend towards concentration in the lower-income sectors; in the higher-income sectors the Francophones tend to be scattered fairly widely among the heavy majority of English speakers.

Another way of looking at the distribution of Francophones and non-Francophones of various income levels may be found in Diagram 1.2. In this scatter diagram each dot represents a sector and is placed vertically according to the average income and horizontally according to the percentage of the population of French mother tongue in the sector. Higher-income sectors appear in the upper portion of the diagram and lower-income ones at the bottom. Sectors on the left-hand side have proportionally a small Francophone population; those on the right, a large one.

In this way it is possible to see that there are many more sectors with few people of French mother tongue living in them than sectors with a high percentage. While virtually all the high-income areas have a relatively low percentage of French-speaking people, there is far less tendency for the low-income sectors to concentrate at any single part of the scale. Indeed, among the lower-income sectors one finds a distribution stretching right

DIAGRAM 1.2

LINGUISTIC CONCENTRATIONS and AVERAGE INCOME of CENSUS TRACTS, OTTAWA METROPOLITAN AREA, 1961

oc	Ottawa (central part)
oe	Ottawa (east part)
ow	Ottawa (west part)
os	Ottawa (south part)
h	Hull
e	Eastview
g	Gatineau
a	Aylmer
pg	Pointe - Gatineau
luc	Lucerne
t	Templeton
wt	West Templeton
d	Deschênes
r	Rockcliffe Park
gl	Gloucester
n	Nepean

across all levels of linguistic concentration, from areas of very high French concentration to sectors of high to moderately high concentration of English plus other languages. Owing to the general socio-economic structure of the capital area, however, these latter sectors are less numerous at the lower end of the income scale than are the sectors of high French-speaking concentration.

While the residential pattern of the population at large may be analyzed only in terms of the average income of each census tract, we can examine that of federal public servants in terms of specific income levels. We have noted in the preceding section that Ottawa and Eastview show a higher percentage of their labour force employed in the governmental sector than do the Quebec municipalities of Hull or Gatineau. It is hardly surprising then to find that federal public servants show a stronger tendency to reside on the Ontario side than

THE NATIONAL CAPITAL REGION

- —··—··— BOUNDARY OF THE NATIONAL CAPITAL REGION
- ———— METROPOLITAN OTTAWA BOUNDARY
- CITY OF OTTAWA AND BUILT-UP AREAS
- GREENBELT
- GATINEAU PARK

Map 1.1. THE NATIONAL CAPITAL REGION

OTTAWA METROPOLITAN AREA, 1961

Map 1.2. OTTAWA METROPOLITAN AREA, 1961

CENSUS TRACTS OF OTTAWA METROPOLITAN AREA, 1961

**Map 1.3. CENSUS TRACTS,
OTTAWA METROPOLITAN AREA, 1961**

LINGUISTIC CONCENTRATIONS OTTAWA METROPOLITAN AREA, 1961

Tracts Where:

- 70 Percent and Over of Population is of English Mother Tongue
- 10 Percent and Over of Population is of Other Mother Tongue
- 70 Percent of Population is of English Mother Tongue and 10 Percent of Other Mother Tongue
- 70 Percent of Population is of French Mother Tongue
- Linguistic Concentrations are Lower than the above

Map 1.4. LINGUISTIC CONCENTRATIONS,
OTTAWA METROPOLITAN AREA, 1961

RICHEST and POOREST SECTORS,
OTTAWA METROPOLITAN AREA, 1961

Twenty Highest Average Income Sectors
Twenty Lowest Average Income Sectors

Map 1.5. RICHEST AND POOREST SECTORS,
OTTAWA METROPOLITAN AREA, 1961

DEGREE of BILINGUALISM
OTTAWA METROPOLITAN AREA, 1961

Tracts

50 % and Over of Population Bilingual

25 to 49.9 % of Population Bilingual

Map 1.6. DEGREE OF BILINGUALISM,
OTTAWA METROPOLITAN AREA, 1961

does the population at large. The proportions for all public servants and for high-income public servants are compared to the figures for the general population in Table 1.24.

Table 1.24. Percentages* of various populations living on the Ontario and Quebec sides of the Ottawa metropolitan area, by mother tongue, 1961

Population	Total		Mother tongue					
			English		French		Others	
	Ont.	Que.	Ont.	Que.	Ont.	Que.	Ont.	Que.
Total M.A. population N=429,750	77.5	22.5	94.4	5.6	49.4	50.6	94.7	5.3
Total federal public service N=45,619	85.4	14.6	95.9	4.1	61.3	38.7	97.5	2.5
Federal public service earning over $10,000 N=2,017	96.2	3.8	98.1	1.9	78.6	21.4	97.1	2.9

Sources: Table A, Appendix A; Tape 1, Table 3 (this tape is based on a 100-per-cent sample of federal public servants).

* Percentages run horizontally, the figures for Ontario and Quebec adding to 100 for each mother tongue by population category.

For those of English and other mother tongues, who are already very heavily concentrated on the Ontario side, the difference between public servants and the general public is rather small; for those of French mother tongue, the difference is greater, and it becomes greater still for higher-income public servants. In the capital area some six out of every 10 French-speaking public servants reside in Ontario, and this proportion rises to almost eight out of 10 among those reporting earnings over $10,000 in 1961.

It is possible to analyze in more detail the residential pattern of federal public servants, though the source of these data does not permit a study by individual census tracts. Two tables in Appendix A give the number and percentage of federal public servants living in each of 12 zones of the metropolitan area, each zone representing a cluster of contiguous census sectors. Table J refers to all federal public servants resident in the metropolitan area, Table K to the group of just over 2,000 officials who in 1961 had earnings of $10,000 or more. Each table taken separately allows us to see the residential pattern for those of English, French, and other mother tongues, while a comparison of one table against the other enables us to identify more clearly the tendencies of the upper income group as compared to the total number. Though the analysis could be carried much further, it seems necessary here only to indicate the broad tendencies suggested by the data.

To compare first those of high income against the total public service (*see* Tables J and K, Appendix A), it will be noted that those earning over $10,000 in 1961 tend to be more concentrated than the others in the suburban ring around the urban core, specifically in the eastern, south-eastern, south-western, and western sectors of the city of Ottawa, and in the zone composed of Rockcliffe Park, Nepean, and Gloucester. Those earning less tend to be more concentrated in central Ottawa, Eastview, Hull, and the zone comprising the remaining Quebec municipalities. In broad terms this pattern holds true for public servants of French, English, or other mother tongues alike; the only major discrepancy is a further tendency for some upper-income Francophone public servants to concentrate in sectors 11 to 15 of east-central Ottawa, the Sandy Hill area.

When we compare more closely the residential patterns for the different language groups in the total public service (Table J, Appendix A) we find, as might be expected, some general tendencies not unlike the residential pattern for the total population. Francophones tend to be more concentrated than the others in Eastview, Hull, the remaining Quebec munipalities, and Ottawa Lower Town (Zone B). Anglophones tend to be more concentrated in the outer edges of Ottawa (Zones D, G, and H), in the other Ontario municipalities (except Eastview), and in the central part of downtown Ottawa (Zone E). (*See* Map 1.4, which shows an analogous pattern for the total population.) Public servants of other mother tongues follow much the same pattern as the Anglophone group.

Public servants earning over $10,000, regardless of their mother tongue, seem to show a more pronounced similarity of residential pattern, at least within the city of Ottawa itself. In six of the eight Ottawa zones in Table K, the percentage distributions for French, English, and other mother tongues are closely comparable. For the remaining zones, Francophones tend to be more concentrated than the others in the east-central areas of the city, and are far less concentrated than either the English or others in the west end. Outside the city of Ottawa, high-income Francophone public servants are more concentrated than the other groups in Hull and in Quebec generally, but less so in the zone comprising Rockcliffe Park, Nepean, and Gloucester.

The overall impression left by Table K, however, is of substantially similar residential patterns for high-income public servants of all language groups. This suggests that for large numbers of upper-level civil servants the choice of residence is influenced less by linguistic or cultural factors than by other considerations. The same may well hold true for the higher-income levels of the general population also but the available data do not enable us to say so with certainty.

Summary. The residential pattern of the federal capital area shows that roughly two thirds of both the French-speaking and the English-speaking population live in census sectors of substantial linguistic concentration. The population of non-English, non-French mother tongues tends, to a striking degree, to live in primarily Anglophone sectors. Further analysis by income levels reveals a wide range of linguistic proportions for low-income census tracts, from high French-speaking concentration to high English-speaking concentration. In upper-income tracts there is a tendency for those of French mother tongue to be fairly widely scattered throughout the metropolitan area. The pattern for federal public servants points in much the same direction. For the group as a whole there are clear tendencies towards linguistic concentration; for the upper echelon the residential pattern is far less directly linked to mother tongue. In other words, there is little tendency for the middle and upper income French-speaking population of the federal capital area to form a residential concentration of their own, analogous, for example, to one of the English-speaking suburbs of Montreal.

It is perhaps wise to conclude this section with a caveat. The tendency of upper-level public servants to live dispersed among their English-speaking counterparts may be due to their relatively small numbers. In 1961, public servants of French mother tongue accounted for only 9.0 per cent of those earning over $10,000 per year and 8.7 per cent of those earning $8,000 to $10,000, compared to 15.4 per cent of those earning $6,000 to $8,000 and 34.9 per cent of those earning less than $6,000 (Tape 1, Table 3, Part I, 225). The residential tendencies described in this section might well be modified by any significant increase in the number of French-speaking residents at the middle- or upper-income levels.

E. Bilingualism

To what extent is the population of the capital of Canada bilingual? While the following chapters will attempt to answer this question in some detail and especially in relation to specific areas, this section is concerned to give a broad statistical measurement of the ability of the local population to speak the two official languages. The basic data on bilingualism may be related in turn to some of the characteristics analyzed in preceding sections; we can study the incidence of bilingualism as it relates to ethnic origin, to geographical and residential factors, and to the working world. This particular aspect of our inquiry is important because the bilingual population plays a vital role as a bridge between the two major linguistic communities, not only for the federal capital alone, but also to some degree for Canada at large.

In 1961, 30.8 per cent of the Ottawa metropolitan area population reported a knowledge of the two official languages. This is between two and three times the national average, the figure for Canada as a whole being 12.2 per cent. As may be seen in Table 1.25, the Ottawa area ranks second among the major metropolitan areas in Canada in its degree of bilingualism, following Montreal where the proportion of bilingual persons is 36.8 per cent. Among the other major metropolitan areas, Quebec City alone contains a substantial proportion of people knowing both French and English—24.3 per cent of the population. For the remainder, well under 10 per cent reported a knowledge of the two languages.[7]

Table 1.25. Percentage distribution of population, Canada and principal metropolitan areas (population of 200,000 or more), by official language, 1961

Region	Total	Official language			
		English only	French only	Both	Neither
Canada	100	67.4	19.1	12.2	1.3
Ottawa	100	55.0	13.2	30.8	1.0
Montreal	100	21.9	39.2	36.8	2.1
Toronto	100	92.6	0.2	4.3	2.9
Vancouver	100	94.9	0.2	3.9	1.0
Winnipeg	100	90.9	0.6	7.4	1.1
Hamilton	100	94.9	0.2	3.4	1.5
Quebec	100	1.4	74.1	24.3	0.2
Edmonton	100	93.7	0.3	5.1	0.9
Calgary	100	95.9	0.1	3.3	0.7

Source: Census of Canada, 1961; Catalogue 92-549.

As in most other parts of Canada, the overall level of bilingualism in the Ottawa metropolitan area is considerably higher for Canadians of French origin than for those of British origin. In the Ottawa area some 60.1 per cent of the population of French origin reported in 1961 they were bilingual as compared to 9.6 per cent of those of British origin. These percentages were more than twice as high as those for the country as a whole, the comparable figures for Canada being 30.0 and 4.0 per cent respectively. Clearly, while the French-origin population is considerably more bilingual than the British, both groups contribute to the higher-than-average level of bilingualism in the capital.

Knowledge of the two official languages among those of other than French or British origin in the Ottawa area is at a lower level than that for the population of French origin, but is generally higher than the British-origin figure. Some groups, such as those of German,

---

[7]Bilingualism can, of course, be measured in relation to other languages besides French and English, but Canadian census data are very incomplete in this respect. Nevertheless, some material is available with regard to those whose reported mother tongue is other than the two official languages. Thus, the population speaking English *or* French *plus* one other language (as indicated by the question on mother tongue) accounts for about 5.7 per cent of the population aged 15 years and over of the Ottawa metropolitan area; those who speak English *and* French *plus* another language (on the same basis) add another 1.0 per cent to this figure. The corresponding figures for the Canadian population at large are 11.0 and 0.7 per cent respectively. Actual bilingualism of this type may be much higher, for these are minimum levels revealed by the census. Thus while official bilingualism in the capital is well above the national average, the incidence of bilingualism with respect to other languages may be less widespread than in the country as a whole. Ottawa data: Tape 3, Table 5 (20-per-cent sample of population aged 15 years or over); Canada data: Tape 5, Table 1 (1-per-cent sample of all households).

Dutch, and Scandinavian backgrounds, are as low or lower than the British group in their level of official bilingualism. Others, such as those of Jewish, Italian, and other European origins, have perceptibly higher levels. However, even the most bilingual of the non-British, non-French groups falls far below the level of official bilingualism reported by those of French origin (*see* Table L, Appendix A).

The incidence of bilingualism also varies widely for individual municipalities in the metropolitan area. From a high of 54.4 per cent in Deschênes, the range extends to a low of 8.7 per cent in Nepean. Table 1.26 presents the detailed distribution. The percentages for Eastview and Hull, 52.4 and 49.1 per cent respectively, suggest they are among the most highly bilingual municipalities of their size in Canada (*see* Table L, Appendix A). While Ottawa has the second lowest percentage of bilingual persons among the municipalities of the area, it does have by far the largest absolute number as a result of its relative size. The proportion by provinces should also be noted: 26.5 per cent of the population on the Ontario side of the metropolitan area is bilingual, as against 45.8 per cent on the Quebec side.

Table 1.26. Percentage distribution of population, Ottawa metropolitan area, by official language, 1961

Municipality	Population		Official language			
	N	%	English only	French only	Both	Neither
Total M.A.	429,750	100	55.0	13.2	30.8	1.0
Ottawa	268,206	100	70.4	3.3	25.0	1.3
Eastview	24,555	100	32.0	14.5	52.4	1.1
Gloucester	18,301	100	54.5	12.2	32.8	0.5
Nepean	19,753	100	90.7	0.4	8.7	0.2
Rockcliffe Park	2,084	100	69.0	1.5	29.6	0.1
Total Ontario	332,899	100	67.9	4.5	26.5	1.2
Hull	56,929	100	5.6	44.7	49.1	0.6
Aylmer	6,286	100	34.3	17.6	48.0	0.1
Deschênes	2,090	100	25.0	20.3	54.4	0.3
Gatineau	13,022	100	8.1	52.7	39.1	0.1
Lucerne	5,762	100	45.7	14.5	39.6	0.2
Pointe-Gatineau	8,854	100	1.8	59.4	38.7	0.1
Templeton	2,965	100	8.1	52.7	39.1	0.1
West Templeton	943	100	31.9	40.0	28.0	0.1
Total Quebec	96,851	100	10.6	43.2	45.8	0.4

Source: Census of Canada, 1961; Catalogue 95-528.

City-wide averages tend to hide very wide variations from one census sector to another (*see* Table M, Appendix A). Within Ottawa itself the percentage of bilingual persons living in the various census tracts varies from a low of 7.8 per cent to a high of 68.8 per cent.

Map 1.6 shows the location of the sectors characterized by high and low levels of bilingualism. It will be noted that of the 17 sectors in the metropolitan area where over 50 per cent of the population is bilingual, seven are in Ottawa, six in Hull, and three in Eastview. As might be expected, there is a high correlation between the level of bilingualism and the number of persons of French mother tongue living in the sector. Of the 17 most bilingual sectors, 12 contain populations over 70 per cent French-speaking; of the 39 sectors where less than 25 per cent of the population is bilingual, 34 are over 70 per cent English-speaking. (A comparison between Map 1.4 and Map 1.6 illustrates the relationship between mother-tongue concentration and bilingualism.) A further inverse correlation exists between the income level of the sector and the extent of bilingualism. Sixteen of the 17 most bilingual tracts are among the lower 40 in terms of average income, while 30 of the 39 least bilingual sectors are among the upper 40.

It is also interesting to compare the rates of official bilingualism in the federal capital area between 1951 and 1961. Table 1.27 indicates the percentage of the total population speaking one or both or neither of the official languages in these years. The figures suggest that the level of bilingualism in the capital revealed by the 1961 census is not a development of recent years; indeed it has decreased slightly since the 1951 census. While the proportion of those speaking French only has not changed very much, the proportion of those speaking English only has increased very slightly, as has the relatively small group speaking neither official language. Because of the limitations of the 1951 data we cannot analyze these figures further. Presumably the declining percentage of those of French origin, the most bilingual element, and the influx of population from less bilingual areas are the major factors in the change.

Table 1.27. Percentage distribution of population, Ottawa metropolitan area, by official language, 1951 and 1961*

Official language		1951	1961
Total	N	281,908	429,750
	%	100	100
English only		53.2	55.0
French only		13.6	13.2
Both		33.0	30.8
Neither		0.2	1.0

Source: Censuses of Canada, 1951, I, Table 58; 1961, Catalogue 92-549.
* The 1941 figures are not available for the metropolitan area.

Bilingualism and the working world. A closer approximation to the language that will be used in the public life of the capital may be obtained from an examination of the degree of bilingualism to be found within the local labour force. Not only does this body exclude young children who have not yet learned to speak any language, but also such persons as students, housewives and pensioners whose role in the provision of goods and services to the public is marginal.

The total labour force in the capital is considerably more bilingual than the population as a whole (40.8 per cent as against 30.8 per cent) and, as may be seen in Table 1.28, the same holds true for those of French, British, and other origins considered separately. Clearly, the contribution of those of French origin to the bilingual labour force is a substantial one: in fact, in the labour force roughly four out of five of those who reported an ability to speak the two official languages are of French origin.

Table 1.28. Percentage of population officially bilingual by ethnic origin, Ottawa metropolitan area, total population and labour force, 1961

	Total	Ethnic origin		
		British	French	Others
Total population	30.8	9.6	60.1	13.6
Labour force	40.8	12.4	83.8	18.1

Sources: Census of Canada, 1961; Catalogue 95-528 (total population). Tape 3, Table 1 (labour force).

The main focus of our inquiry should be to establish whether bilingual persons currently play any special part in the working life of the capital. This involves two basic questions. First, are bilingual members of the labour force concentrated in special areas—by industry, occupation, or educational level? Second, is the pattern of remuneration of bilingual persons such as to encourage them to utilize their language skills in any special way in the economy of the region?

To consider the first question first, none of the statistical tabulations at our disposal enables us to study bilingualism by industry structure, but we can analyze the incidence of bilingualism by educational level and by occupational category. From the point of view of education, Table 1.29 shows the proportion of the bilingual population to the total labour force at each level of schooling, for those of French, British, and other origins. It will be noted that for the three groups taken side by side no very pronounced pattern emerges, except that for each origin those with some university education report significantly higher levels of bilingualism than the rest. But the differences in levels of bilingualism between groups remain far greater than differences between educational levels.

Table 1.29. Bilingual members of the labour force expressed as a percentage of the total in each category by ethnic origin and level of schooling,* Ottawa metropolitan area, 1961

Level of schooling	All origins	Origin		
		British	French	Others
All levels	40.8	12.4	83.8	18.1
Elementary	51.5	13.3	79.8	14.4
Secondary (1-2 years)	44.1	10.5	86.2	16.3
Secondary (3-5 years)	31.7	9.8	83.4	17.3
University (1 year or more)	37.6	20.0	91.6	27.8

Source: Tape 3, Table 8, Parts I and II.
*"No schooling" column omitted as the numbers are too small to be significant in a 20-per-cent sample.

More interesting, perhaps, is the distribution of bilingual persons by occupational category. Table 1.30 shows the percentage of bilingual persons in each occupational sector for those of French, British, and other origins. What stands out in this table is the relatively uniform distribution of bilingual persons across the whole occupational range, and the persistence of major differences by ethnic origin in every occupational group. It seems significant that managers and sales personnel of British origin, for example, are not significantly more bilingual than labourers of British origin, and neither group is strikingly different from the labour force of British origin as a whole. On the other hand, the labour force of French origin shows high levels of bilingualism in almost all occupational categories, dropping significantly only in the categories of labourers and workers in primary industry. Even the degree of bilingualism in these categories, however, is very high in relation to all occupational categories for those of non-French origin.

Table 1.30. Bilingual members of the labour force expressed as a percentage of the total in each category by ethnic origin and occupation group,* Ottawa metropolitan area, 1961

Occupation	All origins	Ethnic origin		
		British	French	Others
Total	40.8	12.4	83.8	18.1
Managerial	36.7	14.7	90.6	25.3
Professional and technical	33.4	14.2	86.9	24.5
Clerical	39.5	10.1	88.9	16.9
Sales	43.9	15.9	86.7	21.0
Service and recreation	37.2	11.1	77.0	14.4
Transport and communication	54.3	14.2	88.5	19.6
Other primary	33.3	15.6	64.9	14.4
Craftsmen	48.6	13.2	82.5	14.0
Labourers	50.3	15.3	72.7	12.3

Source: Tape 3, Table 8, Parts I and II.
* Excluding categories of "farmers" and "not stated."

Only in the column for those of non-French, non-British origins do the variations between occupation groups become very pronounced. Managers and professionals of other origins show roughly twice the proportion of bilingual persons as do labourers of other origins. But this may reflect, at least in part, an educational experience gained outside Canada, or it may reflect the ethnic diversity represented by the "other origins" column.

The pattern of remuneration for bilingual persons may best be studied by comparing their incomes with the incomes of unilingual persons having the same educational and occupational characteristics. This has been done in full in Table N, Appendix A for ethnic origin and educational level, and in Table O for ethnic origin and occupational category. A simpler way of presenting the relationship is to calculate the difference, positive or negative, between the average income of bilingual persons and of the *total* group having the same characteristics. It may then be said that bilingual persons enjoy a premium or suffer an income disadvantage when compared to the rest of the group, though we must be careful to state that this premium or penalty need not be a direct result of bilingual skills, but can arise rather from other factors not made clear by our data.

Table 1.31 shows these differences calculated by educational level, with differences in favour of bilingual persons as plus values and against them as negative ones. It will be seen that bilingual persons of French origin tend to earn a little more than the average for the whole group at every educational level, though the differences remain small because so large a percentage of those of French origin are in fact bilingual. Bilingual persons of British origin in 1961 tended to earn a little less than their unilingual counterparts, except for those with upper-level secondary education. For all levels together, however, bilingual persons of British origin earned more than unilingual persons because of their greater concentration at the upper educational level. Only for those of other origins do the income advantages of bilingual persons become very pronounced and, even for them, there is an exception for the group with two years or less of secondary education.

Table 1.31. Differences in average income between bilingual members of the labour force and total labour force for each level of schooling,* by ethnic origin, Ottawa metropolitan area, 1961

Level of schooling	All origins	Ethnic origin		
		British	French	Others
All levels	− $204.	+$324.	+$132.	+$711.
Elementary	+ 40.	− 290.	+ 151.	+ 452.
Secondary (1-2 years)	− 176.	− 12.	+ 64.	− 154.
Secondary (3-5 years)	− 122.	+ 158.	+ 42.	+ 678.
University (1 or more years)	− 183.	− 85.	+ 140.	+ 337.

Source: Tape 3, Table 8, Parts I and II.
* Excluding category of "no schooling."

The pattern of differences for each occupational category is more complex. Table 1.32 shows some income differences of considerable size in favour of bilingual persons, particularly at the managerial and professional levels for those of British and other origins. For French, British, and other origins alike all the differences are positive, and sometimes moderately large, in the managerial, professional, sales, and service and recreation categories, which suggests that bilingualism in these sectors may produce tangible monetary advantages. On the other hand, some negative values are encountered too, and the overall pattern for all occupations is somewhat mixed.

From the standpoint of the working world, then, the 1961 census data do not point very clearly towards any special role for bilingual persons in the life of the capital area. They are not notably concentrated in areas either of administrative responsibility or of public contact. Their income advantages tend, with a few exceptions, to be rather small, and sometimes even negative. In any case, bilingualism appears to play a smaller part in accounting for income differences than do factors such as sex, education, occupation, and ethnic origin. (See for example, the average income of bilingual persons of French and British origins in Tables N and O, Appendix A.)

Table 1.32. Differences in average income between bilingual members of the labour force and total labour force for each occupation group,* by ethnic origin, Ottawa metropolitan area, 1961

Occupation	All origins	Ethnic origin		
		British	French	Others
Managerial	− $223.	+$658.	+$ 51.	+$846.
Professional and technical	− 7.	+ 253.	+ 200.	+ 410.
Clerical	− 74.	− 22.	+ 21.	+ 30.
Sales	− 114.	+ 142.	+ 88.	+ 681.
Service and recreation	− 419.	+ 50.	+ 204.	+ 448.
Transport and communication	− 172.	− 600.	+ 63.	− 286.
Other primary	− 44.	− 333.	− 129.	+ 154.
Craftsmen	+ 17.	− 80.	+ 110.	+ 116.
Labourers	+ 98.	+ 387.	+ 51.	− 41.

Source: Tape 3, Table 8, Parts I and II.
* Excluding categories of "farmers" and "not stated."

On balance it must be concluded that bilingualism was not a major determinant of employment income in the Ottawa metropolitan area labour force at the time of the 1961 census. Rather it tended to be an accidental characteristic, seemingly irrelevant to most areas of the working world. This may simply mean that in the circumstances then prevailing the demand for bilingual persons in the labour market was less than the supply, so that language skills as such could command little or no premium. This is not to say, however, that this will be a permanent characteristic of the labour market of the capital. Both the place of bilingual persons in the occupational structure and their relative remuneration might alter significantly as a result of any major change in public policy with respect to language.

Summary. The population of the capital is at present one of the most highly bilingual in the country, and it has been so for some time. Those of French origin are considerably more bilingual than the population of British and other origins. This same pattern also holds true for the labour force, although the labour force as a whole has a higher level of knowledge of the two official languages than has the general population. What this means in practical terms is that the working population has language resources considerably superior to the Canadian average. The data on average incomes suggest that the demand for bilingualism in the capital has not yet created any significant pressure upon the supply of bilingual persons, and that language skills in the past have commanded no significant premium in the labour market. In terms of the existing labour force in the federal capital area, there may well be a considerably greater potential for serving the public in both languages than has yet been utilized.

Chapter II

The Provincial Framework

A. Introduction

We now turn to an examination of the governments active in the area. To talk of the National Capital Region or the Ottawa metropolitan area is perhaps to give a false sense of administrative unity to the capital area. It must be remembered that some 72 municipalities fall within the Region, 13 of them forming the metropolitan area; that two provinces exercise jurisdiction over it; and that the federal government plays a not inconsiderable role as well. The government and administration of the capital area are, then, extremely complex. In this chapter and the three that follow, we shall attempt to sort out the respective jurisdictions of the municipal, provincial, and federal authorities and to describe in some detail the language practices of each.

This chapter is concerned with the two provinces, Ontario and Quebec, whose influence in the capital area is pervasive. To some it might perhaps have seemed more logical to begin a study of government and inter-governmental relations in the capital with either the federal or local authorities, rather than with the provincial governments. Yet municipalities in Canada cannot be seen apart from the provinces in which they are situated, and also the circumstances peculiar to the Ottawa area require some prior consideration of the local municipalities if the federal role therein is to be appreciated. Thus the actualities of Canadian government and politics point toward a treatment of first the provincial factor, then the local administrations, and finally the federal government.

The basic delineation of provincial powers is provided by the British North America Act. Sections 92 and 93 of the Act need not be produced in full here, although, as we are primarily concerned with the influence of the provinces on the capital area, the articles having to do with local affairs may be noted. Section 93 relating to education clearly falls within this category, as do eight of the 16 subsections under section 92. These are:

92 (2): Direct taxation for provincial purposes
92 (7): Hospitals
92 (8): Municipal institutions

92 (9):   Licences for raising revenues for provincial, local, or municipal purposes
92 (10): Local works and undertakings
92 (13): Property and civil rights
92 (14): Administration of justice
92 (16): Generally, all local or private matters.

Not all of these areas are administered in the same way, for the province may choose to delegate some of its powers to another body. In Section B of this chapter, "Provincial Government and the Citizen," those areas administered by the province are studied. These include both provincial statutes which speak directly to the individual citizen and also programmes administered by the various government departments. Section C, "Provincial Government and the Municipalities," is concerned with the province and the bodies to which it delegates authority, the most important class of which are the municipal corporations.

Data for this study were gathered throughout 1966. Individual departments of the provincial governments served as a principal source of information. Most of the Ontario departments were reached, at their request, by means of a written questionnaire sent to Queen's Park. On the Quebec side, telephone interviews with the heads of local government offices were used.

Of the 13 local offices of the Ontario government in the capital area that we approached, 11 returned usable replies. These were Agriculture, Education, Health, the Hospital Services Commission, Highways, Labour, Lands and Forests, the Liquor Control Board, Public Welfare, Reform Institutions, and Transport. One department did not reply to the questionnaire; another had no contact with the local population and was excluded from the analysis for this reason. On the Quebec side, 12 local offices were identified and interviewed. These were Agriculture, Family and Social Welfare, Health, Highways, Industry and Commerce, Justice (Probation Service), Labour, Lands and Forests, the Liquor Commission, Revenue, Tourism, Hunting and Fishing, and Transport.

The various aspects of the Ontario Department of the Attorney-General are dealt with in Chapter VI of this study, "The Legal Systems," with the exception of the Ontario Provincial Police. This body and the Quebec Provincial Police are not included, as police functions within the metropolitan area are largely carried out by the municipal protective services.

B. Provincial Government and the Citizen

The practical consequences of living in Ontario or Quebec are for the most part very much the same. An important exception to this, however, lies in the area of provincial linguistic usage. A number of examples will be found, both in this chapter and elsewhere in the study, in which Quebec has used or permitted the use of both English and French, and Ontario, in contrast, has made provision for the English language alone. Because of this dichotomy, the relationship of the citizens of Ontario and Quebec with their respective governments will be considered separately. In both cases, we shall describe: a) the effect of provincial statutes on the citizen body, b) the practices of the provincial government departments at both the central and the local level, and c) the linguistic competence of the provincial public servants with whom the citizen has to deal.

1. Ontario

a) Effect of provincial statutes

A province in its general legislative role permits, requires, or prohibits activity by individuals in the province. Examples of this sort of provincial regulation are innumerable: mandatory returns of corporations and individuals; the form of a registrable conveyance of land or conditional sale contract; the claims of wives and widows against their husbands and their husbands' estates; the regulation of liquor consumption; the rights of parents concerning their children; family matters in general and especially divorce and separation; employment discrimination, fair employment practices, and minimum wages; and so on.

Several of these and other areas may be subject to some form of regulation as to the language of their conduct, although there is a wide variation from province to province in this respect. The matters that from time to time have been involved are outlined by C-A. Sheppard:

> The language in which the authorities must communicate with the citizens or advise the public at large; the language of the official forms and returns a citizen must submit to the authorities; the language in which certain products which are toxic or dangerous must be labelled; is frequently regulated by law. Even the linguistic aspects of a number of professional activities can lead to legislation: the language qualifications for admission to the practice of a given profession; the minimum knowledge of the current language needed for certain trades, particularly those, such as mining, requiring the observance of safety measures; and the language in which qualifying examinations can or must be passed. Even private papers—when their importance to society at large warrants it—can require linguistic regulation: for example, the documents, bills of lading, and notices issued by public carriers; labour contracts; and trade marks.[1]

In Ontario, however, the provincial government has taken few steps to legislate on linguistic practice. A few laws have required the use of the English language. For example, the Judicature Act, first passed in 1881, calls for all writs, pleadings, and proceedings in all Ontario courts to be in the English language, while the Mining Amendment Act, 1961-62, requires certain types of mineworkers to have a sufficient knowledge of English for their work. A degree of indirect recognition is accorded the French language in some statutes relating to education. The Ontario School Trustees' Council Act, 1960, states that the council shall consist of representatives of L'Association des commissaires des écoles bilingues d'Ontario, among others.

In a number of cases, while English is not specifically required, it is difficult to see how its use could be avoided. Thus some statutes specify the precise use of certain forms, samples of which are provided only in English. The use of both English and French is nowhere obligatory.

The statutes themselves are always published in English. Very recently some legislation has been translated into French, including the 1965 Act relating to the University of Ottawa. However, the French versions in these cases have no legal status.

---

[1] C.-A. Sheppard, "The Law of Languages in Canada" (study prepared for the Royal Commission on Bilingualism and Biculturalism, 1966).

b) Language practices

The degree of French-language service varies in the different regions of Ontario. At headquarters most departments are called upon to handle requests in languages other than English. The language called for, while most frequently French, is by no means invariably so, for Ontario is a linguistically diverse province. It should be stressed that the proportion of non-English communications with Queen's Park is very small indeed: most departments estimated that less than 1 per cent of letters received from the public were not in English.[2]

For provincial public servants in the province as a whole, 13.5 per cent use languages other than English in their work. However, if the public servants in the five south-eastern counties (Carleton, Glengarry, Prescott, Russell, and Stormont) are considered alone, this proportion jumps to 25.6 per cent (Bryan study). In the capital area itself there is a higher than average call for French-language service. Of the 11 decentralized offices in the area, six reported that over 15 per cent of their work was conducted in French.

More particularly, the Ottawa area offices estimated their use of the French language as follows. The Departments of Education and Transport stated that they used French whenever they were dealing with a Francophone. The Department of Health has three offices in the area: a tuberculosis clinic, an inspectorate under the stuffed articles and pesticides regulations, and a public health laboratory. French was not used at all in the latter two, but was employed 40 per cent of the time in the clinic. Lands and Forests reported that 30 per cent of its business was conducted in French. The Liquor Control Board stated that 25 per cent of the business in its stores was in French but only 1 per cent in its office. The Hospital Services Commission estimated that its bilingual clerk spends 25 per cent of his time working in French. (As there are five persons working in this department's Ottawa office, perhaps 5 per cent would be a better figure for comparative purposes.) Public Welfare gave an estimate of 15 per cent and Labour of less than 5 per cent. The latter department was seeking a bilingual person to replace an office manager who had left; it had found that the amount of business conducted in French increased with the number of Francophones on the staff. Reform Institutions felt that only 2 per cent of its business was in French: "The majority of people dealt with by the Ottawa office are English-speaking, but when other languages are required our staff are usually able to use interpreters."[3] Highways stated that French was rarely used while Agriculture simply reported that its contacts were primarily in English.

The Bryan study found that the occasions on which service in a language other than English is offered by the government of Ontario appear to be subject to wide variations from department to department. Although each department determines its own policy and practice with regard to linguistic usage, two general conclusions did emerge: "The concessions made to other languages by the Ontario Government are determined by the kind of contact involved—whether personal or written—and by the kind of person involved in the contact—whether the general public, business organizations, or other governments."

---

[2] N. Bryan, "Ethnic Participation and Language Use in the Public Service of Ontario" (study prepared for the Royal Commission on Bilingualism and Biculturalism, 1966).

[3] Unless otherwise specified, all quotations in this section are taken from the questionnaires completed by the departments.

In the province generally, members of the public are more likely to receive linguistic concessions than are business organizations or other governments. Moreover, for the general public, the use of languages other than English is more common in personal than in written contacts. Concerning written communication, some seven agencies reported that they answer a letter in the language in which it is sent; six regularly use other languages in addition to English in their public notices and advertising; five do the same for their publications; and one employs multilingual forms. Contacts with business organizations are almost entirely in English, whether oral or written. The same applies to communications between Ontario and the federal government and all the provinces but Quebec. In the case of the latter, Ontario departments sometimes use French in their replies.

For the local provincial offices in the capital area, the same general pattern can be seen, although it tends to be obscured by the diversity of practice from one department to another. The Liquor Control Board, the Hospital Services Commission and the Department of Education reported that their Ottawa offices offer service in both English and French over the telephone, in interviews, and also in written communications. The Liquor Control Board stated that on rare occasions it receives letters from a foreign country, "in which case the local Embassy is usually contacted for translation." The Hospital Services Commission noted that practically all its letters are sent to Toronto for handling, but even so all French letters are answered in French. Occasionally the Commission is called upon to deal with a person who can speak neither English nor French, although such persons usually have friends or neighbours who can telephone on their behalf or who will accompany them and provide interpretation.

Four offices—Public Welfare, Transport, Labour, and Reform Institutions—while answering their letters in English only, handled telephone calls or interviews in French as well. Public Welfare commented that it receives very few letters; and Labour remarked that a non-English letter coming into the office would be translated into English, either by the office staff or, if need be, by a translation bureau. This department also noted that its bilingual service depended on the presence of a bilingual staff member.

The Department of Health, it will be remembered, operates three offices in the region— a tuberculosis clinic, a public health laboratory, and an inspectorate under the stuffed articles and pesticides regulations. All three answer letters in English. In the first two the Department reported that telephone calls can be answered in French, although English is the preferred working language; the inspectors can only take calls in English. The clinic can conduct interviews in French; the other two request that interpreters accompany the non-Anglophone.

In the Department of Lands and Forests, practically all communications leaving the Ottawa office are in English. However, it was indicated that the bilingual staff member was employed in answering letters in French. The office of the Department of Agriculture initiates all communications in English. Nevertheless, in interviews, telephone calls, and correspondence French is used if the one bilingual stenographer is involved in the work.

The Department of Highways reported that its office uses English only in letters and over the telephone, and by preference in interviews.

To sum up, the Ottawa offices of the Department of Education, the Liquor Control Board, and the Hospital Services Commission would appear to make extensive provision for service in both French and English. In other departments the range of service available in the two languages varies from considerable to limited. All seem to be aware of some demand for French-language service, but few offer an equal range of service in the second language.

All 11 local offices distribute printed documents. Seven of them (Education, the Liquor Control Board, Reform Institutions, Lands and Forests, Transport, Agriculture, and Highways) had documents in English only. Of these, only Reform Institutions was aware of demands for non-English language documents coming from the Francophone population. According to the Department's statement, "such demands are infrequent and we encounter little difficulty in dealing with them in English." Such an attitude would seem to place administrative convenience above the preferences of the public being served.

The Department of Health reported that it translated locally only the documents relating to the tuberculosis clinic. It did not know whether there was any demand for non-English documents in relation to the public health laboratory, but the Department was aware of a "slight" demand by the French and Italian groups for documents in their languages relating to the clinic and inspection services. According to the Department: "The Ottawa offices have found that they can carry out their work satisfactorily using only English, as most French-speaking residents are bilingual; however the inspectors working under the Stuffed Articles and Pesticides regulations can see more need for pamphlets re pesticides being printed in Italian or German than French for the same reason as above." Again, administrative convenience appears to be the main criterion of language usage.

The Department of Public Welfare recognizes a "not too great" demand for non-English documents originating primarily with the French-language group. It does in fact make informational pamphlets available in French.

The Department of Labour and the Hospital Services Commission are perhaps the most language-conscious of all Ontario departments. The former publishes pamphlets in several languages besides English even though "there is no real pressure for non-English-language documents." The Hospital Services Commission has one combined literature folder available in 13 languages, and most of its other documents appear to be available at least in French in addition to English. The reason for this multilingualism was explained by the Commission: "There is no province-wide great public demand, although we hear mostly from French-speaking areas. Public demand played only a small part in motivating the production of non-English literature. We were concerned that the language barrier would not cause a resident to be vulnerable to hospital expense. A survey of 12 ethnic groups in the Province revealed that the greatest problems were amongst the Italian and Portuguese."

All 11 local agencies apart from the Department of Transport reported they were in contact with the federal government, although for the Departments of Education and Lands and Forests, this was an infrequent affair. Agriculture, Health, Highways, Labour, Lands and Forests, and Reform Institutions always used English in their contacts. The other four reported the use of both French and English.

Five local offices (Education, Health, Labour, Transport, and the Liquor Control Board) had no contacts with the Quebec government. Of the remaining six, only Public Welfare and Reform Institutions got in touch with Quebec once a month or more often. The Department of Public Welfare alone used English and French in both initiating and responding to contacts; the others used English on all occasions.

Four departments (Agriculture, Lands and Forests, Transport, and the Liquor Control Board) stated that their Ottawa offices had no contacts with French-language municipalities in Ontario, such as Eastview. Of the other seven agencies, Highways, Labour, and the Hospital Services Commission are in less than weekly contact with the municipalities. Four of the seven use English only in their communications (Health, Highways, Labour, and Reform Institutions). Public Welfare and Education use both English and French, while the Hospital Services Commission uses English "except where contact could be by telephone with our bilingual field clerk."

Only four offices stated they had contacts with French-language groups and institutions (Health, Public Welfare, Education, and Hospital Services Commission). The first uses only English in these contacts. The next two use both languages, while the Commission uses English except when the bilingual field clerk is available.

The internal language of work in the Ontario government is English. File systems are kept in this language in all but two departments. Agriculture files communications in their original language, and Education does the same with routine letters—provided that a note in English as to content is attached. Non-routine letters are first translated. Forms for civil servants to fill out are in English with the exception of the Department of Education's statistical returns required of inspectors of bilingual schools. All internal manuals and circulars are again available only in English. The language of work is English, apart from those officials in the Department of Education who deal with bilingual schools and French courses of study; they work in French.

c) Provincial public servants

According to Ontario government sources, the total number of public servants in the province (including provincial police) at the end of December 1965 was 43,141. They received an average income of $4978 and one-third worked in metropolitan Toronto. Some 690 public servants were located in the five south-eastern counties.

As may be seen in Table 2.1, the percentage distribution by mother tongue of those parts of the Ontario public service covered by the census and by the Bryan study does not accord with the general population figures. In 1961, those of English mother tongue in the public service of Ontario as a whole were over-represented in comparison with their place in the population; those of French and other mother tongues were correspondingly under-represented. The Bryan study found a similar pattern. In the south-eastern counties, public servants of French mother tongue form four times the percentage they do at the provincial level, although they still remain under-represented in relation to their population strength in the area.

Table 2.2 shows the knowledge of English and French revealed by the 1961 census for the Ontario public service as a whole. The vast majority of employees reported English as their sole official language: only about one in 12 claimed they could speak both English

Table 2.1. Percentage distribution of Ontario population, 1961, and provincial public servants, 1961 and 1966, by mother tongue

Mother tongue		Ontario			Five eastern counties	
		Population (1961)*	Public servants (1961)**	Public servants (1966)***	Population (1961)*	Public servants (1966)***
Total	N	6,236,092	21,647	24,897	478,134	690
	%	100	100	100	100	100
English		77.5	87.2	85.1	62.0	81.4
French		6.8	3.3	3.1	31.3	12.3
Others		15.6	9.6	11.8	6.6	6.2

Sources: * Census of Canada, 1961; Catalogue 92-549.
** Census of Canada, 1961; Tape 2, Table 1, 18 (tape based on a 100-per-cent sample).
*** Bryan, "Ethnic Participation and Language Use."

Table 2.2. Ontario public servants, mother tongue by official language, 1961

1. Numbers

Mother tongue	Total	Official language			
		English only	French only	Both	Neither
Total	21,647	19,815	39	1,777	16
English	18,868	17,980	–	888	–
French	711	–	39	672	–
Others	2,068	1,835	–	217	16

2. Percentages

Mother tongue	Total	Official language			
		English only	French only	Both	Neither
Total	100	91.5	0.2	8.2	0.1
English	100	95.3	–	4.7	–
French	100	–	5.5	94.5	–
Others	100	88.7	–	10.5	0.8

Source: Tape 2, Table 1, 18.

and French. This pattern is subject to wide variations when the mother-tongue factor is introduced. It will be seen that whereas roughly 19 of every 20 public servants of French mother tongue stated they were bilingual, the proportion for those of other mother tongues drops to one in 10, and falls still further to one in 20 for those of English mother tongue. Despite this low proportion, public servants of English mother tongue still provide the largest absolute number of bilingual persons, on account of their predominance within the Ontario public service.[4]

By combining the "English" and "Both" columns in Table 2.2, we find that an ability to use English, and presumably to serve the public in this language, is possessed by virtually all Ontario public servants. An indication of the relatively rare ability to give service in French is gained by combining the "French" and "Both" columns: only about one in 12 is able to do so. According to unpublished material prepared for the Bryan study, nearly one in six Ontario officials could give service in a language other than French or English.

In the Ottawa area, slightly over one-fifth of the provincial public servants were reported to be bilingual, a proportion somewhat lower than that for the population as a whole. (The population of the Ontario side of the metropolitan area was 26.5 per cent bilingual in 1961; for Carleton county the figure was 25.3 per cent—Census of Canada, 1961.) While the percentage of bilingual staff varied from office to office, in all but a single case at least one staff member was sufficiently bilingual to carry out his duties in both English and French. The composition and language skills of the staff in the local provincial offices are presented in detail below.

The Department of Highways employs locally 12 professionals, 35 administrators (two of whom are bilingual), 20 clerical staff, and 444 labourers, operators and others (of whom 55 are bilingual). The Department of Lands and Forests estimates that virtually all its Ottawa staff speak English only. The number of its staff is usually 62, although seasonally this may rise to a maximum of 350. In its Ottawa office there are four bilingual persons, while all three members of the office in Plantagenet—situated some 40 miles from Ottawa and outside the National Capital Region—can speak the two languages. According to the Department, several of its staff members are developing their bilingual skills. The Department of Health has a total staff of 39 in the area: seven professionals, two inspectors, eight in the clerical and 22 in the technical and maintenance categories. Of these, only one clerical employee and three in the last category are bilingual.

The Department of Labour has two professional employees out of 20 who are fully bilingual, while one of its four-member clerical staff "understands spoken French, but

---

[4] While the census question asks about ability to *speak* the second language, the results of the Bryan study indicated that public servants of English mother tongue could *read* French a little more frequently, but actually *speak* it less frequently, than the census figures suggest. For those of English and other mother tongues the percentages of respondents reporting language skills in French were as follows:

Mother tongue	Read French	Write French	Understand spoken French	Speak French
English	6.4	2.9	4.2	2.6
Other languages	11.8	4.6	10.1	6.2

For both groups the so-called passive language skills (reading and understanding) seem to be further developed than the more active ones (speaking and writing). (Unpublished material prepared for the Bryan study.)

does not speak it." Among the Hospital Services Commission staff, of one district supervisor, two field office clerks and two field service representatives, one of the clerks is bilingual. The Department of Transport has 39 administrative and clerical employees, of whom eight are bilingual. Among the Department of Agriculture's four employees, there is one bilingual stenographer. Working for Public Welfare are two persons in the professional category (one of whom is bilingual), one bilingual person as an administrator, three in the clerical class (two being bilingual), and 17 semi-professional welfare workers (of whom four are bilingual).

Of the employees with the Liquor Control Board, one of two administrative staff, none of the six clerical staff, seven of 21 in the managerial category, and 35 of the 80 store clerks are bilingual. Eighteen of Education's 45 inspectors are bilingual. Of the two district inspectors, the one dealing with East Ottawa is bilingual, while the other, who is concerned with West Ottawa, speaks English only. Three of the six clerical personnel are bilingual, including the telephonist and two of the four secretaries. The Department of Reform Institutions has one clerical employee and three rehabilitation officers. None of the four is bilingual, although two of the officers and the clerk have a limited grasp of French. These data for local offices in Ontario are summarized in Table 2.3.

Table 2.3. Language capabilities of Ontario public servants in the Ottawa area, 1966

Department	Total employees	Bilingual	Some knowledge of French	English only	
				Number	As % of total
Total	429	95	5	329	76.6
Highways*	67	2		65	97.0
Lands and Forests	62	4		58	93.5
Health	39	4		35	89.7
Labour	24	2	1	21	87.5
Hospital Services Commission	5	1		4	80.0
Transport	39	8		31	79.5
Agriculture	4	1		3	75.0
Public Welfare	23	8		15	65.2
Liquor Control Board	109	43		66	60.6
Education	53	22	1	30	56.6
Reform Institutions	4		3	1	25.0

Source: Questionnaires filled out by the provincial departments.
* Excluding the 444 labourers and others who would have little or no contact with the public.

Staffing policy. Some of the bilingual staff in Ottawa offices are there as a result of deliberate departmental policy; some are there for other reasons. Before looking at departmental practice in this respect three points might be noted. The official personnel policy of the Ontario government is to employ and promote staff on the basis of merit alone: ethnic, religious, political, or other comparable factors would not be considered as determinants of merit. Also, in no position (with the exception of a few in the Departments of Education and of the Provincial Secretary) is a knowledge of another language besides English a formal requirement. Finally, the province does not reward bilingualism financially (Bryan study).

On the other hand, the specific selection of linguistically gifted public servants would appear to be implied as a result of the recent statement made by the Provincial Secretary and Minister of Citizenship: "I accept as government policy of this administration that no person need ever be aggrieved, need ever be deprived of any right or of any privilege or anything which any one of his co-citizens is entitled to by reason of not being able to communicate in a language which will make him and his problem understood. Any such person appearing on the scene in any department of this government will have his wants attended to completely and fully" (Ontario Legislature, *Debates,* 1966, 3309). One may note that the Minister's statement places the burden of communication on the public and not on the public servants: only when the citizen has shown he cannot use English will the province make an effort to communicate with him in his own language. In other words, the effort and the uncertainties of using an unfamiliar language rest on the shoulders of the private citizen.

Notwithstanding the official personnel policy of selection by merit alone, examples of the deliberate placing or promotion of bilingual persons may be found.[5] The practice in this respect is erratic, as it varies not only from department to department, but also from branch to branch.

The Department of Agriculture permits its local offices to set their own policy as to the linguistic skills of candidates. The Ottawa office, as a result, has decided to employ a bilingual stenographer, who can do the necessary translation and interpretation. The Department of Health leaves its decentralized offices a similar option, although its Ottawa branches have not in fact decided on any policy. While the Liquor Control Board has a long-standing policy of placing bilingual personnel in appropriate parts of the province such as Ottawa, the lower level staff are recruited locally, store managers deciding what languages they need among their staffs. The Ottawa branches reported having no set policy.

The Department of Labour has a general policy of matching district officers to the language of the district. According to an interview with a departmental official in Toronto, Ottawa is something of a special case: in addition to Francophone personnel, there must also be staff acceptable to the Ottawa valley Irish community. Beyond this, it has a policy of preferring bilingual people if all other qualifications meet accepted standards.

The Department of Lands and Forests usually recruits local people who could, according to the Department, be expected to speak the local languages. All three employees in its Plantagenet office must be bilingual, and bilingual personnel were being sought for the Fitzroy Harbour office. The Department reported difficulties, however, in acquiring suitably qualified officials who were also competent in the two languages.

---

[5] Although not included in our study, it might be noted that the Ontario Provincial Police conducted a successful campaign in the fall of 1966 to attract bilingual recruits for service in eastern Ontario and elsewhere in the province, as it was felt they were "needed" in these areas. *The Globe and Mail,* December 6, 1966.

The Department of Public Welfare hires people locally when it can, stating in its advertisements a strong preference for bilingual recruits. As a general rule, it is departmental policy to place in its Ottawa office at least one bilingual person in each category of employment (professional, clerical, and others). One of the three stenographers must be bilingual.

The Department of Transport especially selects bilingual driver-examiners for 10 Ontario centres, one of which is Ottawa. The Ottawa office of the Department of Education must have bilingual inspectors for the bilingual schools in the area. It also ensures that its telephonist is bilingual. Reform Institutions has no policy with regard to the language skills of recruits. The policies of the Department of Highways and the Hospital Services Commission are somewhat ambiguous.[6]

Generally speaking, there does seem to be an awareness that a knowledge of French and other languages besides English is of value in certain positions in the Ontario public service, especially in the eastern and northern parts of the province. Before turning to a study of the situation in Quebec, a further substantiation of this point is in order. Asked whether they thought another language besides English would be useful in their work, fully 54 per cent of Ontario public servants answered affirmatively (Bryan study). Some 40.7 per cent specifically named French as the language which would be useful. Taking the south-eastern counties alone, 71.4 per cent considered another language would be useful, and practically all of these chose French. Clearly many Ontario public servants are aware of a greater need for the French language in their work than they can presently supply. Yet our study has found no current language-training programmes undertaken by the government of Ontario to meet these perceived demands.

2. *Quebec*

a) Effect of provincial statutes

By section 133 of the B.N.A. Act, provincial statutes in Quebec must be published in both English and French. In contrast to Ontario, Quebec legislation also frequently mentions language use. The following examples, taken from the Sheppard study ("The Law of Languages in Canada"), will give some idea of the range of activities subject to linguistic regulation by statute or subordinate legislation.

(1) By the Unclaimed Goods Act, notices in newspapers of the sale of unclaimed goods by launderers or dyers and fur merchants are to be published in both English and French.
(2) Article 1682c of the Civil Code reads: "The following shall be printed in French and in English: passenger tickets, baggage checks, way bills, bills of lading, printed telegraph

---

[6] Interviews in Toronto with representatives of these two agencies indicated the deliberate placing of bilingual staff in the Ottawa area. In their written answers to the question of whether or not there was a set policy of having bilingual people in certain positions in their Ottawa offices, the two gave negative replies.

forms, and contract forms, made, furnished or delivered by a railway, navigation, telegraph, telephone, transportation, express or electric power company, as well as all notices or regulations posted in its stations, carriages, boats, offices, factories or workshops."

(3) By the Election Act, enumerators are to wear a badge bearing the words "Enumérateur Québec Enumerator."

(4) The Fire Investigations Act demands that the Secretary of the Fire Commissioner of Montreal speak and write "the French and English languages correctly."

(5) The Medical Act provides that examiners assigned by the Provincial Medical Board to Laval University and the University of Montreal be French-speaking and those assigned to McGill University be English-speaking.

(6) The Act respecting the Board of Roman Catholic School Commissioners of Quebec states that the Board shall consist of seven members, one of whom is to be English-speaking.

(7) Examinations under the Veterinary Surgeons Act shall be in French and English.

(8) Ordinance No. 39 of 1962 (dealing with forest operations), made under the Minimum Wage Act, stipulates that: "The employer must take the necessary steps in French or English, according to the language of the employee concerned."

(9) The Quebec Companies Act lays down that: "If the company has a French and an English name, or a name consisting of a French and an English version, it may be legally designated by its French name or its French version thereof, or by its English name or the English version thereof, or by both names or both versions."

A recent example relating to the labelling of foods is the Order-in-Council, adopted March 15, 1967, providing that "the use of French is obligatory in all inscriptions [on all foods consumed by humans or animals, except alcoholic beverages] and inscriptions in another language must not take precedence over those in French" (quoted in *The Globe and Mail,* April 18, 1967). In addition, practically all official forms are in both languages and it is usual practice to permit them to be filled out in either French or English. Clearly language, in both the public and private spheres, has been a matter of concern to the Quebec legislature.

b) Language practices

For Quebec public servants as a whole, some 66.9 per cent use only French in their work, 32.0 per cent use both English and French, and 1.1 per cent use only English.[7] Taking as the general provincial average that roughly one-third of public servants are sometimes called upon to work in English, we find that eight of the 12 decentralized offices in the Hull area are above the average. As in Ontario, the local offices showed marked differences from one to another. This seems to be the result of the varying geographical areas and clienteles they serve.

The local offices of five departments (Tourism, Lands and Forests, Industry and Commerce, Highways, and Agriculture) felt that roughly half of the people coming to them

---

[7] G. Lapointe, "Essais sur la fonction publique québécoise" (study prepared for the Royal Commission on Bilingualism and Biculturalism, 1966).

were English-speaking. Tourism and Lands and Forests attributed this to the large influx of tourists from Ontario and the United States during the summer months. According to the Department of Industry and Commerce, its public consists mostly of company directors, many of whom are English-speaking. Also, as this department is seeking to attract new Canadian, American, and European plants to the area, the need for English is clear. The Department of Highways felt that, all in all, it uses the two languages equally, but it noted some geographical variations: English is the main language used in the county of Pontiac, the two are about equally employed in Gatineau county, while in Hull itself French is the dominant tongue. Lastly, the Department of Agriculture mentioned that it serves many English-speaking municipalities in the area, particularly in Pontiac county. The offices of the Departments of Transport and Revenue, and also the Liquor Commission all estimated that between 35 and 40 per cent of their contacts are with Anglophones.

Falling below the provincial average is the Family and Social Welfare office. Here the proportion of English-language contacts was down to between 15 and 20 per cent, but even this figure, the office felt, was unusually high on account of the inclusion of Gatineau and Pontiac counties within its jurisdiction. Three departments have relatively little contact with the English-speaking population. The Department of Health pointed out that the area it serves is made up of the municipalities along the Ottawa River (from Gatineau to Aylmer), which taken together are primarily French-speaking. The Department of Labour felt that, of the people seeking jobs at its employment office, only 1 per cent are Anglophones, while of the employers contacting them some 5 to 6 per cent are English. The probation service of the Department of Justice found only 5 per cent of its clientele to be English-speaking, although it estimated that some 10 per cent of the population of the area it serves speak English.

Table 2.4 shows that language use for the Quebec public service as a whole differs according to the kind of person with whom communication has been established. One Quebec public servant addressing another will almost invariably do so in French. Communications with municipalities and other such bodies are also conducted mainly in French. Next in the extent to which French is employed comes the general public, followed by business concerns and the federal government. Apparently French is used only rarely in contacts with other provincial governments, and this applies with particular emphasis to Ontario-Quebec relations. Table 2.4 also shows that written communications are slightly more likely to be in French than oral ones.

Variations from this general pattern occur among the departments. At the provincial level generally, in their external aspects at least, departments dealing largely with the general public, such as Revenue and Health, offer a completely bilingual service. Departments whose contacts with the general public are restricted do not necessarily feel themselves under the same obligation. Some will use only French when initiating communication with an individual or business (in replying to a letter, only the Civil Service Commission does not make it a rule to use the language of the correspondent). Calls for tenders by the Departments of Public Works and Highways in some cases will be published in French alone. These, however, are exceptions to the general rule that the public can

The Provincial Framework 55

expect service in either language from Quebec public servants.[8] The decentralized offices situated in the Hull area follow this general rule: every one of the 12 reported that service can be obtained in either French or English.

Table 2.4. Language usage of Quebec public servants, 1965

	1. External language usage					
Communications to:	Oral communication			Written communication		
	Mainly French	English and French	Mainly English	Mainly French	French and English	Mainly English
General public	78.6	20.2	1.2	79.6	18.5	1.8
Municipalities; school commissions; social and hospital services	90.0	8.6	1.4	90.3	7.8	1.8
Industrial and commercial enterprises	64.3	32.6	3.0	65.7	30.6	3.7
Federal government	63.8	25.0	11.2	61.0	27.0	12.0
Government of Ontario	12.4	19.6	68.0	16.5	17.8	65.7
Governments of other provinces	30.9	23.4	45.6	26.2	19.2	54.5
	2. Internal language usage					
Same department	96.0	3.1	0.9	96.9	2.1	1.0
Other departments	96.0	3.5	0.5	96.7	2.6	0.7

Source: Lapointe, "Essais sur la fonction publique québécoise."

Asked what was their policy and practice with regard to language usage in correspondence, telephone conversations and face-to-face interviews, nine local offices replied that they employ the language of the person being addressed. In initiating communications, the general practice seems to be to select the language according to the name of the person involved. These nine are the Departments of Agriculture, Health, Highways, Justice, Labour, Revenue, Tourism, Transport, and the Liquor Commission.

The Family and Social Welfare and Industry and Commerce offices make the first initiative in French, but switch to English if the respondent is of that tongue. In Lands and Forests the policy is to use French "except where this is impossible."

---

[8] J. LaRivière, "Le bilinguisme dans la fonction publique québécoise" (working paper prepared for the Royal Commission on Bilingualism and Biculturalism, 1965).

As for documents sent or given to the public, most appear to be available in the two languages. Where the French and English versions are printed separately, the language of the request or the name of the recipient determines which version is to be handed out.

There are some exceptions to this general practice. Written material for the Department of Labour comes from Quebec City and is in French only. However, the local staff translate where necessary. The Department of Agriculture's office expressed the opinion that not enough English-language documents are sent to the Hull region, which because of its strong English-speaking minority is something of a special case. To fill this gap, the office makes use of federal government and Ontario documents. Some of the material issued by the Department of Industry and Commerce is in French only.

Language use when communicating with the federal government varies considerably from office to office. Two (Highways and the Liquor Commission) are never in touch with Ottawa. Three report the use of French only (Health, Labour, Lands and Forests). The Justice office uses the language of the respondent. Those of the Departments of Industry and Commerce, Revenue, and Transport initiate communication in French, but switch language if the respondent is English-speaking. Unless they know they will be talking or writing to a French-speaking civil servant, Agriculture and Family and Social Welfare use English only. Tourism does business with the National Capital Commission and the federal Department of Forestry: in the former case it always uses French, in the latter, English.

Four offices have no dealings with the Ontario government (Highways, Industry and Commerce, Labour, and the Liquor Commission). Of those that do have such contacts, the Transport and Revenue offices use the language of the respondent. Agriculture, Health, and Justice employ English unless they know that the person being addressed is a Francophone. Lands and Forests uses English, lest the use of French result in misunderstanding. Tourism always makes the initiating communication to the Ontario Lands and Forests Department in French. The replies that come back are sometimes in French, sometimes in English. At one time Family and Social Welfare always used to write in English to the Ontario Workmen's Compensation Board; today it uses only French. The responses are sometimes in one language, sometimes in the other.

In their dealings with the English-language municipalities on the Quebec side of the National Capital Region, the local Quebec public servants generally use English. Agriculture, Family and Social Welfare, Highways, Labour, Lands and Forests, Revenue, and Transport offices reported they use the language of the respondent. Industry and Commerce uses the language of the municipality. It gave the example of Lucerne, whose population and municipal administration are half Anglophone, half Francophone. Thus in its contacts with the administration it would use one or the other language according to whom it was addressing. The Department of Health uses French unless the municipality is English-speaking, while Tourism only uses English when it is dealing with a municipal employee who does not speak French. Justice and the Liquor Commission stated they have no contacts with English-language municipalities.

Only seven offices mentioned language usage with respect to English-speaking groups and schools. Agriculture, Family and Social Welfare, Health, Justice, and the Liquor Commission use the language of the respondent. Tourism only employs English when it is dealing with unilingual persons, and Industry and Commerce, which is in contact with the Chambers of Commerce, reports the use of French only.

The use of languages other than English or French does not appear to reach any significant level in the Quebec public service. Asked if they thought such languages would be useful in their work, only 3.5 per cent of provincial servants concurred, as against 67.2 per cent who thought a knowledge of English would be useful (Lapointe study). None of the local offices in the Hull area mentioned the employment of other languages in documents and other official papers, as is done in the provincial offices in Ottawa. It will be recalled from Chapter I, however, that the percentage of those having neither French nor English as mother tongue on the Quebec side of the metropolitan area is only 1.6, compared to 8.1 on the Ontario side, and that the proportion unable to speak either French or English was only 0.4 per cent, as against 1.2 per cent in Ontario.

The internal language of the Quebec government is French. The card-indexes of files are all in this language except for the Department of Finance where they are bilingual. With the exception of this Department and Quebec Hydro, internal forms are in French only. Manuals and circulars are published exclusively in French (LaRivière study). As shown in Table 2.4, very few public servants make use of English in communications within the public service. In short, while the Quebec administration presents a bilingual aspect to the public, its internal language is almost exclusively French.

c) Provincial public servants

The Quebec public service employs some 47,000 persons, 24,000 of whom are under the Civil Service Commission. In 1965, the average income of the whole group was $4343. The previous year found 46.6 per cent working in the Quebec metropolitan area, 23.2 per cent in the Montreal metropolitan area, and 30.2 per cent elsewhere in the province. In the city of Hull the census showed 144 persons working for the provincial government in 1961, or 0.69 per cent of the total provincial public service. In 1941 there were 69 provincial servants in Hull; in 1951 there were 92. These formed 0.78 and 0.82 per cent respectively of the total Quebec administration.

From Table 2.5, we can see that both the English and the other non-French mother-tongue groups are under-represented in the public service in relation to their position in the population at large. The French mother-tongue group is correspondingly over-represented.

Table 2.5. Percentage distribution of Quebec population and provincial public servants by mother tongue, 1961

Mother tongue		Population*	Public servants**
Total	N	5,259,211	22,155
	%	100	100
French		81.2	95.9
English		13.3	3.4
Others		5.6	0.7

Sources: * Census of Canada, 1961; Catalogue 92-549.   ** Tape 2, Table 1, 15.

In Table 2.6, the distribution by official language of Quebec public servants is given. Contrasting with the largely unilingual Ontario public service, that of Quebec is extensively bilingual. Moreover, no one mother-tongue group provides a disproportionately high number of bilinguals, although it should perhaps be noted that the most highly bilingual group in the Quebec public service is of English mother tongue. Of course, as a reflection of their overwhelming numerical superiority in the public service as a whole, those of French mother tongue provide the bulk of the bilingual personnel.

Combining the "French" and "Both" columns in Table 2.6 to obtain an indicator of the ability to give service in French, we find that, as in Ontario, virtually all Quebec public servants can give service in the majority language of the administration—in this case, French. A combination of the "English" and "Both" columns shows that close to two-thirds can do so in English also.[9]

Provincial public servants employed in the Hull area were reported to be bilingual in greater proportions than the general provincial average. Although one cannot give precise figures, approximately 90 per cent were reported able to give service in the two languages. Again there were departmental variations in this pattern.

In the case of five offices, all the staff were stated to be fully bilingual. These are Labour (with three employees), the Liquor Commission (with an estimated staff of 41 in the area), Revenue (with two employees), Agriculture (with 10) and Industry (with two). In a further three, all but one of the staff were said to be fully bilingual, and this one person in each case does have some knowledge of the other language. These are the offices of the Departments of Justice (employing 11 persons), Family and Social Welfare (with 20) and Transport (with 12).

Twenty of the 22 employees in the Department of Health were reported able to give service in either language. Tourism has a staff of 17, one or two of whom were said not to be bilingual and the rest having varying degrees of proficiency in the two languages. Highways has a staff of approximately 200, of whom 150 are labourers not in contact with

---

[9] Some further detail on language skills of Quebec public servants may be found in the Lapointe study, which classified respondents as Francophone or Anglophone according to the language in which they filled out the questionnaire (rather than by reported mother tongue). It also attempted to grade each of the skills on a four-point scale: little or no difficulty, some difficulty, great difficulty, and no knowledge at all. If we take the two upper categories combined as representing sufficient ability to give service in both languages, the percentage of civil servants effectively bilingual in each skill is as follows:

	Reading	Writing	Understanding	Speaking
Francophones' capacity in English	83.1	74.3	77.1	72.8
Anglophones' capacity in French	90.2	74.0	86.1	81.8

It will be noted that by this definition the level of bilingualism is higher than the 1961 census figures indicate. As in Ontario (see 49, fn 4), the passive language skills of reading and understanding are stronger than the active skills of writing and speaking, though in this case only marginally so. (Source: Lapointe study.)

The Provincial Framework 59

the public. Of the remaining 50, 10 are in the administrative category and all, it was indicated, are bilingual. The other 40 are technicians, almost all of whom are also bilingual.

Table 2.6. Quebec public servants, mother tongue by official language, 1961

1. Numbers

Mother tongue	Total	Official language			
		English only	French only	Both	Neither
Total	22,196	229	8,270	13,685	12
English	757	205	–	552	–
French	21,265	–	8,243	13,022	–
Others	174	24	27	111	12

2. Percentages

Mother tongue	Total	Official language			
		English only	French only	Both	Neither
Total	100	1.0	37.3	61.7	0.1
English	100	27.1	–	72.9	–
French	100	–	38.8	61.2	–
Others	100	13.8	15.5	63.8	6.9

Source: Tape 2, Table 1, 15.

The local office of the Department of Lands and Forests services an area extending some 300 miles north of the Ottawa River, and employs a staff of 50 (60 in the summer). However, only 15 persons (20 in the summer) are concerned with the territory falling within the National Capital Region. Nine of these work in the Hull office. Most of the 15 employees were reported to be bilingual, at least to some extent, although the quality varies widely.

Clearly there is a high level of bilingualism among the staff of the provincial offices in the Hull area. However, with 49.1 per cent of the population of Hull reporting both French and English as their official languages in 1961, a question arises: to what extent is the large number of bilingual persons in the local offices the result of accident or design?

Staffing policy. For Quebec public servants as a whole, 38.1 per cent reported they were required to be bilingual for their present post. Among Anglophone officials the percentage who were required to have a knowledge of French was 69.5; among Francophone public servants 37.6 per cent were required to know English (Lapointe study). At the local level, there was again variation among the departmental offices in the Hull area.

In the case of five offices, bilingualism was stated to be a required qualification for employment. Agriculture, Revenue, Transport, and the Liquor Commission all fall within this category. The first of these noted it experiences some difficulty in recruiting suitably qualified bilingual personnel, pointing out that the province of Quebec does not offer any financial reward for bilingualism. The fifth office, Justice, requires a "sufficient" number, but not necessarily all, of its probation officers in each division to be bilingual.

Three offices—Tourism, Health, and Lands and Forests—do not attach very much importance to bilingual qualifications, although in the case of the last it is regarded as "useful."

In their attitude to language requirements, four offices fall between these two extremes. While there is no formal policy as such favouring bilingualism, a knowledge of the two languages is required in one way or another. Industry and Commerce said its employees had to be bilingual "because of necessity." Family and Social Welfare followed a similar pattern in that, all other conditions being equal, the bilingual candidate will be preferred to the unilingual one "because of the requirements of the job." This department also mentioned that it tests the candidate's knowledge of English. Highways, while stating that language requirements are not imposed on technicians and labourers "as they have little or nothing to do with the public," noted that for the administrative class a knowledge of the two languages is necessary. No problem had actually ever arisen, however, as no unilingual French-speaking person had hitherto presented himself as a candidate for an administrative post. Labour prefers to hire bilingual persons "because of the region."

However, the absence of a definite policy of bilingualism seems to have little effect on the language abilities of the departmental staffs. As noted previously, all offices in practice have a high percentage of their employees able to give service in the two languages. This seems to be the result of a recognition of the need for bilingualism in the area, and the highly bilingual population from which the locally-based employees are drawn.

3. Ontario and Quebec: comparison and evaluation

In their patterns of linguistic usage the provinces of Ontario and Quebec today are evidently fairly far apart. The main differences may be quickly recapitulated by way of a summary and comparison.

a) In provincial legislation Ontario rarely makes reference to language and makes no direct provision for bilingualism; Quebec has frequently legislated on linguistic matters and has required the use of the two languages.
b) Ontario statutes are published officially in English only; Quebec statutes are required to be published in both English and French.
c) In Ontario, 13.5 per cent of public servants sometimes use a language other than English in their work; in Quebec 33.1 per cent employ a language other than French.
d) A reasonably complete service in French as well as English is offered by three of the 11 Ontario offices in the federal capital area; in all 12 local Quebec offices service in English as well as French is virtually always available.
e) Although more printed material is available in the two languages in Quebec than in Ontario, neither province is fully bilingual in this respect.
f) The internal language of work is almost exclusively English in the Ontario administration and French in the Quebec administration.

g) Occasional use of languages other than French and English was recorded in the Ottawa offices, but not in the Hull ones.
h) Considerable variation in linguistic practice within each province may be found. Four distinct variables are: geographic location (service in areas where the population is linguistically heterogeneous is more bilingual than elsewhere in the province); departments (generally, socially-oriented departments such as Education seem more bilingual than technical ones like Highways); clientele (in Ontario, at least, the general public is more likely to receive bilingual service than are commercial enterprises); and the medium used (written communications are more likely to be in English in Ontario and French in Quebec than are oral communications).
i) In the federal capital area, roughly twice as many provincial servants are employed in the Ontario as in the Quebec sector.
j) In both the Ontario and the Quebec public services, the largest language group is over-represented in relation to its position in the provincial population. The smaller groups are under-represented. In other words, both public services are more strongly representative of the majority culture of their province than is the population as a whole.
k) In Ontario, 8.2 per cent of officials can understand both English and French; in Quebec 61.7 per cent can do so. In the Ottawa and Hull areas, the equivalent percentages are much higher, being roughly 22 and 90 per cent respectively.
l) Among Ontario officials, 40.7 per cent thought a knowledge of French would be useful in their work; some 67.2 per cent of Quebec officials thought English would be useful.
m) Bilingual staff is deliberately recruited in the capital area by both provinces, although in the case of Ontario such policies are rather sporadic.
n) Both provinces leave language policy in the federal capital substantially undefined. Most of the decisions in this area appear to be made by local officials according to the exigencies of their departmental working situations. This may well account for the extensive variations from department to department revealed by our inquiries.

The local offices in the Quebec sector of the capital area are clearly far better equipped to give service in the two languages than are those in the Ontario sector. Quebec public servants do not expect the English-speaking population to use French in communicating with them. One local official told of his surprise in encountering an Anglophone citizen who attempted to speak French to him. There seems to be a corresponding expectation (which is almost wholly satisfied) on the part of English-speaking persons in Quebec of being able to deal with the provincial government in their own language.

In Ontario, on the other hand, the assumption is that the Francophones can generally speak English, and that service in French is consequently more or less unnecessary. Although the Ontario government is far from the monolithically unilingual structure it is sometimes made out to be, the aspirations of Francophones to be served in their own language, notwithstanding their facility in English, have not been recognized by the province, either in principle or in practice. Rather, the province appears to look on service in another language as an exceptional practice, to be used only in cases of demonstrated need. The general impression given is that administrative efficiency tends to rank before public convenience as a determinant of language use in the Ontario administration.

It must be remembered, of course, that Ontario is under no constitutional obligation to provide administrative services in French, either in the federal capital area or elsewhere. However, apart from the requirement that its statutes be published in English as well as French, Quebec is constitutionally no further bound than is Ontario to provide administrative services in a second language.

C. Provincial Government and the Municipalities

In this section, the powers delegated by the provincial governments rather than those exercised directly are considered. The extent of delegation depends entirely on the provinces. It seems clear that a province may delegate, but not abdicate, any of the powers it possesses. This means that a province must be able to resume its jurisdiction over any area that has been given to another body to handle, and that in many cases it will retain for itself a general supervisory capacity.

The use of local institutions as agents to carry out provincially-determined programmes is fairly widespread. School boards, police commissions, planning boards, committees of adjustment, boards of health, hospital management boards and the like all fall within this category.

To some extent these bodies may be locally responsive, particularly when they are composed wholly or in part of locally elected or appointed persons. They enjoy greater freedom from provincial control than do the local offices of Ontario and Quebec government departments discussed in the preceding section. At the same time, such bodies must keep within the bounds of their powers and duties as delineated by the provinces.

Legislation governing the language of the regulations, notices, forms and returns of these bodies is essentially the same as that applying to municipal institutions and is examined below. Briefly, occasional requirements for bilingualism will be found in Quebec, while Ontario is silent on this matter.

The major institution that the province employs to carry out its objectives is, of course, the municipality. Numerous examples could be cited of obligatory functions imposed on municipal corporations by the provinces: maintenance of streets and bridges, the sharing of such costs as the upkeep of county court-houses and jails, the establishment of a police force. All these form part of the functions of a municipality.

Municipalities in Canada have no independent existence. Their creation, enlargement, boundaries, and forms of government are all dependent on provincial enactments. (Municipalities in the Northwest Territories and the Yukon form an exception in that they are subject to the ordinances of the territorial government instead of provincial law.) The very powers they exercise are those that the province chooses to delegate to them. Moreover, with the increasing complexity, costliness, and extent of government, the municipalities' dependence on the provinces is growing.

Yet it would be wrong to look on municipal government as being completely subservient to the provincial. Within the limits set by the provinces, municipalities do have considerable freedom of manoeuvre. This is necessary: the resources of the provincial apparatus are not such that the affairs of the province can be managed without extensive delegation. It is also desirable, for not only have municipal institutions been called, in the words of de Tocqueville, the strength of free nations, but also, more prosaically, it may be said that only they can provide the knowledge of local conditions that is essential to successful administration. Among these local conditions, the specific cultural and linguistic needs of the people are an important consideration, particularly in the federal capital, where the population served may include not only local residents but visitors from all over Canada.

General empowering acts. The major influence on the shape and powers of municipalities in both provinces is the general empowering act. In Ontario, there is the Municipal Act which covers all municipalities, although some of its provisions apply only to authorities of a certain size, while in Quebec there are two bodies of law, the Cities and Towns Act and the Municipal Code. The former applies to those local government areas containing 4,000 or more inhabitants whose authorities have made a special application to Quebec City to come under the Act rather than the Code. A quick summary of the contents of these three pieces of legislation will reveal the detailed control exercised by the provinces over municipal institutions.

The Ontario Municipal Act commences with a chapter bearing the self-explanatory title of "Formation, Erection, Alteration of Boundaries, and Dissolution of Municipalities, Etc." Next, the Act considers various aspects of municipal councils: their composition, qualifications for membership, vacancies thereon and rules of procedure for meetings. It goes on to deal with qualifications for voters and procedures to be followed at municipal elections. The duties of a Board of Control, which must be set up in all cities with a population of over 100,000, are outlined. The Act also provides for the officers of municipal corporations (for example, section 215 (1): "The Council shall appoint a clerk"); methods of passing by-laws; finances of municipalities; and the power to acquire land. The duties of local government in regard to police forces and administration of justice, and the maintenance of highways and bridges are specified.

By section 243, "Every council may pass such by-laws and make such regulations for the health, safety, morality and welfare of the inhabitants in matters not specifically provided for by this Act as may be deemed expedient and are not contrary to law, and for governing the proceedings of the council, the conduct of its members and the calling of meetings." The areas of municipal activity envisioned in this general clause are "the health, safety, morality and welfare of the inhabitants." The matters specifically provided for by the Act fall within these four categories. Filling some 30-odd sections and 96 pages, these areas are specified in a detailed fashion, and while extensive, they are rarely of great importance.[10] In short, Ontario municipalities are charged with the regulation of a host of minor, though undoubtedly necessary, functions which affect our daily lives.

Of the eight Quebec municipalities within the Ottawa metropolitan area, four (Aylmer, Hull, Gatineau, and Pointe-Gatineau) are subject to the provisions of the Cities and Towns Act. Deschênes, Lucerne, Templeton, and West Templeton fall under the Municipal Code.

The main difference between the Act and the Code is that the latter is adapted to the needs of smaller municipalities and rural communities. The Code's grant of power to pass

---

[10] Some of the areas covered by the Act are: drainage and floods; exhibitions; parks; fire matters; animals and birds; food and fuel; nuisances and signs; and markets. Such examples give a good idea of the local nature of the matters concerning which municipalities may pass by-laws.

by-laws to control the fencing of animals would be of little use to Hull, for example. While the structures of municipal government vary between the two, they are, on the whole, substantially the same. We shall, therefore, only look in detail at the Act.

Comparing the Quebec Cities and Towns Act and the Ontario Municipal Act, we find that both follow more or less the same pattern, although there are some variations. For example, only the Ontario Act provides for a board of control while provision for a municipal court is only made in the Quebec Act. If anything, the Quebec legislation is more detailed than its Ontario counterpart, especially in the provisions concerning municipal elections. The sections in the two Acts dealing with areas over which the city or town has powers to pass by-laws appear to be similar. One difference between the two is in the general clause which appears to be wider in Quebec: section 424(1) reads, "The council may make by-laws to secure the peace, order and good government, health, general welfare and improvement of the municipality, provided such by-laws are not contrary to the laws of Canada, or of this province, nor inconsistent with any special provision of this act or of the charter."

What does mark off the two Quebec pieces of legislation from the Ontario Act is the question of language. The latter is wholly silent on the matter, while the two Quebec laws make some detailed provisions. To take the Municipal Code first, some eight articles refer to the two languages. Article 15 provides that in case of conflict between the French and the English texts of the Code, "that version shall prevail which is most consistent with the provision of existing laws." Article 127 permits the use of both languages at council meetings. The following article stipulates that either French or English must be used for all documents deposited or filed in the office of the corporation. Article 129 states that, as a general rule, all public notices must be published in the two languages, while under article 339 "every special notice . . . must be given in the language of the person to whom it is addressed." Where the person addressed speaks neither English nor French, notice may be given in either language.

Exceptions to article 129 are provided for under article 130. The minister of Municipal Affairs is empowered to exempt municipalities from the rule of publication in the two languages. Until permission to use a single language is obtained, by-laws are only valid if published in both English and French. The minister may revoke any exemption. The general rule, then, is that all municipalities under the Code are officially bilingual, unless the minister, looking at each case individually, decides, presumably on the basis of the linguistic composition of the municipality's population, to make an exception. Of the four municipalities under the Code in the Ottawa metropolitan area, only Lucerne appears to have been authorized to publish in a sole language—English—although the municipality reports that it does in fact publish in both.[11]

The language provisions in the Cities and Towns Act are rather different from those in the Code. There is, for instance, nothing on the use of language at council meetings. Moreover, no section provides for the possibility of exemptions to be made by the minister of

---

[11] Information supplied by the municipality of Lucerne. When the municipality received its exemption in 1927 the population was predominantly Anglophone. By 1961, however, those of French mother tongue had grown to 45.1 per cent of the population.

Municipal Affairs from the linguistic provisions of the Act. Public notices must still be published in English and French (section 362). If a notice is provided in a newspaper rather than posted in a public place, this must be done by inserting the notice in both a French and an English paper circulating in the municipality (section 373). Documents, orders or proceedings of a council, the publication of which is required by law or by the council, as well as by-laws, follow the same procedure as outlined in section 362. The municipal courts provided for by the Act fall under section 133 of the B.N.A. Act.

In all three of these general empowering acts, certain forms, such as ballot papers, are prescribed. In the two Quebec laws an English and a French version are provided: in the Ontario Municipal Act they are given in English alone. The question arises in Ontario whether the use of French in addition to, or in substitution for, the English version would render a form invalid. An analogy may be found in the case of traffic signs erected by municipalities: there is still some disagreement, at least among Ottawa civic authorities, as to whether the use of French in addition to English on signs is legally acceptable in Ontario (see Appendix C).

Further, an opinion has been given in one legal study that "there does not appear to exist any legal impediment to any municipality anywhere in Canada, no matter how small its linguistic minority, which desires to use a minority language in the conduct of its affairs" (Sheppard study). This is to say that an Ontario municipality such as Ottawa, for instance, should find no legal impediment barring the way to the provision of bilingual services; and that, while the province can impose such a requirement on a municipality, the silence of the province in this matter does not preclude the municipality from acting on its own initiative.

Municipal charters. Language provisions may also be inserted into a city's charter. A charter is an act of a provincial legislature granting a city certain powers which, to the extent that they coincide with areas covered by the general empowering acts, such as the Cities and Towns Act, replace the latter. Where the charter is silent, the general acts apply.

The only municipality in the Ottawa metropolitan area that reported specific linguistic provisions in its charter is Hull. Granted in 1893, Hull's charter makes several references to the English and French languages. Some of these have been since amended; the sections quoted below take into account such amendments up to the year 1965.

In Hull, by-laws may, on the decision of the council, be translated into English, although in case of conflict between the two versions, the French text prevails (section 72). Until its amendment some years ago,[12] this section had required the translation of by-laws into English. By-laws enter into effect after publication of notices in French and English in a newspaper indicating their nature and object (section 76).

Public notices are given by means of an announcement in French and English inserted at least twice in a newspaper published within 25 miles of the city (section 401). Originally no language requirement was made in this respect.[13] Publication of any documents, orders, and proceedings of the council must be in accordance with section 401 (section 67). Three other sections dealing with the construction of roads, the provision of water, and the collection of taxes also call for a public notice (sections 144, 311, and 442b).

---

[12] S.Q. 1953-4, 2-3 Eliz. II, c. 68, s. 14.
[13] The 1893 provision was amended by S.Q. 1955-6, 4-5 Eliz. II, c. 73, s. 29.

Section 21 requires the publication of a notice concerning municipal elections in English and French. Sections 151d and 349 call for the publication in both languages in the *Quebec Official Gazette* of notices in respect to the city's ownership of roads and the sale of immovables for non-payment of taxes respectively.

Generally, the charter's linguistic provisions are similar to those in the Cities and Towns Act, although some differences may be found, notably in the publication requirements for by-laws. The role of municipal charters in adapting the general acts to the special requirements of an area is, however, worthy of notice.

Other means of provincial influence. Apart from the general empowering acts and charters, there are many other ways, both formal and informal, in which provinces bring their influence to bear on municipalities. Some of these may be mentioned, but only briefly, since their linguistic implications are less obvious than the provincial controls discussed previously.

Special provincial legislation may be passed, such as the Act Respecting the City of Ottawa, 1952. This law covered a number of points peculiar to Ottawa which the city could not handle without provincial enabling legislation. These points (questions arising from decisions of the Ontario Municipal Board, and powers to pass by-laws in regard to housing standards, the Ottawa Firemen's Superannuation Fund, and the exterior design of certain buildings) clearly show the detailed matters that are subject in the first instance to provincial control.

Many municipal by-laws require the approval of the provincial government before going into effect. In Ontario, for instance, by-laws relating to public health and traffic must be submitted to the provincial Departments of Health and Highways respectively. Municipal finances are also closely supervised provincially by means of audits, inspections and limitations on borrowing. The minister of Municipal Affairs may call for a commission of inquiry into municipal finance if he feels this to be necessary.

Provincial influence may be of a less formal nature. Persuasion, advice, assistance, training programmes for municipal employees, and the provision of such services as the crime laboratory of the Ontario Provincial Police, all play their part in provincial-municipal relations.

Perhaps the most fundamental of all provincial controls is the power to revise the whole structure of local government in a region. In Ontario the problems associated with growing urbanization and outworn municipal institutions have led the provincial government to pass under review several areas, including Ottawa, Kitchener-Waterloo, and the Lakehead. In the case of the Ottawa area, the provincial government established a special commission of inquiry, the Ottawa, Eastview, and Carleton County Local Government Review (the Jones Commission), to study the matter. The Commission's final report, published in June 1965, was followed in February 1967 by a preliminary proposal from the provincial government for a metropolitan system of government that would more or less comprise the Ontario portion of the National Capital Region. This proposal would transfer certain municipal powers presently exercised individually by the city of Ottawa and 16 other Ontario municipalities to a "super-council" responsible for the whole of the Ontario sector.

To sum up this section, Ontario has no provisions requiring municipalities to use the two languages. But neither has it formally barred any municipal authority from doing so at local option. Quebec legislation, on the other hand, contains certain explicit requirements as to language use covering a fairly extensive range of municipal activities and situations. These too seem to constitute a minimum legal requirement, to be enlarged by any municipality which sees fit to do so.

Looking at provincial-municipal affairs from a more general point of view, we find a rather complex relationship between the two governments. Together they form a partnership and, while there can be no doubt as to who is the senior partner, it would be wrong to think of them as master and servant. For reasons of flexibility and efficiency, the municipality performs not only necessary but vital functions that the province could not easily undertake itself. In short, while a municipality outside of the provincial framework would be inconceivable under the present arrangement of government in Canada, a province the size of Ontario or Quebec without municipal authorities to assist it would be equally improbable. The two need and complement each other. (In the case of the Northwest Territories and the Yukon, the territorial government provides the framework.) In the two following chapters we shall look more closely at the manner in which municipalities in the capital area operate within the framework provided by the provinces of Quebec and Ontario.

D. Summary

The influence of the provincial governments of Ontario and Quebec in the federal capital area is very extensive. The schools to which a resident sends his children, the local government institutions which play so large a part in his daily life, the courts before which he is called to appear, all bear the imprint of one province or the other. To the citizen, the province means taxes, laws, and bothersome regulations; he may also sometimes recognize it as a valuable source of services and advice.

From another point of view, one may ask how the people of the federal capital area are viewed by the provincial administrations in Toronto and Quebec City. The answer to this would seem to be that they are seen and treated in the same way as the other millions of provincial inhabitants. That the area is the seat of the federal government has made no discernible impact on provincial practice. To a certain extent, the linguistic dualism of the region has required special administrative provisions, but the adjustments have been limited, practical, and pragmatic, particularly in Ontario. It would appear that in the first hundred years of Confederation no significant consideration has been given by either province to the peculiar linguistic and cultural needs of the Ottawa area in its role as the capital of Canada.

Chapter III   Municipal Administration: Ottawa

A. Introduction

In this and the next chapter we are concerned with two major areas: first, the language practices of the municipal administrations in the Ottawa metropolitan area, particularly the language of service to the public; and second, the composition and language skills of civic staff members. Our interest in the second question stems primarily from its relevance to the first: if the public is to be served in French and English, as a matter of policy, the civic staff must clearly be competent to do so. But this consideration leads to others. If a municipality is to provide services in both languages, it must recruit bilingual personnel in sufficient numbers; it must utilize them appropriately in positions of public contact; yet if able bilingual personnel are to be attracted and retained, it must also offer them full opportunities for advancement and career development. Failing this, it will risk grave deficiencies in the quality of service that it can provide in the second language. We mention these ramifications in passing simply to indicate that the question of providing effective bilingual municipal services at once involves complex problems of public administration.

Because of the complexity and variety of the existing structures, each of the major municipalities will be described separately. In this chapter the city of Ottawa only will be examined. Though its size alone entitles it to priority status, there is also its significance on the national level: in the minds of many, "city of Ottawa" and "capital of Canada" appear to be synonymous terms. Further, the attitudes encountered during the study of Ottawa were quite distinct from those met in the other municipalities of the area.

In the data-gathering phase of the study, several research methods were attempted. Some of these ran into difficulties which reduced their value. For an accurate understanding of the description of the Ottawa administration that follows, it seems important to list and describe these various research approaches so as to indicate both their validity and their limitations.

Interviews and personnel records. When the Commission first formally approached the three core cities of Ottawa, Hull and Eastview[1] in February 1965, it was anticipated that an analysis of personnel records, along with a series of face-to-face interviews with selected municipal employees would yield sufficient data to present an adequate picture of the language practices and composition of the three administrations. Although this assumption was largely justified in the case of Hull and Eastview, the request to study Ottawa by means of these methods encountered a number of obstacles. While the mayor at first agreed orally to the research proposal, the two senior civic officials to whom he referred the matter insisted on a formal authorization from Board of Control before proceeding further. Accordingly, on March 8, 1965, the research staff sent the city clerk, at his request, a short written description of the proposed study. The project was debated by Board of Control on March 9, challenged as to its legality in the House of Commons and before the Ontario Human Rights Commission, and referred to City Council for consideration. From City Council it was referred back to Board of Control (which then requested from the Commission a "completely itemized report" on the study); referred again from Board to Council with a narrowly restrictive Board recommendation; approved by Council on April 5, with the Board's restriction removed; moved immediately for reconsideration at the next Council meeting by a member of Board of Control; and finally authorized by Council at its meeting of April 20—some seven weeks after the initial request (*see* documentation in Appendix D).

As amended by Council, the authorization permitted the Commission's staff to confer with the city clerk, the director of personnel, and any elected representative and employee who agreed to be interviewed. No explicit reference was made to the Commission's request for access to personnel data. However, it soon became apparent that Commission staff would not be allowed to examine any civic personnel records. In spite of Council's general authorization and the Commission's guarantee that confidential information would be treated as such, the director of personnel maintained that permitting any access to his files would violate his professional responsibilities.[2]

Checklists of salaried employees. As a result, the research staff was faced with the prospect of conducting a study without a firm or up-to-date documentary basis. To overcome this difficulty, checklists—based on a personnel list supplied by the city—of all salaried municipal employees were developed. These lists, intended for completion by civic departments, were designed to provide basic information on each employee's mother tongue, knowledge of French, English, and other languages, job classification, and frequency of contact with the public. The lists were aimed at the salaried categories only—about 1,000 persons or 28 per cent of the city's total labour force of approximately 3,700—because it was felt that the salaried group was responsible for most of the significant areas of verbal contact with the public.

---

[1] Copies of the relevant correspondence and documentation are included as Appendix D.

[2] The Commission's experience with the administrations of other cities was quite different. In neither Winnipeg nor Montreal, where similar studies were carried out, were any problems encountered concerning access to personnel records.

During the summer of 1965 we proceeded on the basis of checklists and interviews. In both these techniques certain difficulties were encountered, and the results, while useful in a preliminary way, were simply not adequate even in combination. Although the majority of civic departments supplied all the information requested, a few returned incomplete or carelessly filled out lists. One question on the list proved somewhat ambiguous in its wording, and the heads of two small but strategically placed departments—those of the City Clerk and of Secretary to Board of Control—refused any employee data at all. These gaps left the overall picture somewhat vague. Moreover, the checklists were designed primarily to yield data on the city's capacity to provide service to the public in both English and French. To this end, most of the data obtained dealt with the employee's degree of public contact and his language skills. No attempt was made through the checklists to determine the present level of demand for bilingual services, employee attitudes, or the language of work within the administration, on the assumption that these areas would be dealt with adequately in the interviews.

However, the interviews held at this stage with 29 senior civic officials yielded a picture lacking a solid documentary basis and marred by inconsistencies. The prolonged and often acrimonious public debate that preceded the authorization to conduct the study may have generated an atmosphere that created mistrust and inhibited open discussion. In any case, there were marked divergences among various respondents, particularly between Francophones and Anglophones, on such basic questions as whether the city does in fact offer adequate service to the public in French, and whether French-speaking employees at City Hall have career opportunities comparable with those open to Anglophones. Of the 30 senior officials approached during this phase, only one refused to be interviewed.

A written questionnaire. Since the first techniques had proved insufficient, the Commission decided in the autumn of 1965 to gather more precise data by means of a comprehensive questionnaire. In this way we hoped to obtain a more exact and reliable picture of the city administration in all its relevant aspects—including language capabilities of employees; current language policies and practices; public demand for service in French, English, and other languages; representation of language groups at various levels within the civic administration; career patterns, remuneration, and educational levels; and finally employee attitudes towards language questions.[3]

During the winter of 1965-66, the questionnaire was designed and pre-tested, the trained personnel for its administration and interpretation were assembled, and approval of the final text was obtained from the associations of civic employees. In the later stages close liaison was maintained with the city's director of personnel, and indeed several changes in the instrument were introduced at his suggestion. He approved the final version of the text but felt that he could not personally authorize its administration.

Accordingly, on April 25, 1966, the Commission once again wrote Board of Control to make the text of the questionnaire available to them and to request permission to

---

[3] The Commission made no firm decision as to the need for a questionnaire until the late summer of 1965, though Board of Control requested a copy of any questionnaire that might be proposed as early as April 14 (*see* Appendix D).

administer it on May 10. For six weeks no reply was received. Finally, after a further letter from the Commission, the Board wrote on June 9, refusing permission. This was the only instance among the 35 major surveys conducted during the Commission's research programme in which permission to administer a questionnaire was denied.

The rejection of the questionnaire represented a major setback to the research staff, who then had to look for alternative methods of inquiry. On June 29 the Commission proposed to Board of Control a meeting to discuss possible alternatives, putting forward as one suggestion the preparation of a programmed computer print-out of certain personnel data that might be available in the Personnel Department. However, the Board rejected this idea on July 18, and even ruled out a meeting to discuss any other research methods until the alternatives were spelled out. At this stage an attempt was made to add precision to the study by interviewing a slightly wider range of civic employees, but this was abandoned owing to the high proportion of refusals encountered.

Samples of documentation. In the meantime, before matters had reached this impasse, the research staff had asked the heads of 18 municipal departments and agencies for examples of the printed forms normally used both within the administration and in dealing with the public. This, it was felt, would give some insight into the language or languages of the administration's printed documentation. Eight agencies replied, though the director of one of them called the next day to request the return of his submission unopened. Ten did not reply. Once again the data clarified the practice of some departments, while leaving the overall picture somewhat nebulous.

A telephone survey. At this point we had very little precise evidence on oral language usage. We therefore decided to explore this question by means of a small telephone survey, which would pose in French to the appropriate departments a series of questions such as might normally be asked by members of the public in dealing with the city.[4] Since the capacity of the city to give service in English has never been questioned, the purpose was to test the availability and quality of services that could be provided in French. In all, 50 calls were directed in French[5] to the city administration by several members of the Commission staff over a period of approximately four months. Although the sample was small, questions were carefully selected so as to involve a wide range of departments and agencies giving service to the public and, indeed, every civic department was contacted at least once.

Limited though it was, the telephone survey provided some useful data and general insights into the oral capacities and language attitudes of civic employees. While the sample was too small to give a reliable picture of any single department, the aggregate result for the city as a whole is probably accurate.

---

[4] Sample questions: When are the next municipal elections? At what hours is Laurier House open to the public? Where can one obtain inoculations? What are the taxes on a certain house? When will the work on a certain street be completed?

[5] Early in the survey it was found that several departments were being effectively shielded from calls in French by unilingual English-speaking telephone operators at the city's central switchboard. In such cases interviewers were instructed to use enough English to get past the switchboard and then revert to French.

Census data, 1961. Finally, the Commission had arranged, at the beginning of its research programme, to obtain special tabulations of data from the Dominion Bureau of Statistics, based upon the 1961 Census of Canada. Among the groups so selected for close study were employees of the federal and provincial governments, and also municipal employees in selected municipalities. Thus, for a 100-per-cent sample of municipal employees resident in Ottawa in 1961, and similarly for Hull, the research staff had tabulations relating to ethnic origin, mother tongue, official language, age, sex, education, income, occupational category, and other characteristics. Although these figures refer to 1961, they acquired added importance from the fact that more up-to-date information on Ottawa could not be obtained directly from the city.[6]

For Hull the figures proved less valuable. This was principally because the very high proportion of employees of French origin (96.5 per cent) and the extremely small number who listed English as their mother tongue made intergroup comparisons of very doubtful validity.

All in all, some seven different research phases were employed in assembling the following picture of the Ottawa municipal administration. Virtually all revealed certain limitations and imperfections as the study proceeded. While we tried to be as thorough and as resourceful as possible, there is no doubt that a more detailed and perhaps a more convincing picture could have been produced if a greater degree of co-operation had been forthcoming from Board of Control and senior civic officials. This was the only part of the study that met substantial resistance to the very idea of examining the present language situation in the capital area. However, one approach corroborates another and, even if incomplete on points of detail, the picture of Ottawa that emerges is, we believe, broadly accurate.

B. *Language of Service to the Public*

As might be expected in a city where approximately seven out of every 10 residents have English as their mother tongue, the bulk of civic business involving members of the Ottawa public is conducted in English. Communication in English may be called the norm; in a formal sense it is also the language of work within the Ottawa municipal administration. The chief task of this section is, therefore, to delineate the degree to which services are equally available in French. Since the area to be treated is rather large, a distinction is drawn between oral usage, which involves direct, interpersonal contact, and written usage, in which an intermediary stage—be it a letter, form, circular or some

---

[6] These data refer to employees of municipal governments who *resided* in Ottawa at the time of the census, but in fact the city has required its employees to reside within the city limits since May 1931. Certain other area municipalities have the same requirement; others are too small to affect the Ottawa picture. One can, therefore, count on a fairly high correlation between municipal employees *resident* in Ottawa and those *employed* by the city. It should also be noted that to preserve the anonymity of individuals, tabulations were programmed by the Dominion Bureau of Statistics so as to suppress any line where the total represented one person only. Consequently totals vary slightly from table to table.

other document—is inherent in the communication process. It might be noted at once that there is considerable variation in language usage from agency to agency. What follows represents the general pattern. For a more detailed look at certain agencies which are especially important from the standpoint of public contact, *see* Appendix E.

According to the interviews with department and branch heads, a very low percentage of civic business is conducted in French. Only six of the 29 persons interviewed maintained that French-language transactions comprised more than 15 per cent of their total business with the public. At first glance this appears rather surprising, in view of the proportional size of Ottawa's French-speaking community, but there was general agreement that the current demand for services in French is relatively low.

Oral usage. Oral communications between civic employees and members of the general public occur both in face-to-face situations and by telephone. Unfortunately, little can be said with any accuracy concerning face-to-face contacts. This was one of the areas which the questionnaire refused by Board of Control was designed to elucidate.

In the field of telephone contacts, more specific information is available. First, the main listing of municipal agencies in the 1965, 1966, and 1967 telephone directories appears only in English[7] under the heading "City Hall Corp. of Ottawa." Thus at least a minimal knowledge of English appears to be required before a correct contact can be made.

Second, of the 29 civic officials interviewed, 26 reported that their agencies were identified by the person answering the call in English only. Two others failed to reply to the question, while one reported that a bilingual salutation was sometimes used.

The results yielded by the telephone survey were largely similar. Of the 50 calls placed, 47, including those made through the central switchboard, met with an initial response in English only. In one instance the telephone surveyor did not record the response; in another, the language of response could not be identified; while in the one remaining case a French-language salutation was employed. No bilingual responses were encountered. Thus, in the two stages preceding the actual request for service—the individual's location of the relevant agency in the telephone directory, and the city's initial response—English is employed almost exclusively.

Once the actual communication begins, however, the use of French rises considerably, though not as much as the interview results had led us to expect. In 26 of the interviews, it was reported that either telephone operators were bilingual or French-language calls were directed to bilingual employees. Two respondents failed to reply to this question; only one said that the operator in his agency asks the caller to speak English. As the agencies of two of these last three respondents were not included in the telephone survey and the department of the third was called only once, it is clear that the interview responses point to a distinctly higher number of successful calls than the survey, conducted about a year later, in fact obtained.

In Table 3.1 the overall results of the telephone survey are presented. There are several points concerning this table which require explanation. French language service, in

---

[7] The main Hull listings are in French only, while under the heading "Eastview, ville de" the departmental listings are bilingual. All three cities have a cross-listing in the other language. Thus Ottawa has "Ottawa Cité de — see City Hall."

one form or another, was available in some 34 cases, or 68 per cent of the total. However, had we rigidly adhered to our original assumption—that we were unilingual members of the French-speaking public—and employed no English at all, this figure would have been considerably lower. Because of the presence of telephone operators speaking English only on the city's central switchboard, the telephone surveyors were obliged on seven occasions to employ a few words of English in order to reach the agencies thus "curtained off." Had the above figures been calculated taking this phenomenon into account, the proportion of calls in which some form of French-language service was obtained would have been 54 per cent, instead of 68 per cent.

Table 3.1. Availability of Ottawa municipal services in French, 1966

Total (N=50)	100 %
Service available immediately	20
Service available though involving a marginal delay	22
Service available but only after insistence	16
Service available but involving major delays or linguistic difficulties	10
Service unavailable	32

Source: Telephone survey.

Although some form of French-language service was obtained in approximately two of every three calls, an important qualitative reservation must be stated. If the criterion of adequate service in French is the citizen's ability to use French as a full and real alternative to English without substantial delay or less expert service, only those calls in the first two categories of the table so qualify. That is, in only 42 per cent of the calls could the services rendered in French be considered adequate.

In 13 of the calls made, or 26 per cent of the total, the quality of service in French was distinctly inferior to that available to the English-speaking caller. In some instances the employee attempted to persuade the caller to speak English, thus occasioning a definite time loss; in others the information was given in garbled form because the employee's facility in French was inadequate; while in a few cases there were delays of up to five minutes because a French-speaking employee was not immediately available.

Despite the absence of French from the telephone directory and from the salutations employed by receptionists, it is fair to say that the ability of the civic administration to provide adequate telephone service in French, once contact is made with the relevant agency, is perhaps greater than many members of the public might suspect. But in about six of every 10 telephone calls placed, the research team was unable to obtain service in French equivalent to that available in English. There is one further consideration. The telephone survey consisted of simple, direct questions, such as could be answered by most employees in the department concerned. Whether the same ratio of success would be maintained if the questions were more complex or technical is difficult to say.

Written usage. In order to present the data in as thorough a manner as possible, three different types of written usage will be analyzed: correspondence, information distributed through the mass media, and public forms. The first of these, correspondence, differs quite markedly from the other two to the extent that the role of the administration may often be a passive one from a linguistic standpoint. Frequently the citizen, rather than the city, initiates the contact.

According to the interviews, the proportion of French-language correspondence received by the city is quite low. Of the 29 departmental and branch spokesmen interviewed, four reported receiving letters in French every day or almost every day, and two suggested that this occurred about once a week. Of the remaining 23 spokesmen, three reported that their agencies received letters in French only once a month, 19 maintained they were contacted in French "very rarely," and one said his agency never received French-language communications. Despite the low proportion of letters received, some municipal agencies appear to have reasonably well-developed techniques to handle French-language correspondence. Thus 11 of the 29 agencies, including two of the four reporting daily contact, maintained that letters in French were handled completely in French. Seven, including one with daily and another with weekly contact, reported that letters were translated internally but did not specify whether or not a French-language reply was sent. Seven other agencies did not respond or maintained that the procedure varied with circumstances. Four agencies, including one reporting daily reception of French correspondence, stated that they replied to French-language letters in English.

Information distributed through the mass media, the second type of written usage, is generally handled in the following manner. Announcements to be made are either submitted to, or originate in, the City Clerk's office, in English. Representatives of both the French- and English-language newspapers, television or radio stations are then informed, and it is left to the French-language media to make the necessary translation. Thus, when the announcements reach the public they are generally available in either language, but this is due rather to the presence in Ottawa of well-developed French-language media than to City Hall policy. The spokesmen of six agencies, however, reported that at least some translation was done by their own staff.

With respect to printed matter distributed by the city, such as public forms, notices and promotional material, the extent of the administration's bilingualism is open to rather serious doubt. Some 14 of the 29 agencies reported that 5 per cent or more of their business with the public was conducted in French. Of these 14, only six reported that they employed bilingual forms or forms available separately in French and English. The forms of seven other agencies appear to be available only in English. The remaining case, that of the Tax and Water Revenue Branch of the Treasury Department, is rather interesting. When the interview was carried out in 1965, this agency reported that forms were printed in English only but that prior to 1958 bills had been printed in both French and English. French was dropped, the agency said, because the adoption of I.B.M. cards for billing left insufficient space for both languages. In June 1966 City Council passed a resolution approving bilingual city tax and water bills, to take effect in 1967. This has now been implemented, space for French having been found on the same size of data processing cards as used previously.[8]

---

[8] The Ottawa Hydro-Electric Commission has used bilingual data processing cards for its electricity accounts for several years.

Of the remaining 15 agencies surveyed, five reported the use of some bilingual forms or forms for which a separate French version exists. Thus, of the 29 agencies, 12 have at least some forms available in both English and French, while 17 employ only English forms. However, in the 12 agencies reporting the use of some bilingual forms, the stress should be placed on the word "some." In most instances the range of material available in English appears to be considerably wider than that available in French.

If the interviews gave the impression that the printed matter destined for public use is only occasionally available in the two languages, analysis of the sample documentation submitted by civic agencies tends to bear this out. It strongly suggests that in no department is the full range of departmental services as open to the person wishing to conduct his written civic business in French, as it is to the person using English.

The promotional material distributed by the city seems to be rather more bilingual than is normally the case with public forms and notices. However, French is still very far indeed from occupying equal status with English. For example, the Fire Prevention Branch of the Fire Department, which disseminates literature designed to foster fire safety measures, is one of the most successful municipal agencies in providing bilingual service. Nevertheless even here, according to an inventory submitted by this agency of the various types of promotional material used, the range of topics dealt with in the material available in French is roughly half that handled in English.

One case typifying the relative positions of the two languages is their use in the city's official tourist map. This document, distributed free at the Tourist and Convention Bureau's information kiosques, has a French as well as an English heading; most of the material included on the map, however, appears in English only.

Not all the printed material employed by the city originates within the administration—several civic agencies reported using documents prepared by the senior levels of government. It is interesting to note here that the institutional context in which the city operates appears to pull, gently but visibly, in two directions: while only one French-language version of an Ontario document was reported, those produced by federal agencies appear to be largely bilingual. In at least two civic agencies, the only bilingual forms reported were those made available by federal authorities.

To sum up, it is only in the information disseminated by the mass media—thanks to the presence of French-language press, radio and television facilities—that the French language is a full alternative to English. In none of the other categories of oral or written usage does it seem possible for the Francophone to obtain in his own language the same range of services as are available to the Anglophone.

The position of languages other than English and French. Earlier in this study we pointed out that while English and French are, in a numerical sense, by far the most significant languages spoken in Ottawa (*see* 8) other languages are also found and some are spoken fairly widely. In the course of the interviews, 10 languages other than English or French were reported by municipal spokesmen as having been encountered during the course of their work. These languages, listed by the frequency with which they were mentioned, were: Italian, 15 times; German, six times; Greek, Polish, Spanish, Ukrainian, Slavic (*sic*), twice each; Arabic, Russian, and Jewish (*sic*), once each.

Contacts in this category appear to be fairly rare, although four civic agencies[9] reported that their business with members of other language groups—particularly the Italian community—comprised up to 15 per cent of their workload. While most city departments seem to believe that in the provision of service to members of these communities their usual procedures are adequate, a few agencies evidently go to considerable lengths to accommodate requests for service in languages other than French or English. Spokesmen for the Tax and Water Revenue Branch, and the Urban Redevelopment, Conservation, and Housing Branch both reported that their agencies had hired Italian-speaking employees specifically to deal with requests for service in that tongue.

The Health Department, in response to our request for sample documentation, submitted copies of forms available in Italian and Dutch (the Dutch-language forms, as well as one of the three Italian samples, had evidently been obtained from a federal agency). The director of this agency reported that his department also distributed a few forms on hygiene in restaurant kitchens, printed in Arabic, Cantonese, and Greek, and, in the post-1956 period, had "produced quite an amount of material in Hungarian"[10] for those who had come to Ottawa in the aftermath of the revolution in Hungary. On a slightly different note, a spokesman for the Tourist and Convention Bureau reported that arrangements had on occasion been made to provide interpreters for tourist parties speaking languages other than French and English.

Although it is clear that these four agencies make specific efforts to serve members of other language groups, no other agencies can be added to their number on the basis of the data available—perhaps because of the low demand that is considered to exist for such services.

Internal language usage. There remains to be mentioned the language of work and communication within the administration. None of the various sources for this study reported the existence of any French-language or bilingual internal forms or documents. This applies on the departmental as well as the inter-departmental level, and is equally true of those agencies headed by Francophones as of those headed by Anglophones.

The position of French as an oral language of work appears to be almost as weak as it is on the written level. In only three of the 29 interviews was French mentioned as a language of oral communication among municipal employees. In communications between French- and English-speaking municipal servants, it is the general practice for the French to speak English, not the English to speak French. On the basis of the limited data available to us, no other conclusion is possible but that the language of work of the Ottawa municipal administration is almost exclusively English.

C. Attitudes towards the Provision of Bilingual Service

Of major importance to the presentation of an adequate picture of the Ottawa municipal administration are the attitudes encountered in the course of the study. The

---

[9] The Public Welfare Department, the Tax and Water Revenue Branch of the Treasury Department, the Office of the Assessment Commissioner, and the Urban Redevelopment, Conservation and Housing Branch of the Property Administration Department.

[10] Letter from head of Health Department, June 30, 1966.

main source of data for this section was necessarily the interviews with heads of the various municipal departments and branches. Members of this group, however, are important as they exert an influence on the policies and general attitudes of the administration far stronger than their numbers would suggest.

Of the 30 department and branch heads whom we attempted to interview, only four reported French as their mother tongue. This distribution is significant. Indeed, perhaps the most striking aspect of the analysis was that the French-speaking respondents, together with one or two of those having English as mother tongue, reacted in markedly different ways to the majority.

Most Anglophones tended to feel that the present level of services provided by the city in French is, by and large, adequate. Very few saw any need to seek improvements. In a few cases, references—veiled and otherwise—were made to former agency heads[11] who were reputedly anti-French or anti-Roman Catholic or both, but this situation was said to have changed.

On the other hand, the Francophone respondents, supported by a small minority of the Anglophones, looked at fundamentally the same situation and found it wanting. The general consensus of this group was that, while some isolated efforts were made to serve the French-speaking public, these services were basically inadequate. More than once it was suggested that a Francophone had to speak English if he wished to obtain the level of service available to Anglophones.

The key point to be noted here is the different concepts of "adequacy" which seem to underlie the views of both groups. Most of the English-speaking respondents appear to see themselves involved in the administration of a predominantly English-speaking Ontario municipality. The provision of services in English is to them the norm. Other languages, including French, have, if anything, a secondary status. Since French-speaking citizens are the most numerous of the non-English groups, greater accommodation is extended to French than to any language other than English. Thus, if French is seen as a secondary language with no official status, it is readily understandable that many of these respondents should see the present level of French service as adequate, or even liberal.

The position of the Francophones, and a small minority of Anglophones, appears to have been based on quite a different criterion. To them the French language is or should be a practical alternative to English for the citizen in his relations with the city authorities. From this perspective it is immediately apparent that the level of services in French described above is very far from satisfactory.

There is, however, another aspect of the attitudes encountered which is not fully explained by differences in the perspectives of the two groups. Several members of the English-language group greeted the interviewers with hostility, latent or overt. Reference has already been made to one department head who refused to be interviewed at all. In several other cases the interviewers came away with the unmistakable impression that the respondent was antagonistic to the entire study: it was asserted, almost belligerently, that no problems of bilingualism existed in agency X *yet*. In some instances it was suggested that the Commission, by conducting research on these topics, was accomplishing nothing and

---

[11] None of whom, apparently, was still employed by the city at the time the interviews took place.

simply "stirring up a storm" within a basically satisfactory situation. This attitude seemed to indicate a reluctance among some civic officials to contemplate changes in linguistic arrangements, and perhaps a tacit acknowledgement that the present situation is not universally regarded as satisfactory.

To ascertain the relative weight assigned to bilingualism by members of the administrative elite, the 29 senior officials interviewed were asked whether they thought it important that some of their employees be bilingual and, if so, why, and more specifically for what types of positions facility in both French and English was important.

Three of the respondents felt that the importance of having bilingual staff members was negligible. Three others considered it might be of some importance but were unable to designate specific job categories that should be filled by bilingual personnel. The remaining 23 believed it was important to have some bilingual staff members and identified specific types of positions to be staffed with bilingual personnel.

Table 3.2 lists by frequency the job categories so identified. It will be noted that a few posts common throughout the administration are mentioned several times; the majority are more specialized, and often limited to one or two agencies. Further, most respondents did not suggest that all employees within these job categories should be bilingual. They usually observed that it would be desirable to have "a few" or "some" bilingual staff in category X.

Table 3.2. List of positions identified as preferably bilingual, Ottawa municipal administration

Type of position	Number of times mentioned
Telephone receptionist	8
Clerical staff dealing with the public	7
Inspectors	6
Work crew foremen (in specified wards)	3
Recreation programmer	1
Applicant interviewer	1
Health instruction staff	1
Food service staff	1
Nursing staff	1
Case worker	1
Social worker	1
Buyer	1
Town planner	1
Engineer	1
Lawyer	1
Agency supervisor	1

Source: Interviews with departmental heads.

Yet the table does imply some interesting attitudinal trends. The frequency with which the receptionist and clerical categories were identified suggests a broad awareness of a need for bilingual personnel on this level. The same degree of awareness in regard to professional categories, however, is not evident. Even when they are taken as one group, professional positions were identified only half as frequently as the receptionist and clerical categories.

On the level of the administrative elite itself, very little importance appears to be attributed to the presence or absence of bilingual staff. Only one respondent identified his own position as a post which should be held by a bilingual person. The remainder appear to have felt that competence in French was not relevant to their personal efficiency as municipal administrators.

In short, although approximately 80 per cent of those interviewed attributed some importance to bilingualism in the civic administration, the positions most frequently identified were relatively low-status, low-reward posts, such as receptionists and clerks. Seemingly less important was the linguistic ability of professional employees, while almost no importance was attributed by members of the elite to the presence or absence of bilingual persons at their own level. As will be seen in the following chapter, this scale of values contrasts visibly with the conception of bilingual service encountered in the city of Hull and elsewhere.

D. Composition and Language Skills of Administration

The range and quality of services that any institution can provide are directly related to the abilities of its staff. This is to say that no study of a local government would be complete without an examination of its municipal servants. In this section we shall be looking at the employees of the city of Ottawa primarily from two broad standpoints: the composition and structure of the administration in terms of linguistic groups; and the incidence of bilingualism and the roles played by bilingual employees.

No single comprehensive body of information, such as the questionnaires would have produced, was available to us. Instead several sources have been used, the three main ones being:

1) A city of Ottawa personnel list for the spring of 1965. This list covers all 3,742 persons employed by the city at that time and is broken down as between salaried and wage-earning staff. A name analysis technique was applied to the list in order to obtain in approximate terms the presumed ethnic origin of the total administration. A separate print-out of those earning a salary of over $9600 was also obtained.

2) Checklists prepared during the summer of 1965. These lists were filled out with respect to some 900 salaried employees, representing the administrative core of the city. The fire and police services, those employed directly by judicial agencies, and a very small group whose functions could not be ascertained, are not covered by the checklists. No information was obtained from the offices of the City Clerk and of the Secretary to Board of Control. This, along with a number of partial responses and non-responses from other agencies, brought the overall response rate to about 90 per cent of the group approached. From these checklists information was supplied on four points only: job classification, degree of public contact, mother tongue, and fluency in the French language.

3) Census material for 1961. The Dominion Bureau of Statistics supplied the Commission with tabulations of census data for municipal public servants resident in the city of Ottawa. These data on some 2,700 employees relate to ethnic origin, official language, mother tongue, schooling, occupation, age, sex, earned income, and a number of other variables.

Linguistic composition. Table 3.3 compares the linguistic proportions by mother tongue of the Ottawa administration with the city population at large. The group of French mother tongue is over-represented in the administration in relation to its position in the city at large. Those of English mother tongue are slightly under-represented, while those of other mother tongues are considerably so.

Table 3.3. Ottawa, mother tongue of city population and administration, 1961

Mother tongue	City		Administration	
	N	%	N	%
Total	268,206	100	2,676	100
English	188,072	70.1	1,780	66.5
French	56,882	21.2	791	29.6
Others	23,252	8.7	105	3.9

Sources: City: Census of Canada, 1961; Catalogue 95-528.
Administration: Tape 2, Table 1, 42.

More recent data on mother-tongue composition of the administration are not available. However, using a name analysis technique, the distribution by presumed ethnic origin for the spring of 1965 may be obtained. This is given in Table 3.4. In the same table are also presented the 1961 census figures on ethnic origin. These two sets of percentages are closely comparable, even though some names had to be classified as doubtful in the name analysis. (For example, surnames such as "Albert" and "Martin," could indicate either French or British origin. Surnames of non-French, non-British origins are often difficult to identify as such, and may consequently be underestimated.) That there should be such slight variation between 1961 and 1965 in the ethnic distribution suggests strongly a linguistic stability that would also leave the mother-tongue figures changed very little over this period.

Table 3.4. Ottawa municipal employees by ethnic origin, percentages, 1961 and 1965

	1961	1965
Total	100	100
British	54.7	54.1
French	33.1	32.9
Others	12.2	10.2
Doubtful	–	2.8

Sources: 1961: Tape 2, Table 1, 42.
1965: Name analysis of city of Ottawa's personnel list.

While it is clear that the city has a relatively high proportion of employees of both French origin and French mother tongue, it is of equal importance to note that they are not evenly distributed throughout the administration. On the contrary, as Table 3.5 indicates, employees of French ethnic origin exhibit a marked tendency to cluster near the bottom of the hierarchy.

Table 3.5. City of Ottawa municipal employees, ethnic origin by income category, 1965

Ethnic origin	Total		Hourly paid		Salaried		High salaried	
	N	%	N	%	N	%	N	%
Total	3,742	100	1,702	100	1,991	100	49	100
British	2,024	54.1	745	43.8	1,244	62.5	38	77.6
French	1,232	32.9	787	46.2	441	22.1	4	8.2
Others	382	10.2	156	9.2	219	10.9	3	6.1
Doubtful	104	2.8	14	0.8	87	4.4	4	8.2

Sources: Name analysis of the city of Ottawa's personnel list and of its print-out of those earning $9600 + per annum.

For the two major ethnic groupings, it is apparent that those of British origin, some 55 per cent of the total work force, include rather less than 45 per cent of the hourly paid workers, over 60 per cent of the salaried employees, and over 75 per cent of those drawing a salary of $9600 or more per annum. On the other hand, those of French ethnic origin, though about 33 per cent of the total civic work force, contribute more than 45 per cent of the city's hourly paid workers, 22 per cent of its salaried employees and less than 10 per cent of those in highly rewarded positions.

A more precise measurement of income distribution is supplied by census data. As presented in Table 3.6, these indicate a pattern similar to that of the previous table. In the income categories below $5000 the employees of British origin are under-represented and those of French origin over-represented. In the upper income levels the positions are reversed. It is important to note that in 1961 one out of five city employees of British origin had an income of $5000 or more, while only one out of 10 of French origin and one out of seven of other origins were in this income category.

Table 3.6. Municipal employees in Ottawa, by ethnic origin and employment income, percentages, 1961

Ethnic origin	Total		Employment income			
	N	%	Under $3000	$3000-$4999	$5000-$9999	Over $10,000
Total	2,677	100	24.8	59.0	15.1	1.1
British	1,465	100	21.9	57.7	19.0	1.4
French	885	100	29.6	60.5	9.4	0.6
Others	327	100	25.1	60.9	13.1	0.9

Source: Tape 2, Table 9.

The disproportionate weight of the employees of British origin in the upper echelons is again apparent when we look at the names appearing on the city's organization chart for the upper levels of its administrative departments. On the chart appear 76 persons earning $6500 or over. This group, which includes the department heads, can fairly be termed the city's administrative elite; it almost certainly includes the senior personnel who are important from a broad policy-making standpoint. Table 3.7 provides further evidence of the pre-eminence of employees of British origin in the decision-making circles of the city. The 18 department heads appearing here showed a distribution in 1965 roughly similar to the top administrative structure as a whole. As of December 1967, however, all three heads of non-British origin had retired or resigned, and the city apparently had at this point no department heads of French or other mother tongues.

Table 3.7. City of Ottawa municipal employees appearing on the organization chart and earning $6500 or over, by ethnic origin, 1965

Origin	All senior positions		Department heads only	
	N	%	N	%
Total	76	100	18	100
British	63	82.9	14	77.7
French	8	10.5	2	11.1
Others	2	2.6	1	5.6
Doubtful	3	3.9	1	5.6

Source: Name analysis of city of Ottawa organization chart.

The over-representation of employees of British origin at the top of the city's work force and of employees of French origin at the lower end may be seen in yet another way by looking at the occupational distribution of municipal employees. Table 3.8 illustrates the occuptational pattern revealed by the 1961 census.

Table 3.8. Municipal employees in Ottawa, ethnic origin by occupation group, percentages, 1961

Occupation		Ethnic origin			
		Total	British	French	Others
Total	N	2,673	1,462	885	326
	%	100	100	100	100
Managerial		5.3	6.4	3.7	4.6
Professional and technical		11.1	13.3	5.8	16.0
Clerical		14.4	16.4	11.5	13.5
Service and recreation		31.7	37.5	24.4	25.8
Transport and communication		4.1	3.4	5.5	3.4
Craftsmen		15.4	13.1	19.1	16.0
Labourers		15.4	7.7	27.3	17.5
All others*		2.5	2.3	2.6	3.4

Source: Tape 2, Table 7, Parts I and II, 36.
* Comprising census categories of Sales, Farmers and "not stated."

The first two occupation categories, both of which are of relatively high status, encompass some 20 per cent each of those of British and other ethnic origins but only 10 per cent of those whose origin is French. At the lower end of the occupational scale, the categories of craftsmen and labourers account for over 46 per cent of those of French origin as compared to only 21 per cent of those of British origin, while those of other origins fall in between at 33.5 per cent. Despite the fact that Ottawa civic employees of French origin are only 60 per cent as numerous as those of British origin, they actually outweigh the latter in sheer numbers (411 against 304) in these lower-status occupations.

Bilingualism. In 1961, 36 per cent of all municipal employees in Ottawa were bilingual. This compares favourably with the level for the city population of 25 per cent. Correspondingly the figures for those speaking English only, French only, and neither of the two official languages were lower in the municipal administration (62, 1, and 0 per cent respectively) than those for the total Ottawa population (70, 3, and 1 per cent respectively).

The bilingual personnel, however, are not distributed evenly throughout the city's work force, mainly because most of them are French-speaking by mother tongue and, as we have seen, most Francophones are clustered in the lower-status positions. Table 3.9 presents the mother tongue by official language correlation for municipal servants in Ottawa in 1961. Two points emerge clearly. First, whereas only one in nine of those of English mother tongue could speak the two languages, over 19 in every 20 of those of French mother tongue could do so. The high level of bilingualism in the latter group serves to emphasize an earlier conclusion—that English is the language of work in the Ottawa administration. Second, the staff of French mother tongue supplies the great majority (78 per cent) of bilingual personnel, even though it is less than half the size of the combined non-French groups.

Table 3.9. Municipal employees in Ottawa, mother tongue by official language, percentages, 1961

Mother tongue	Total		Official language		
	N	%	English only	French only	Both
Total	2,644	100	62.5	1.2	36.3
English	1,772	100	89.1	–	10.9
French	783	100	–	4.0	96.0
Others	89	100	83.1	–	16.9

Source: Tape 2, Table 4, 177-80.

In the light of this latter point, it is not surprising to find a close correlation in the occupational distribution by ethnic origin (Table 3.8) with that by official language (Table 3.10). A comparison of the two tables shows that the four categories where French-origin employees form a higher percentage than the British (transport, craftsmen, labourers, and "all others") are the same four categories with a higher than average level of bilingualism. Conversely, the four categories with lower than average levels of bilingualism (managerial, professional, clerical, and service) are those where employees of British origin are in a higher proportion than those of French origin.

Table 3.10. Municipal employees in Ottawa, occupation group by official language, 1961

Occupation	Total		Official language			
	N	%	English only	French only	Both	Neither
Total	2,673	100	62.2	1.2	36.5	0.1
Managerial	142	100	69.0	–	31.0	–
Professional and technical	297	100	74.1	1.0	24.9	–
Clerical	386	100	71.2	0.3	28.5	–
Service and recreation	848	100	71.7	0.6	27.7	–
Transport and communication	109	100	48.6	0.9	50.5	–
Craftsmen	412	100	54.1	1.0	44.9	–
Labourers	412	100	36.9	3.9	58.7	0.5
All others*	67	100	50.7	4.5	44.8	–

Source: Tape 2, Table 7, Parts I and II, 36.
* Comprising census categories of Sales, Farmers and "not stated."

The influence of ethnic origin on bilingualism and occupation is further analyzed in Table 3.11. Instead of examining all four official-language categories as in the previous table, only the proportion formed by those having a knowledge of both languages is given. The resulting figures are noteworthy on two counts. First, it is clear that the level of bilingualism among those of British origin shows no tendency to rise with the status of the occupation. Second, the fluctuations in the percentages for those of French origin give us a clue to the whereabouts of two small but interesting groups—those municipal employees of French origin who speak only English, and those who speak French only. The latter, numbering only 31, are mostly concentrated in the labouring and "all other" categories. The former group, those of French origin speaking only English, has 87 members, of whom 60 are in the professional and technical, clerical, and service and recreation categories (Tape 2, Table 2). It is their strong presence here that explains the lower than average rates of bilingualism for employees of French origin in these three categories.

Clearly, bilingualism is more likely to be found in the lower than in the upper ranks of the Ottawa administration. The checklist material, which includes only those salaried employees who form the administrative core of the city, reinforces this fact: for the latter group the overall level of bilingualism drops from 36 to around 29 per cent.

The checklists employed a simpler approach than the census in determining linguistic ability. As the city's ability to provide service in English was not in question, the salaried staff were only asked to state their degree of fluency in French. A rating of either "fluent" or "considerable" has been taken to indicate a sufficient knowledge of the second language for a municipal employee to use it in the performance of his normal duties.

Municipal Administration: Ottawa

Table 3.11. Municipal employees in Ottawa, total number and percentage of the total who are bilingual for each ethnic origin and occupation category, 1961

Occupation	Total		Ethnic origin					
			British		French		Others	
	Total	% bil.	Total	% bil.	Total	% bil.	Total	% bil.
Total	2,661	36.6	1,462	9.5	885	86.7	314	21.7
Managerial	142	31.0	94	7.4	33	100.0	15	26.7
Prof. and tech.	294	25.2	193	11.9	51	78.4	50	22.0
Clerical	386	28.5	241	8.7	102	81.4	43	14.0
Serv. and rec.	843	27.6	548	6.8	216	82.4	79	22.8
Trans. and comm.	109	50.5	49	10.2	49	93.9	11	36.4
Craftsmen	412	45.4	191	11.5	170	91.8	51	17.6
Labourers	409	58.9	113	16.8	242	87.6	54	18.5
All others*	66	45.5	33	15.2	22	86.4	11	54.5

Source: Tape 2, Table 2, 210.
* Comprising Sales, Farmers and "not stated."

Table 3.12 presents the salaried group's facility in French according to mother tongue. The important contribution of Francophone municipal servants to the bilingual corps is immediately apparent. By the above criterion, only 9 per cent of the Anglophones are functionally bilingual. Even with the addition of those of other mother tongues, the combined level of bilingualism for non-Francophones rises only to 10 per cent. The staff of French mother tongue, which makes up 22 per cent of the total salaried group, supplies 74 per cent, or 204 of the 276 bilingual municipal servants.

Table 3.12. City of Ottawa salaried employees, mother tongue by French-language facility, 1965

Mother tongue	Total		French-language facility			
	N	%	None	A little	Considerable	Fluent
Total*	935	100	63.7	6.7	4.6	24.9
English	679	100	82.6	8.2	5.9	3.2
Others	52	100	67.3	13.5	5.8	13.5
French	204	100	–	–	–	100**

Source: Checklists.
* Partial responses and non-responses excluded.
**Owing to an ambiguity on the checklists, the degree of fluency in French for those of French mother tongue could not be calculated from the returns. In this and the following tables we have had to make the rather arbitrary assumption that those of French mother tongue have retained a fluent command of their language. This was one of the topics which the questionnaire was designed to measure with greater accuracy.

Because of the relatively low proportion of bilingual staff in the salaried group, an extremely important area to examine is the location of these people in the administration. Do they play any special role with respect to the citizen's communication with City Hall? The first aspect of this question is the departmental distribution of the salaried employees, as given in Table 3.13. While it is apparent that at least one person in each department has a fluent knowledge of French, rarely does the proportion of those having a little or no knowledge of French fall below 60 per cent. Only three agencies (Health, Island Lodge and Geriatric Centre, and Property) had as many as two out of five staff members able to give service in French.

Table 3.13. City of Ottawa salaried employees, French-language facility by department, 1965

Department	Total		French-language facility				
	N	%	Fluent	Considerable	A little	None	No answer
Total	990	100	23.5	4.3	6.4	60.2	5.6
Assessment	50	100	14.0	10.0	–	74.0	2.0
Community Renewal	10	100	10.0	10.0	40.0	40.0	–
Health	85	100	28.2	12.9	5.9	52.9	–
Island Lodge	103	100	39.8	1.9	2.9	55.3	–
Legal	17	100	11.8	11.8	23.5	41.2	11.8
Personnel	15	100	20.0	20.0	–	60.0	–
Planning and Works	288	100	17.4	4.2	5.9	64.6	8.0
Property	24	100	33.3	–	4.2	54.2	8.3
Public Welfare	66	100	21.2	1.5	3.0	72.7	1.5
Recreation and Parks	43	100	27.9	2.3	11.6	48.8	9.3
Tourist	4	100	50.0	–	–	50.0	–
Traffic	20	100	30.0	–	5.0	65.0	–
Treasury	132	100	20.5	2.3	15.9	45.5	15.9
Water Works	133	100	27.1	1.5	–	70.7	0.8

Source: Checklists. Information not available for offices of the City Clerk or the Secretary to Board of Control.

According to the checklists, some 12 per cent of the administrative core have no public contact whatsoever, while a further 20 per cent are in less than daily contact. As Table 3.14 shows, however, there seems to be no positive link between increased public contact and increased fluency in French. Indeed the combined proportion of those having a fluent and considerable knowledge of French scarcely differs between the staff with no public contact (29.5 per cent) and those in more than daily contact (30.2 per cent). In other words, there is no clear statistical evidence of any overall policy of staffing positions requiring public contact with bilingual personnel. Indeed, if the "fluent" column alone is considered, facility in French decreases as public contact increases.

Table 3.14. City of Ottawa salaried employees, French-language facility by degree of public contact, 1965

Degree of public contact	Total		French-language facility				
	N	%	Fluent	Considerable	A little	None	No answer
Total	990	100	23.5	4.3	6.4	60.2	5.6
None	122	100	28.7	0.8	4.9	64.8	0.8
Less than once a day	195	100	24.6	2.1	4.1	69.2	–
More than once a day	599	100	24.2	6.0	7.5	61.8	0.5
No answer	74	100	6.8	2.7	5.4	16.2	68.9

Source: Checklists.

Another way of looking at the position of bilingual personnel in the administration is to see in what kinds of work they are engaged. On the checklists employees were listed under one of six job classifications: wage-earning (although those reported under this heading were salaried employees, most were apparently in occupations normally associated with wage employment), secretarial, clerical, technical, professional and supervisory. Although broadly similar to the census occupation groupings, these job classifications were established so as to correspond to the city's personnel structure.

Classified according to the degree of French-language facility, the job classification distribution is given in Table 3.15. When the "fluent" and "considerable" percentages are combined, no one distribution by job classification is startlingly different from another. Approximately 10 percentage points separate the group with proportionally the greatest French-language ability—the wage-earners—from the one with the least—the secretarial staff. This differs from the situation which emerged when the total municipal labour force was examined by occupation group: in that case there was a distinct tendency for the lower-status positions to show a greater than average number of bilingual employees (*see* Table 3.10).

Table 3.15. City of Ottawa salaried employees, French-language facility by job classification, 1965

Job classification	Total		French-language facility				
	N	%	Fluent	Considerable	A little	None	No answer
Total	990	100	23.5	4.3	6.4	60.2	5.6
Wage-earning	72	100	33.3	–	1.4	65.3	–
Secretarial	66	100	18.2	4.5	3.0	74.2	–
Clerical	180	100	26.1	4.4	5.6	62.8	1.1
Technical	300	100	26.3	2.7	6.3	64.3	0.3
Professional	149	100	18.8	11.4	8.1	59.7	2.0
Supervisory	174	100	24.7	4.0	10.9	59.8	0.6
No answer	49	100	–	–	–	2.0	98.0

Source: Checklists.

The information presented above on the distribution of personnel able to speak French by department, by public contact, and by job classification all points to the conclusion that, among the salaried group at City Hall, employees able to give service in French are not concentrated in any special areas. There is no evidence in our statistical analysis of any conscious policy to locate bilingual staff at strategic positions in the organization—on the contrary, the relatively even distribution of bilingual personnel suggests a complete absence of any differentiation of function according to linguistic ability.

It is necessary, however, to add to this last statement some element of qualification. Various departments have made efforts to recruit bilingual personnel for certain posts— for example, receptionists or public health nurses. The usual procedure is that the department concerned states its preference for a bilingual candidate when the post is advertised. Two cases were reported to us—the post of secretary to the city's Centennial Committee and that of a receptionist in the Personnel Department—in which bilingualism was made a formal requirement for the job, but this is the exception rather than the rule. For the vast majority of posts, the only linguistic requirement appears to be a sufficient knowledge of English to work in that language.

Finally, we inquired whether the city had any programmes to improve and develop the linguistic abilities of its employees. One specialized training programme was reported in the Ottawa Police Department (*see* Appendix F). Up to 1967, however, the civic administration itself has had no language training schemes of any kind.

E. Summary

The following are the major points that may be abstracted from the study of Ottawa:
1) Most communications between the administration of the city of Ottawa and members of the public are conducted in English, the current demand for services in French being relatively low.
2) The telephone survey indicated that in the field of oral usage, adequate service in French could be obtained on approximately two out of five occasions.
3) As to written correspondence, whether a letter sent to the administration in French will be answered in the same language seems to depend largely on the agency contacted. Some agencies reply in French as a matter of policy; others invariably in English; still others reported that procedures varied with the circumstances.
4) Information is distributed through the mass media in both languages, with translation into French usually provided by the media themselves.
5) Public notices, forms, and promotional material are available to a limited degree in French as well as English. On the whole, bilingualism in this area appears to be rudimentary.
6) Four agencies reported a need to make some provision for service in languages other than French and English.
7) The internal language of work is, from all the evidence available, English only.

8) With respect to the composition of the civic labour force, those of French mother tongue form a higher proportion within the administration than they do in the city at large. The percentages for those of English and other mother tongues are correspondingly lower.
9) However, the statistics on hourly-paid as against salaried employees, on employment income, on the decision-making core, and on occupation groups all point to a preponderance of Francophones in the lower echelons. Anglophones, on the other hand, account for a disproportionate share of the higher-salaried positions.
10) About 36 per cent of the employees were reported to be bilingual, but such personnel are not evenly distributed across the total municipal work force. When only the salaried group is considered, the bilingual proportion drops to around 29 per cent.
11) Approximately three-quarters of the bilingual staff are French by mother tongue.
12) There is no clear evidence that bilingualism among employees of English or other mother tongues is found more frequently in the higher-status, better-paid occupational categories.
13) Within the administrative core, the checklists provided no discernible evidence of a deliberate placing of bilingual personnel by department, by degree of public contact, or by job classification. Nevertheless, it was reported that for some specific positions a knowledge of French and English is a preferred—or in rare instances a required—qualification for the post.
14) Linguistic practice at Ottawa City Hall is characterized by its unevenness. With no overall policy, each department is evidently left considerable latitude in determining the extent to which service is to be offered in French as well as English.

In the light of the findings of this chapter, the general conclusion must be that French does not represent a full alternative to English for the citizen in his dealings with the city. That at present public demand for services in French should be low is probably not unrelated to the administration's poor ability to provide them.

Among department heads, two broadly different attitudes seemed to emerge. One group, which included most of the Anglophones, saw Ottawa as an Ontario city making relatively liberal provision for one of the province's linguistic minorities. The second and smaller group, primarily but not exclusively Francophone, saw considerable room for improvement.

Once again, the consequences of Ottawa's position as an Ontario municipality need to be stressed. In the preceding chapter we pointed out the extensive provincial impact on the framework of local government. The strongest impression that emerges from an examination of the Ottawa administration itself is that it views linguistic and cultural questions from a fundamentally provincial perspective. Nowhere in this phase of the study did we discover any significant sentiment that Ottawa's position as the federal capital should have a bearing on language policy at City Hall.

Chapter IV   Municipal Administration: Other Municipalities

A. Introduction

In the previous chapter, we looked closely at the administration of the city of Ottawa, the major city of the capital region. But the metropolitan area contains 12 other municipalities. A comparison of these with Ottawa by population and linguistic composition will be found in Table A, Appendix G.

The four municipalities, in addition to Ottawa, situated on the Ontario side of the Ottawa River are Eastview, Gloucester, Nepean and Rockcliffe Park. All five, together with several rural municipalities, would come within the borders of the plan for metropolitan government in the Ottawa area proposed by the government of Ontario in February 1967. Similarly, all of the eight Quebec municipalities—Aylmer, Deschênes, Gatineau, Hull, Lucerne, Pointe-Gatineau, Templeton and West Templeton—are included in the plan for a Quebec Commission of the National Capital Region as submitted by the Regional Economic Council for the West of Quebec to the Quebec government. These 12 municipalities were included in the Ottawa metropolitan area for census purposes in 1961.

Ottawa was treated separately from the other municipalities because of the sheer size of its administration and for methodological considerations. Various research methods were used to analyze Ottawa, none of which was completely satisfactory in itself (see 69-73). For the other municipalities, however, the smaller size of their administrations and their greater informality and willingness to co-operate enabled us to gather our material more simply. During a telephone interview a questionnaire[1] on linguistic practice was filled out. The questionnaire was then sent to the municipality for confirmation and further comment, along with checklists similar to those employed in Ottawa to

---

[1] To meet the different situations prevailing in the two provinces, the questionnaires for Ontario and Quebec municipalities varied slightly.

report on the language knowledge of municipal employees.[2] In addition, for the two cities of Hull and Eastview, interviews were conducted with most heads of municipal departments.

The checklists of employees were filled out independently in each municipality, so that the criteria of linguistic fluency may vary somewhat from one municipality to another. We have sought to diminish this effect by defining bilingualism in broad functional terms as the ability of an employee to give service in either French or English. Hence those reported to have either a "fluent" or "considerable" knowledge were for this purpose accounted qualified; those reported to have "little" or "none" were not.

B. The City of Hull

In contrast to Ottawa, Hull is a Quebec municipality and, as such, is faced with a legal obligation to provide many bilingual services to the public. The linguistic provisions of the city's charter must be met, and also those laid down in the provincial Cities and Towns Act *(see* 64, 65–6). However, as we shall see below, Hull goes rather beyond the strict requirements of the law in this respect.

Language practices of the administration. The demand for service in English is small, but not unimportant. In December 1966 an official of the city estimated that some 14 per cent of the letters sent to the administration were in English, 85 per cent were in French and 1 per cent in other languages. He also reported that the language of letters sent out by the administration to members of the public followed the same approximate distribution; so did telephone calls and personal meetings between municipal servants and the general population.

Despite the relatively small demand for English-language service, it is a principle of the administration always to offer service in both French and English. Any citizen can send in a request, orally or in writing, in either official language, and he will be answered in the same language. However, within the administration, an individual's request, forwarded in one language, may be handled in the other. Take, for example, the case of an English-speaking citizen who writes to the city in English objecting to his municipal assessment: the content of the letter will be discussed in French, without being translated, by the Assessment Department. The reply will be sent directly in English.

As far as we can determine, the switchboard operators are sufficiently bilingual to give information in either language and to transfer calls to the right department. They usually acknowledge calls in French only, thus: "Hôtel de Ville," "Bureau du Greffier," etc. Staff at the front desk in the various departments must be bilingual. In general, any individual who needs information will be served in the language which he prefers to use.

---

[2] Templeton failed to return its checklists and the confirmed copy of the questionnaire. Thus the analysis of the language practices of this municipality is based on the telephone interview alone.

Turning now from the municipality's relations with individual members of the public to its broad communications of general interest, we find section 401 of Hull's charter is of direct relevance. It reads:

> When a public notice is ordered to be given, under any provision of this act or any statute concerning the city, without prescribing the form or manner in which such notice shall be published, such notice shall, in such case, be given by an advertisement inserted at least twice in English and in French in a newspaper published and printed within a 25 mile radius of the city.

All city departments appear to obey the law to the letter: the Clerk's Office publishes the by-laws passed by Council in French and English, and notices of expropriation and intention to borrow, issued respectively by the Assessment and Finance Departments, are handled in the same manner.

Hull also uses the two official languages for all official documents—tax bills, police tickets and summonses, municipal traffic signs, safety notices (for example, "Défense de fumer" and "No Smoking"), and applications for building and other permits.

Calls for tenders for the construction of public works are published, in French only, in the newspaper *Le Droit,* if the works are of a local character and to be undertaken by local industry. If the works are on a larger scale, advertisements in both French and English newspapers are used. Annual reports from departments are not all bilingual; in particular, the report of the Police Department is prepared only in French.

Each department does its own translations. There is no translation bureau, and no need for one is considered to exist at present. If there is any conflict between the interpretations given to the French and English versions of a document, the French text prevails.

The usual internal working language is French. Most documents, files and forms intended for internal use (for example, work orders, memoranda, fire reports and assessment reports) are printed in French. The filing systems (file-names, card indexes, letterheads, etc.) of the various departments are in French. Reports from employees and intra- and inter-departmental correspondence are in French. As far back as the present staff can remember, they have always operated in this way. Nevertheless, it is interesting to note that two police officers are allowed to write their daily reports in English; these men are both Anglophone and, while they can handle both languages, they probably express themselves better in English. Forms issued by the government of Quebec for the purpose of obtaining returns are often bilingual, the two versions being printed on opposite sides of the same sheet.

Composition and language skills of the administration. Since the internal working language of the Hull administration is French, a knowledge of this language is clearly essential for recruitment into the municipal service. With regard to a candidate's ability to speak English, however, there is no general rule covering the language requirements of the various departments; practice has been empirically determined, and varies from department to department. It also depends on the nature and importance of the post which has to be filled. In principle all departments ask the applicant to apply in writing, in both French and English, explaining his interest in the competition for the post and the relevance of his qualifications and experience. This written request is used to assess the candidate's language ability—unless he is required to submit to a more detailed written or oral test.

The Police Department is unquestionably the municipal department with the highest language requirements. Would-be entrants have to pass a written examination which includes tests of general knowledge, spelling, vocabulary, and arithmetic. Although these are not difficult, they require considerable knowledge of both French and English. There is also a severe oral test.

The Assessment and Finance Departments appear to be less strict. It is felt that a French-speaking employee can improve his English on the job but, other things being equal, preference in hiring and promotion will be shown to the candidate who proves he has the best language ability.

In other departments (such as Fire or Recreation) requirements are much more loosely stated and harder to define. A candidate is told he must have "some knowledge" of English, a "minimum" which will enable him subsequently to make good any deficiencies in his knowledge. In this third class of municipal services English appears to be an incidental requirement, while a knowledge of French is indispensable.

Even so, a knowledge of English is not without its importance. It might seem that the junior employee who seldom meets the public is faced with a very small bilingual requirement. However, as one municipal employee put it, "Certainly it doesn't matter for an office-worker who doesn't meet the public if he's bilingual or not; but he'll have to be if he wants to get ahead in the city administration." Besides this, the staff of a small city administration like that of Hull has to be mobile; absence, sickness, and holiday-leave frequently make it necessary for one employee to replace another, or to take over from him.

In 1965, the Hull administration employed 225 persons in a full-time capacity. Checklists sent out in early 1967 produced data on 147 municipal servants.[3] It is this body of information on which the following analysis is based. The officials concerned were distributed among the various municipal departments as follows:

Clerk's Office	7	Finance	11
Mayor's Office	1	Library	14
City Manager	2	Maintenance	6
Assessment	10	Tourism	3
Recreation	5	Fire	5
Engineering	7	Police	76

A comparison of the linguistic composition of the city's population and administration (Table 4.1) shows that the population of French mother tongue is slightly over-represented in the administration, with the result that the latter is overwhelmingly composed of Francophones. Anglophones and those of other mother tongues are under-represented at City Hall.

Despite the concentration of personnel whose mother tongue is French, the city's capacity to provide service in English as well as French is widespread. Taking the sum of the "fluent" and "considerable" levels in Table 4.2 as our criterion, we find that more than 90 per cent of Hull municipal servants can give service in English, while a somewhat higher percentage can do so in French.

---

[3] This figure includes only five senior administrative employees of the Fire Department. An interview in 1965 indicated that the full department included about 85 employees, of whom 50 were bilingual.

Table 4.1. Hull, city population and administration by mother tongue

Mother tongue	City (1961)		Administration (1967)	
	N	%	N	%
Total	56,929	100	147	100
English	4,648	8.2	5	3.4
French	51,370	90.2	139	94.5
Others	911	1.6	1	0.7
Not stated	—	—	2	1.4

Sources: Census of Canada, 1961; Catalogue 95-528. Employee checklists, 1967.

Table 4.2. Hull municipal employees, language knowledge

Knowledge of English		Level of knowledge	Knowledge of French	
N	%		N	%
147	100	Total	147	100
107	72.8	Fluent	137	93.2
27	18.4	Considerable	2	1.4
12	8.2	A little	7	4.8
—	—	None	1	0.6
1	0.6	Not stated	—	—

Source: Employee checklists, 1967.

To measure the level of individual bilingualism among civic employees, we have assumed that all are competent to give service in their own mother tongue and that we have merely to consider their facility in the second language. On this basis some 90 per cent of the Hull municipal administrative staff were reported to have a "fluent" or "considerable" second-language knowledge, and may thus be accounted functionally bilingual. As Table 4.3 indicates, unilingualism is obviously the exception among Hull employees.

Table 4.3. Hull municipal employees, second-language knowledge

Second-language knowledge	N	%
Total	147	100
Fluent	107	72.8
Considerable	25	17.0
A little	11	7.5
None	1	0.7
Not stated	3	2.0

Source: Employee checklists, 1967.

Even though French is the internal working language of the Hull administration, not all the municipal servants of mother tongues other than French are functionally bilingual. In fact, four of the six in this category were classed as having "little" or "no" knowledge of French.

In seven of the 12 departments, which between them account for 71 per cent of the Hull administration, every member of the staff has at least a "considerable" grasp of his second language. In a further four departments, a majority of staff members is bilingual.

Finally, we have attempted to establish the position of the bilingual and non-bilingual personnel in the Hull administration by comparing job classification (that is, wage-earner, secretarial, clerical, technical, professional, or supervisory) and frequency of contact with the public against the reported levels of second-language knowledge. Because it has proved impossible to analyze meaningfully the job classification and public contact of the fire and police services, they are excluded from consideration here. This leaves us with a group of 66 employees.

Table 4.4 indicates the placing of bilingual and unilingual staff by job classification. It will be seen that the extent of second-language knowledge is less in the lower-status positions. Less than half of the wage-earning and secretarial staff reported they had a "fluent" or "considerable" command of their second language. In comparison, all the supervisory and professional personnel, and practically all the technical and clerical employees, were reported to be bilingual. This would tend to confirm the fact that bilingualism is a prerequisite to advancement in the Hull administration.

Table 4.4. Hull municipal employees, job classification by second-language knowledge

Second-language knowledge	Total	Job classification					
		W.-E.	Sec.	Clerical	Tech.	Prof.	Sup.
Total	66	10	9	26	6	4	11
Fluent	26	–	1	11	1	3	10
Considerable	25	4	3	13	4	1	–
A little	11	5	4	1	1	–	–
None	1	1	–	–	–	–	–
Not stated	3	–	1	1	–	–	1

Source: Employee checklists, 1967.

Reading across Table 4.5, it appears that all of the "fluently" bilingual officials are in more than daily contact with the public, as also are most of those having a "considerable" knowledge of their second language. Municipal servants having "little" or "no" knowledge of their second language can be found in all three public contact categories. By reading the table downwards, we find that the staff having no contact with the public (all of them wage-earners) have only a limited command of their second language. Five (three wage-earners and two secretaries) of the eight persons having less than daily contact are not functionally bilingual. In contrast, most of those having more than daily contact can give service in both French and English (of the four who cannot, two are secretaries, one is a clerk, and one is a technician).

Table 4.5. Hull municipal employees, degree of public contact by second-language knowledge

Second-language knowledge	Total	Public contact			
		None	Less than once a day	More than once a day	Not stated
Total	66	3	8	54	1
Fluent	26	–	–	26	–
Considerable	25	–	3	22	–
A little	11	3	4	4	–
None	1	–	1	–	–
Not stated	3	–	–	2	1

Source: Employee checklists, 1967.

Thus the likelihood of a member of the public encountering a unilingual municipal servant is remote. Even if this were to happen, it will be remembered that all but one department contains a majority of people able to give service in the two languages. In short, the linguistic resources of the Hull administration are such that service in either French or English is readily obtainable throughout City Hall.

To sum up, we may say that the municipal administration of Hull is basically French; the language of internal administration (working language and language of communication between employees) is French; forms and documents for internal use are in most cases printed in French only. Municipal servants whose mother tongue is English form but a very small minority. However, these factors do not prevent the administration from presenting itself to the public as a bilingual entity. In principle, any member of the public can use French or English in his dealings with the municipal authorities, and his choice of language will determine the language of their reply, whether it be oral or in writing.

To prevent any misunderstanding about the extent of bilingualism in the city government, let it be emphasized that we are dealing with a state of functional bilingualism rather than complete fluency in both languages. Moreover, this bilingualism varies from one department to another, depending on departmental responsibilities and degree of contact with the public. Arrangements are *ad hoc;* bilingualism is flexible, but it is real. Our study did not discover any complaint from the Anglophone population of Hull concerning inequitable treatment from the city authorities as far as language is concerned. We found in Hull a situation of "linguistic peace"; the city government serves the population in French and English without conflict or collision and apparently with a minimum of administrative difficulty.

C. *The City of Eastview*

In many respects Eastview is a unique Ontario municipality. Working within the same provincial framework as Ottawa, it has nevertheless managed to provide service in both

French and English with few apparent difficulties, legal or otherwise. This administrative bilingualism has been brought about, on the one hand, by the needs of the local population (61 per cent French by mother tongue in 1961) and, on the other, by the geographical and political setting of Eastview in a predominantly English-speaking province.

Language practices of the administration. In providing bilingual service, the administration of Eastview is answering a clear need. It was estimated that of the letters sent both to the city and by the city to the public, and of face-to-face interviews between municipal servants and citizens, roughly half are in French and half in English. This distribution changes for telephone calls to and from City Hall. Here an estimated 60 to 75 per cent are in French. Oral contacts appear to outweigh written communications by a considerable margin and, of the former, the more usual medium is the telephone. Communications from individual citizens are most often in French, while those emanating from enterprises, organizations, and institutions tend to be in English.

There is thus a need to give service in both French and English and, in fact, this is the principle on which the administration operates. In practice Eastview appears to be completely bilingual in its pattern of oral communication, and in written communication also as far as the institutional context permits.

On telephoning to the municipality, the first voice that greets the caller employs the formula, "Hôtel de Ville–City Hall." The operators on the central switchboard are all bilingual. Most of the individual departments also employ a bilingual salutation. All of them can accommodate a caller in either language. Rarely is a municipal employee obliged, because of a language barrier, to pass the caller on to someone else—in the vast majority of cases the accommodation is immediate.

Much the same condition obtains in the area of written communications. All eight department heads who were interviewed reported that the language of the original inquiry is respected—incoming letters written in French are answered in French, English in English.

When the city initiates the communication process, the same policy of bilingualism applies. The practice with respect to oral contacts was only mentioned by two department heads during the interviews. One suggested that there was a tendency to use English as the language of approach; the other maintained that his staff attempted first to determine the language of the person being addressed.

As to letters originating from the administration, if the language of the recipient is known, the letter is invariably written in that tongue. If it is not known, several departments appear to make a definite attempt to determine it. When the language cannot be discovered, there appears to be a slight tendency towards using English in preference to French. This tendency may be explained by the assumption, frequently encountered in Eastview, that most of the Francophones understand English, while considerably fewer Anglophones understand French.

The area of forms and public documents presents a different picture. The English language is used more extensively than French. While most documents are bilingual, a significant number of forms are in English only, though no documents destined for the public in French only were reported.

In general, those forms and documents originating with the city are bilingual or in each language separately. Thus one finds available in the two languages all public announcements such as those concerning elections; tax notices and similar official forms; traffic tickets; road signs (although these are to be replaced with graphic, universal traffic symbols); safety signs; permits for construction or business operations; and requests for tenders.

The forms not available in both languages are those relating to the Ontario court system or to the municipality's relations with the province. Legal forms such as subpoenas are in English only. By-laws, because of the provincial context, are drafted in English, although they are translated into French prior to publication.

It might be noted that only recently has French reached a position of equality vis-à-vis English in the documents issued by the city. Prior to 1953 the annual report of the assessment commissioner was issued in English only. It was not until 1957-58 that tax forms and assessment notices became bilingual. Thus the status of the French language in Eastview appears to have improved in the past 15 years. In 1966 the language practice of the city was to some extent formalized and confirmed by a resolution of City Council which provided that all correspondence coming from the public be answered in French or English according to the language in which it originates, and that all communications "addressed to the public in general" be sent out in both French and English (Minutes of City Council, Motion 66-241, passed April 6, 1966).

Internally, the Eastview administration uses both languages on a roughly equal basis. Some distinctions may be made. As we shall see below, a large majority of municipal servants are of French mother tongue, and so most oral contacts take place in French. However, when technical terms are involved or when a person with a limited knowledge of French is present, English is used. As to written communications, English appears to be the language more frequently employed. Five of eight department heads felt this to be so; one felt French was used more often, one considered the two languages were employed in roughly equal proportions, and one offered no opinion.

Composition and language skills of the administration. Clearly, if an Eastview municipal employee is to be effective, he must be able to communicate in both French and English. However, there does not seem to be any definite policy in regard to recruitment and language skills, perhaps because Eastview has no personnel department. Subject to Council approval, hiring is left largely to each department head.

Six department heads touched upon language and employment during the interviews, four expressing a decided preference for bilingual candidates. Three of these suggested that, at least for those in contact with the public, bilingualism was a prerequisite to employment, while the fourth simply stated that as a rule he preferred to obtain bilingual employees. A fifth, whose department employs a high proportion of professionals, maintained that he tried to keep a balance between Francophones and Anglophones but, because of the paucity of qualified candidates, it was not always possible to achieve this goal. The sixth department head, though dealing only peripherally with the question, suggested that there was a certain preference extended to French-speaking applicants. The two department heads who did not discuss the question both administered departments whose staffs were all bilingual at the time of the interview.

In summary, it may be said that, despite the absence of a centralized recruitment procedure, a very strong emphasis is placed on bilingualism as a prerequisite to employment by the city of Eastview.

The Eastview administration, which had consisted of 110 persons in 1964, had risen to a reported total of 131 by 1966. In December 1966, we sent out checklists and received back replies on 107 employees, distributed among the various departments as follows:

City Clerk	4	Welfare	4
Treasury	7	Recreation	3
Assessment	5	Fire	24
Public Works	27	Police	33

It is this group of 107 municipal servants whom we shall analyze for linguistic distribution and skills.

A comparison of the distribution by mother tongue for the city population as a whole and for the administration (*see* Table 4.6), shows that the Anglophones and other language groups are distinctly under-represented at City Hall. This follows the same pattern that was found in Hull.

Table 4.6. Eastview, city population and administration by mother tongue

Mother tongue	City (1961)		Administration (1966)	
	N	%	N	%
Total	24,555	100	107	100
English	8,355	34.0	13	12.1
French	14,976	61.0	93	86.9
Others	1,224	5.0	1	0.9

Sources: Census of Canada, 1961; Catalogue 95-528. Employee checklists, 1966.

Three of the departments have only persons of French mother tongue on their staff. The Fire and Police Departments each have four English-speaking employees. Excluding these eight persons, the other six Eastview employees of non-French mother tongue all occupy relatively high-status positions—two are supervisors, two professionals, and two technical employees; none are wage-earners, secretaries, or clerks.

Both official languages are widely understood by Eastview municipal employees (*see* Table 4.7). Taking again the "fluent" and "considerable" levels of language knowledge as being indicative of the ability to provide satisfactory service in that language, we find that more than four out of five persons (81.3 per cent) in the administration can give service in English; almost all employees (93.4 per cent) can do so in French.

With regard to individual bilingualism, three out of four Eastview employees (or 74.8 per cent) were reported to have a "fluent" or "considerable" knowledge of the second language (*see* Table 4.8). The vast bulk of this bilingual group is provided by the employees of French mother tongue, and the high level of bilingualism in the Eastview administration as a whole is a reflection of their preponderance in the municipal work force. It might be noted, however, that 50 per cent of the employees of English and other mother tongues also were reported as having a "fluent" or "considerable" knowledge of French, a rate far higher than the same groups reveal in the metropolitan area labour force as a whole (*see* Table 1.28).

Table 4.7. Eastview municipal employees, language knowledge

Knowledge of English		Level of knowledge	Knowledge of French	
N	%		N	%
107	100	Total	107	100
56	52.3	Fluent	96	89.7
31	29.0	Considerable	4	3.7
19	17.8	A little	5	4.7
–	–	None	1	0.9
1	0.9	Not stated	1	0.9

Source: Employee checklists, 1966.

Table 4.8. Eastview municipal employees, second-language knowledge

Second-language knowledge	N	%
Total	107	100
Fluent	46	43.0
Considerable	34	31.8
A little	24	22.4
None	1	0.9
Not stated	2	1.9

Source: Employee checklists, 1966.

Finally, we have attempted to establish the position of the bilingual personnel in the Eastview administration by comparing job classification and degree of public contact with the levels of second-language knowledge. After excluding the protective services, as was done in the case of Hull, a group of 50 employees is left. In Eastview, all but two of the 24 municipal servants in the secretarial, clerical, professional and supervisory categories were reported to have a "fluent" or "considerable" knowledge of their second language. Only two of the 13 wage-earners and five of the 13 technicians were bilingual to this extent. If, however, we introduce the variable of public contact (see Table 4.9), it will be seen that none of the "unilingual" wage-earners and only one of the "unilingual" technicians is in contact with the public.

To revert to a more general level—by omitting from consideration the job classifications and taking only the degree of public contact and second-language knowledge—a high correlation is found between the degree of contact and the degree of linguistic ability (see Table 4.10). Thus, practically all those with a high level of bilingualism are in more than daily contact with the public, while those with a low level scarcely meet the public during the course of their work. This correlation suggests that in Eastview some effort is made to deploy bilingual and unilingual municipal personnel in such a way as to carry out the city's policy of providing bilingual service to its citizens with maximum effect.

Table 4.9. Eastview wage-earning and technical employees, public contact by second-language knowledge

Second-language knowledge	Wage-earners		Technicians	
	No contact	With contact	No contact	With contact
Bilingual*	2	–	1	4
Unilingual**	11	–	7	1

Source: Employee checklists, 1966.
* Defined as having a "fluent" or "considerable" knowledge of their second tongue.
** Defined as having "a little," "no" or "not stated" knowledge of their second tongue.

Table 4.10. Eastview municipal employees, degree of public contact by second-language knowledge

Second-language knowledge	Total	Public contact		
		None	Less than once a day	More than once a day
Total	50	21	1	28
Fluent	14	–	–	14
Considerable	14	2	–	12
A little	20	18	1	1
None	–	–	–	–
Not stated	2	1	–	1

Source: Employee checklists, 1966.

From the study of Eastview three points stand out. First, on the attitudinal level, there seems to exist a real feeling that the provision of services in both languages is not a disagreeable necessity but a positive good: the administration appears to be not only able but willing to use both tongues. In our interviews the claim was often stated that because the rights of citizens of both linguistic groups are respected in Eastview, there is very little friction.

In the second place, Eastview's geographical setting plays an important part in the relative position of the two languages. If English is the language of the minority within the city limits, it should be kept in mind that these limits encompass only one square mile of territory. In the municipalities around its borders English is the language of the majority.

Finally, of at least equal importance is the municipality's relationship with the province of Ontario. All eight department heads who were interviewed either stated or implied that this factor was extremely potent in buttressing the use of English by the administration. Not only are all direct relations with the province carried out in English but, in one department at least, matters which the department head believes might reach the province are dealt with in English.

D. *The Other Administrations*

Ten municipalities in the Ottawa metropolitan area remain to be considered. These are, on the Ontario side, Gloucester, Nepean, and Rockcliffe Park; and on the Quebec side, Aylmer, Deschênes, Gatineau, Lucerne, Pointe-Gatineau, Templeton, and West Templeton. In language practices, the three Ontario municipalities follow a similar pattern, that is, broadly speaking, they employ only English in the course of their work. Variations exist among the Quebec municipalities in that some make more frequent use of the two languages than others. However, all seven offer service to the public in French and English. The main differential between the ten municipalities is the provincial factor, and accordingly we shall divide them on this basis in our analysis.

Language practices of the three Ontario municipalities. Demand for French-language service in letters, over the telephone, or in face-to-face interviews is virtually non-existent in the three municipalities. Nepean recorded none at all, while Gloucester and Rockcliffe Park each felt that less than 1 per cent of incoming letters were in French. Gloucester, however, did mention that while telephone and face-to-face conversations were primarily in English, some French was used in the Tax Department as the head was bilingual.

Reflecting the level of demand, service is given mostly in English. All letters are answered in this language. Nepean did mention that although it had never received a letter written in French, the answer would probably be in French if one were received. By-laws in all three municipalities are drafted and published in English only. Public notices, official forms, traffic tickets and summonses,[4] road signs, safety signs, permits for various operations, and requests for tenders issued by the municipalities are in English only as a general rule. Nevertheless, while the handbills and posters that Gloucester puts out are in this language only, the municipality sends notices that are to be made public through the press to *Le Droit* as well as to the *Ottawa Citizen* and *Ottawa Journal*. The same procedure applies to its requests for tenders. Nepean mentioned that it also had used *Le Droit* for publication of requests for tenders. Rockcliffe Park noted that there had been some tendency to replace the traffic signs in the municipality with those of the universal, wordless type.

Such translation as may be required is provided on an *ad hoc* basis. Notices inserted in *Le Droit* are translated by the staff of the paper. Not surprisingly, the internal working language of the three municipalities is English.

The language of service to the public is clearly related to the demand for such service as perceived by the municipality. Rockcliffe Park reported that the French language was not necessary on the business level. Its respondent could not recall encountering a unilingual Francophone resident. Gloucester, too, felt that the linguistic aspects of service to the public were being adequately met by the municipality. The Ontario municipalities have apparently seen no need for bilingual service, and as a result they have provided service only in English.

---

[4] The Ontario Provincial Police provides police services for Rockcliffe Park. Thus the forms used are those of the O.P.P. and not of the municipality.

Language practices of the seven Quebec municipalities. The relative demand for service in French and in English varies sharply from one municipality to another. Table 4.11 shows the level of demand for the use of English in written correspondence, telephone calls, and face-to-face interviews, as seen by the municipalities themselves. In two municipalities, service is requested in English more frequently than in French, in four the opposite obtains, and one (Aylmer) is on the borderline. This ranking in terms of the level of demand for service in the province's minority language remains roughly the same for all three types of public contact.

Table 4.11. Seven Quebec municipalities, demand for service in English as a percentage of total demand for service

Municipality	Letters sent to administration	Telephone calls	Face-to-face interviews
West Templeton	N/A*	70	70
Lucerne	60	51	55
Aylmer	50	50	35
Deschênes	25	10	25
Gatineau	15	15	15
Templeton	10	10	10
Pointe-Gatineau	1	1	1

Source: Questionnaires sent to municipalities in 1966.
* West Templeton reported very little correspondence.

It will be remembered from Chapter II that Quebec municipalities are subject to certain statutory obligations to give service in the two languages as laid down in the Municipal Code or the Cities and Towns Act, and that exception to the provisions of the Municipal Code can be made by the Quebec minister of Municipal Affairs (*see* 64-5). Of the four towns under the Code in the metropolitan area (Deschênes, Lucerne, Templeton and West Templeton), only Lucerne has received such an exemption, and thus since 1923 this municipality has been allowed to conduct its business in English only. However, presumably as a result of the increasing Francophone proportion of the population, Lucerne Council decided in 1962 to use both languages despite its release from the Code's provisions.

Despite the varying level of demand for service in the two languages and the difference in the applicable legal provisions, the seven Quebec municipalities are all effectively bilingual with regard to service to the public. Letters are answered in the language in which they are sent, and it would seem that telephone calls and interviews are conducted in the language of the citizen. Templeton apparently publishes its by-laws in French only. The remaining six municipalities publish bilingually, either with the two versions facing each other on the page (Gatineau and West Templeton) or in separate texts (Aylmer, Deschênes, Lucerne and Pointe-Gatineau). Templeton's by-laws are of course drafted in French, as also are those of Gatineau and Pointe-Gatineau. Aylmer's practice varies, while Deschênes drafts its by-laws in both English and French. Lucerne and West Templeton draft theirs in English only. (This contrasts with the situation in Ontario, where Eastview felt obliged by the institutional framework to draft its by-laws in English.)

Official documents too are almost universally bilingual. Public notices, official forms, traffic tickets and summonses, road signs, safety signs, permits for various operations, and requests for tenders are generally published in both English and French. Only two exceptions to the general rule were reported. Pointe-Gatineau issues its construction permits in French only, while Templeton does the same for its requests for tenders.[5]

Necessary written translations are usually made within each administration. Aylmer, Deschênes, and Templeton use the secretary-treasurer of the municipality, Pointe-Gatineau its clerk. Lucerne employs the municipality's lawyer or engages translators. West Templeton indicated that the need for written translation had never arisen, while Gatineau noted that an official translator had not proved necessary as the Cities and Towns Act provided sample official forms in both languages, and notices sent to newspapers were translated by the newspaper staff.

Where the French and English versions of an official text clashed, Pointe-Gatineau has a by-law giving priority to the French text and Lucerne one that gives priority to the English text. No other such by-laws were reported.

The internal working language of the administrations of Aylmer, Deschênes, Pointe-Gatineau, Gatineau, and Templeton was stated to be French. Lucerne reported English as its main internal language, while West Templeton considered that the two languages were used about equally.

It would seem that in all seven Quebec municipalities language contacts between the administration and the local citizens function smoothly. Aylmer mentioned that on a few rare occasions it had received a letter of complaint from a person with a French Canadian name who had been sent a letter in French, but who was in fact an Anglophone, or *vice versa*. This is illustrative of what appears to be the general attitude prevailing among both the public and municipal servants—that the citizen can expect to be served in his own language. The proportion that the minority-language group forms of the municipal population does not seem to affect this attitude—bilingual service is as available in Pointe-Gatineau with its 3.0 per cent population of English mother tongue as it is in Lucerne with its 45.1 per cent population of French mother tongue.

Composition and language skills of the ten administrations. Policy as to the linguistic abilities of candidates for the municipal service varies widely. In Ontario, Nepean reported that it had no policy at all. Gloucester, while having no formal policy, considered bilingualism a definite asset in certain job categories such as welfare officers, and also in the Tax, Police, and Fire departments. Rockcliffe Park did not report a formal policy either: English would of course be necessary and if in addition the candidate was bilingual this would be favourably regarded.

On the Quebec side, Gatineau and Lucerne both required a candidate for a post in the administrative or Police departments to be bilingual. Deschênes and Aylmer would recruit a bilingual person if this was possible, but Aylmer stressed that the best qualified candidate would be accepted even if he was unilingual. Pointe-Gatineau had no policy as to bilingualism, but did require all its employees to speak French. Templeton had no policy

---

[5] In a few cases, our questions were not applicable. For example, West Templeton issues no traffic tickets and summonses, road signs, or safety signs.

at all. As West Templeton reported no full-time municipal employees, the question was not applicable; in much of the following analysis, no mention of West Templeton is made for this reason.

That even this much weight should be attached to a candidate's bilingualism seems worthy of comment. These are small municipalities which probably experience some difficulty in attracting suitable recruits. Under these circumstances, to establish even a limited requirement of bilingualism would seem to indicate a very real assumption that ability to give service in French and English is a fundamental aspect of the municipal servant's work.

The relative size of the 13 metropolitan area municipalities and their administrations may be seen in Table 4.12. The ranking is by size of the respective populations. There is a rough correlation between population size and the number of persons employed in the municipal service, but it is by no means a perfect one. One factor underlying these variations is the practice among the smaller towns of buying services from one another. Lucerne, for example, takes part of its fire protection from Aylmer, and thus Lucerne's administration is correspondingly smaller than Aylmer's. The disproportionately large Ottawa staff may also be partially explained on these grounds.

So far as we are aware, no municipal services except bus lines cross the provincial boundary. We may therefore compare the number of municipal servants in Ontario municipalities with those in Quebec. In Ontario there is one municipal servant for every 93 residents; in Quebec the ratio drops to one for every 203 residents.

Table 4.12. Municipalities and their administrations in the Ottawa metropolitan area, 1966

Municipality	Population of municipality	Size of administration
Total M.A.	489,392	4,632
Ottawa, Ont.	288,735	3,742*
Hull, Que.	58,902	147**
Nepean, Ont.	43,420	165
Eastview, Ont.	24,047	107
Gloucester, Ont.	23,002	74
Gatineau, Que.	17,434	73
Pointe-Gatineau, Que.	10,903	43
Lucerne, Que.	8,042	17
Aylmer, Que.	7,150	34
Templeton, Que.	3,219	5
Rockcliffe Park, Ont.	2,155	13
Deschênes, Que.	1,772	4
West Templeton, Que.	611	0
Total Ontario	381,359	4,101
Total Quebec	108,033	531

Sources: Population figures: Interim Census 1966, first compilations.
Administration size: Employee checklists.
* Ottawa figure based on the city's personnel list of 1965.
** Excluding firemen. See 96, fn 3.

Looking at the distribution of the administrations by mother tongue (Table A, Appendix G), it is clear that in most cases one group tends to be preponderant. Anglophones form respectively 74, 85 and 85 per cent of the administrations in Gloucester, Nepean, and Rockcliffe Park. Francophones comprise 88, 97 and 98 per cent of the administrations in Aylmer, Gatineau, and Pointe-Gatineau. Only in Deschênes and Lucerne is no one group in such a strong majority. If we compare the distribution by mother tongue for the municipal populations and their administrations, we find that the Anglophone group is relatively over-represented in only one administration, while the Francophone group is over-represented in six administrations.

Insofar as ability to give service in French and English is concerned, differences emerge between the Ontario and Quebec municipalities. As may be seen in Table 4.13, service in English could be given by over half the municipal servants in all but one Quebec municipality. Service in French, on the other hand, while readily available in Quebec, could be given by approximately a quarter or less of the employees of the three Ontario administrations. Looking at the provincial totals, it will be noticed that whereas roughly one-sixth of Ontario servants can give service in French, nearly two-thirds of the Quebec employees can give service in English.

Table 4.13. Eight municipalities, proportion of municipal servants capable of giving service* in English or French

Municipality	Percentage of municipal servants capable of giving service in:	
	English	French
Total (8)	82	48
Gloucester	94	26
Nepean	95	11
Rockcliffe Park	92	23
Aylmer	100	94
Deschênes	100	50
Gatineau	46	98
Lucerne	94	71
Pointe-Gatineau	56	100
Total Ontario (3)	95	16
Total Quebec (5)	65	94

Source: Employee checklists, 1966.
* Defined as having a "fluent" or "considerable" knowledge of the language.

The total for the eight municipalities taken together only serves further to point out the disparity between the position of the two languages in the capital area. While almost five out of six employees in the suburban municipalities can give service in English, fewer than three out of six can do so in French. If we include the three cities of Ottawa, Hull, and Eastview, the ability of civic employees to give service in English climbs to 96 per cent, while their ability to do so in French drops to 42 per cent (*see* Table B, Appendix G).

Many of the municipal servants who can give service in the minority language of the municipality are individually bilingual. Table C, Appendix G gives municipal servants' degree of facility in their second language as reported by each administration. There can be no doubt that the Quebec municipalities employ a far greater proportion of bilingual staff than do the Ontario ones. Apart from the explicit policy of some of the Quebec municipalities in favour of bilingual candidates, this may also be due to another factor—the high level of language skills of the local population among whom the administrations recruit many of their employees. Roughly 40 per cent of the total population of these five Quebec municipalities in 1961 could speak the two official languages. The comparable figures for Nepean, Rockcliffe Park, and Gloucester were 8.7, 29.6, and 32.8 per cent respectively, or an average of 20.7 per cent for all three together.

Of the 140 bilingual municipal servants in the eight municipalities under discussion, 125, or roughly nine out of ten, are of French mother tongue. This is not to say that "French Canadian" and "bilingual" are necessarily synonymous adjectives. Table 4.14 gives the percentage of each mother-tongue group that is bilingual. An examination of this table permits us to say that in the eight administrations, two out of three Francophones are in fact bilingual. Only some 7 per cent of the English and other mother-tongue groups can speak the two languages.

The provincial comparisons are interesting. Civic employees of French mother tongue are more bilingual in Ontario than Quebec: those of English and other mother tongues are more bilingual in Quebec than in Ontario. Clearly a knowledge of English is necessary to work in an Ontario administration, while a knowledge of French, although not necessary, is at the least preferable for the municipal servant in Quebec.

Table 4.14. Eight municipalities, bilingual* municipal servants by mother tongue

Municipality	English and other mother tongues			French mother tongue		
	Total	of which bilingual		Total	of which bilingual	
	N	N	%	N	N	%
Total (8)	225	15	7	188	125	67
Gloucester	57	4	7	15	13	87
Nepean	143	5	4	12	12	100
Rockcliffe Park	11	1	9	2	1	50
Aylmer	4	2	50	30	30	100
Deschênes	2	0	0	2	2	100
Gatineau	–	–	–	75	35	47
Lucerne	7	2	29	10	9	90
Pointe-Gatineau	1	1	100	42	23	55
Total Ontario (3)	211	10	5	29	26	90
Total Quebec (5)	14	5	36	159	99	62

Source: Employee checklists, 1966.
* Defined as having a "fluent" or "considerable" knowledge of their second language.

The position of the bilingual personnel with respect to job classification and frequency of public contact in the eight administrations may also be noted. Since the protective services do not fit easily into the standard job classifications and are also difficult to categorize by degree of public contact, they are excluded from the following discussion.

Table 4.15 compares the three Ontario and five Quebec municipalities in terms of job classification. On the Ontario side, the bilingual staff tend to form a higher than average concentration in the wage-earner category. The clerical category is close to the average, while the remaining ones are below it. In Quebec, on the other hand, we find that the wage-earner category has proportionally fewer bilingual employees than the others. The supervisory, professional, and secretarial categories show a very high percentage of bilingual persons.

Table 4.15. Eight municipalities, bilingual* municipal servants as percentage of total in each job classification (excluding protective services)

Job classification	Total	Ontario municipalities**	Quebec municipalities***
Total	28	13	47
Wage-earner	22	18	27
Secretarial	39	7	100
Clerical	44	14	65
Technical	27	0	62
Professional	29	9	100
Supervisory	31	11	75

Source: Employee checklists, 1966.
* Defined as having a "fluent" or "considerable" knowledge of their second language.
** Gloucester, Nepean, Rockcliffe Park.
*** Aylmer, Deschênes, Gatineau, Lucerne, Pointe-Gatineau.

Table 4.16. Eight municipalities, bilingual* municipal servants as percentage of total for each level of public contact (excluding protective services)

Degree of public contact	Total	Ontario municipalities**	Quebec municipalities***
Total	28	13	47
None	34	21	38
Less than once a day	20	14	30
More than once a day	32	12	67

Source: Employee checklists, 1966.
* Defined as having a "fluent" or "considerable" knowledge of their second language.
** Gloucester, Nepean, Rockcliffe Park.
*** Aylmer, Deschênes, Gatineau, Lucerne, Pointe-Gatineau.

Table 4.16, showing the percentage of bilingual personnel in the three categories of public contact, points to another striking difference between the Ontario and Quebec municipalities. In accordance with the Quebec administrations' policy of giving bilingual service, the percentage of bilingual staff in frequent public contact is considerably higher than that for the employees with little or no contact. In the case of the Ontario municipalities, bilingualism is most widespread among those with no public contact at all. Both of these factors (job categories and public contact), which are discussed in aggregate terms here, are tabulated in Tables D and E, Appendix G, for each of the 13 municipalities of the metropolitan area.

E. Summary

For the 12 municipalities considered in this chapter, the following points may be made:
1) The provincial framework is clearly of importance. Quebec both obliges and encourages its municipalities to be bilingual; Ontario does not. The example of Eastview, however, shows that an Ontario municipality can use both languages in its work.
2) Apart from Eastview, the Ontario municipalities attach relatively little importance to serving the public in French and English; in Eastview and the Quebec municipalities, this is a major concern.
3) The service available to the public reflects these attitudes. Apart from Eastview, service in the two languages is rare in Ontario; in the Quebec municipalities it is almost universally obtainable.
4) Official documents are for the most part bilingual in Eastview and the Quebec municipalities, but not elsewhere.
5) Broadly speaking, the internal language of work is English in Gloucester, Nepean, Rockcliffe Park, and Lucerne; English and French in Eastview and West Templeton, and French in the remaining six municipalities.
6) Only Hull, Eastview, Gatineau, and Lucerne reported actual policies requiring bilingualism of recruits. Most of the other municipalities would accord preference to a bilingual candidate if all other qualifications were equal.
7) Only in Deschênes and Lucerne are municipal servants not predominantly of one mother tongue. Apart from these two, the position of the majority group is stronger in the administration than in the general population.
8) A majority of employees were reported to be bilingual in all municipalities except Gloucester, Nepean, Rockcliffe Park, and Gatineau.
9) Bilingual municipal servants tend strongly to be of French mother tongue. Those of English mother tongue are more likely to be bilingual if they work in Quebec.
10) In Ontario, with the exception of Eastview, the highest percentages of bilingual employees tend to be in positions of low status and low public contact, whereas in the Quebec municipalities and Eastview the opposite tendency is found.

Following this study of the area municipalities, the position of the city of Ottawa can now be put into context. A clear distinction with regard to language usage may be made between Ottawa, Nepean, Gloucester, and Rockcliffe Park, on the one hand, and Eastview and the eight Quebec municipalities on the other. The presence of Eastview in the latter category serves to show both the importance and the limits of provincial influence on language usage. While this influence is undoubtedly strong, it does not offer a complete explanation, for attitudinal factors also have a role. With the latter group of municipalities, bilingualism is the accepted practice, not simply or even primarily because it is necessary but rather because certain psychological factors work in its favour. These factors, such as the expectation that Anglophones cannot understand French, the belief that bilingualism is no great obstacle but rather a help to efficient service, and the assumption that bilingualism is not an impossibly difficult goal at which to aim, have led to the provision of service in the two languages far beyond the level that purely pragmatic considerations might suggest. Finally, it should be noted that neither the "unilingual" nor the "bilingual" municipalities indicated that their linguistic practices were determined by any awareness of the possible special needs of the federal capital area.

Chapter V   The Impact of the Federal Government

A. The Federal Presence

As we have seen in the preceding chapters, the National Capital Region comprises parts of two provinces—Ontario and Quebec—which exercise their constitutional powers in the Region in much the same way as elsewhere in their respective territories. On the local level, the area is governed by a plethora of municipalities which, like all municipalities, are created by their respective provinces and are answerable to them. What does mark off the Ottawa-Hull area from other metropolitan areas is its position as the national capital, and the rather special interest the federal government has displayed in the area as a result of this.

Notwithstanding its special concern for the area, the government of Canada differs from those of other federal countries such as Australia and the United States in that the Canadian constitution gives no express power to the federal government with relation to the government of its own capital area.[1] It might be noted, however, that certain federal measures to develop the capital have been upheld when challenged in the courts.

Nevertheless, despite the lack of a special constitutional position and even without any specific action on its part, the federal government simply by operating in the area has had a not inconsiderable impact on the development and character of the Ottawa-Hull region. The scope, degree, and diversity of federal operations are such that it in fact wields a great deal of influence on the local scene. Consider for a moment a partial list of the government's activities in the region:

Through government departments or Crown corporations, the federal government at Ottawa, for example, makes films, prints pamphlets, runs transportation companies,

---

[1] Professor D.C. Rowat has noted that, of the 15 countries other than Canada that have federal constitutions, 10 have placed the territory of the federal capital in a special relationship with the federal government. Eight of these 10 capitals seem to have preserved some form of local self-government, the only known exceptions being Washington, D.C., and Canberra, Australia. An eleventh country, Austria, has made its capital one of the states of the Austrian federation. See *Le territoire québecois de la Région de la Capitale nationale,* prepared by Le Conseil économique régional de l'Ouest du Québec (Hull, 1967), Appendix A, 44-5.

makes radioactive isotopes, operates a gigantic broadcasting system, manufactures explosives, runs a design centre, supervises pipeline corporations, controls atomic energy, mines uranium, plans parkways, acts as a patron for the arts, maintains historic buildings, administers the northwest territories, runs airlines, publishes magazines and operates bookstores.[2]

Clearly, not all of these activities directly affect the national capital. Taken together, however, their collective impact lends a particular tone to the area.

One index of the weight of the federal government in the area is the proportion of the local labour market for which it accounts. As we saw in Chapter I, in 1961 the Canadian government was the major employer in the National Capital Region, utilizing as it did the skills of some 30 per cent of the local labour force. Indeed, looking at the situation from another perspective, the number of people employed by the Crown was nearly three times the proportion of those involved in the entire manufacturing sector of the area's economy (see Table 1.10).

A considerable proportion of the money which the federal government puts directly into the pockets of so large a segment of the working population is spent within the Ottawa-Hull area. In this way, the government indirectly acts as a support of the local service industries. It has also largely determined the rate of expansion of these industries, for while the federal government has grown in response to factors external to the National Capital Region, the local service industries, by contrast, have developed primarily as the government has attracted more and more people to the capital.

Indeed, the economic dependence of the area on the federal government is so pronounced as to lend a note of artificiality to the regional economy. Both the present size and anticipated development of the latter are based, not on the natural riches or strategic location of the region, but on the continued presence and future vigour of the Canadian government. In short, if tomorrow the federal pay cheques were by some chance suddenly cut off, not only would that third of the local labour force directly dependent upon them go hungry, but also as much again as a further third of the working population would find their livelihood endangered.

In addition to its role as the region's largest single employer, the federal government occupies the rather interesting position of the area's major landowner. In the realization of two of the more prominent federal projects in the area—Gatineau Park and the Greenbelt—nearly one hundred thousand acres were purchased by the Crown. It is worth noting that land is still being bought for these two projects. When complete, the total area of the two combined will comprise approximately 130,000 acres. (For a fuller discussion of this topic see 123.)

Within the two major municipalities of the region the extent of federal holdings is, to say the least, impressive. Of the land within the city of Ottawa, approximately 28 per cent is owned outright by the federal government, while in the city of Hull federal holdings account for approximately 25 per cent of the total (figures provided by the National Capital Commission).

---

[2] W. Eggleston, *The Queen's Choice* (Queen's Printer, Ottawa, 1961), 37.

The sheer size of federal holdings is readily apparent; of at least equal significance, however, are the uses to which government properties are put. Although much of the federally-owned land within the region is employed in providing parks and recreational facilities, the Crown also owns and leases a large number of buildings. As we shall see in a later section, their incidence and distribution play an important role in shaping federal-municipal relations.

A third aspect of the federal government's presence in the National Capital Region is its impact on the budgets of local municipalities. All of the many federally-owned buildings require the normal range of municipal services (fire protection, water supply, sewage disposal, and the like). Normal practice is, of course, for the municipalities to collect property and other taxes to pay for these services. This they cannot do, however, in respect to government property as, by section 125 of the B.N.A. Act, it is provided that "no lands or property belonging to Canada or any Province shall be liable to taxation." Although under no obligation to do so, the government does in fact offer the municipalities some recompense (for a fuller discussion, see 128-30).

Another aspect of the federal presence in the Ottawa area is to be found in the many government institutions that are established in Ottawa simply because it is the capital. These buildings, the most obvious example of which are the Parliament Buildings, are clearly of local importance in relation to the tourist trade. Of more interest, perhaps, to the local population are the national cultural institutions which, although established in the interests of Canadians generally, benefit most directly and continuously the residents of the capital area. The National Gallery, the National Museum, the National Library, and the National Arts Centre (presently under construction), are but some of the more important manifestations of the central government's participation in the provision of cultural facilities.

The federal government is, then, both the major employer and the major landowner in the area. Primarily as a result of the latter role, it figures largely in the affairs of the local municipalities. It also acts as the major provider of cultural and other facilities in the capital. All these activities, however, are the result of the normal day-to-day operations of the federal government.

This is not to say that the federal government has passively watched the development of the nation's capital. On the contrary, despite its lack of an express constitutional relationship with the capital and the consequent need to avoid infringing upon provincial powers, it has long been actively involved in the area. In the following sections the impact of this federal involvement will be described, with the object of answering two major questions: What role does the federal government play in the administration of the capital area, or more precisely of the National Capital Region? What provisions does the federal government make to meet the linguistic and cultural needs of Canada's capital?

Our approach will be primarily institutional, that is, the various government agencies will be taken in turn and their role and function in the capital described. Many agencies have no particular interest in the capital beyond that extended to all areas of Canada, and these will not be specially considered. Some have occasionally been called upon to play a special role in the affairs of the capital, while others have a continuing special interest in the area as well as other duties. Only one agency is solely concerned with the National Capital

Region—the National Capital Commission. We turn first, then, to this Commission and its predecessors, whose history dates back to the end of the nineteenth century.

B. The National Capital Commission

Historical background. Perhaps the primary point to be noted in discussing the historical evolution of agencies working in the capital is that the present activities of the National Capital Commission are not radically different from those of other federal agencies which have preceded it. Although its powers and resources are wider than those of its predecessors, the National Capital Commission, in its concern with the physical setting of the Canadian capital, is carrying out a federal policy which dates back well over half a century to the days of Sir Wilfrid Laurier. As early as 1893, Canada's future prime minister was on record as wishing to see Ottawa become "the centre of the intellectual development of this country, . . . the Washington of the North" (Eggleston, 155).

The Ottawa Improvement Commission, a body of four members established in December 1899, was the first planning agency in the area. It devoted much of its energies to clearing away the more obvious traces of Ottawa's "sub-arctic lumber village" past. Comprising as it did a group of interested but basically amateur planners, and operating on an annual budget of $60,000,[3] the Commission did not make many far-reaching changes, though it did accomplish much that is praiseworthy. The basis of the present Driveway system, often considered among the more charming of Ottawa's prospects, dates from this era.

As the federal government's concern with the capital increased, so were the geographical dimensions of this interest enlarged. Although initially the Ottawa Improvement Commission was almost exclusively concerned with the development of the city of Ottawa, later events suggest the gradual evolution of federal concern for the city of Hull. For example, the Federal Plan Commission, which was set up in 1913, was instructed to "take all necessary steps to draw up and perfect a comprehensive scheme or plan looking to the future growth and development of the city of Ottawa and the city of Hull, and their environs . . ." (Eggleston, 167). The composition of this Commission also bears witness to the extension of federal interest across the Ottawa River. In addition to the chairman and three other members, the mayors of both Ottawa and Hull were members, *ex officio.*

Referred to by one authority as "one of the outstanding state documents of Canadian history" (Eggleston, 167-8), the Holt Report—as the Federal Plan Commission's recommendations came to be known—was in many ways farsighted. However, it appears to have had little immediate effect on federal planning activities in the capital region. The tremendous outlay of energy and money required by World War I and the reconstruction of the Parliament Buildings after the fire of 1916 combined to sideline this master plan of the capital. As a result, the Ottawa Improvement Commission appears to have continued much as it had before until it was replaced by a new and more powerful federal planning body, the Federal District Commission, in 1927.

---

[3]In 1902 the Commission was authorized to issue debentures up to $250,000 and its membership was increased to eight. Its annual budget was twice increased: to $100,000 in 1910 and $150,000 in 1917. *See* J. Harvey Perry, *Report on the Financial and Administrative Arrangements in Capitals of Federal Countries* (Lagos, 1953), 18; and Eggleston, *The Queen's Choice,* 160 and 166.

The Federal District Commission was the chief vehicle for the expression of federal interest in the capital area, until it was reconstituted in 1959 as the National Capital Commission. Perhaps the most interesting aspect surrounding the establishment of the Federal District Commission was the explicit recognition by the government of the day that its interests extended beyond the boundaries of the city of Ottawa. "The purpose," Mackenzie King told the Commons, "is not to confine the work of the Commission to the City of Ottawa, but to include the suburbs of the city and the City of Hull across the way" (House of Commons, *Debates,* April 6, 1927). As its expanded powers, dating from 1934, stipulated, the Commission was responsible for landscape construction and maintenance of all federal properties in the capital area (Eggleston, 176). Partly in recognition of the agency's enlarged purview, membership of the Federal District Commission was established at 10, one of whom was to be a resident of Hull.

The Commission began its operations in 1927 with an annual grant of $250,000, that is, $100,000 more than the Ottawa Improvement Commission had received. However, a year after its inception, the grant was reduced to $200,000 in return for the provision of an immediate capital sum of $3,000,000 (Eggleston, 173). More than half this amount was used to purchase the site of what was to become Confederation Square, the remainder being spent to extend the Driveway system.

The pressures of World War II, the demand for office space and accommodation, the inability of the Commission to cope with the situation, and most important, the increasingly chaotic financial relationship between the federal government and the city of Ottawa, raised new problems. During the war years a number of "temporary" federal buildings (some of which are still extant in 1967) as well as many permanent structures were built. As Ottawa was obliged to provide the municipal services they required, and yet could not constitutionally collect taxes on them, it found itself in an increasingly difficult financial position. The outcome was the 1944 Joint Parliamentary Committee of Inquiry. The most important result of this Inquiry related, not to town planning, but to federal-municipal financial relations. After hearing the arguments both for and against increasing federal financial assistance to the city of Ottawa, the Committee recommended that the annual federal grant for municipal services be increased from $100,000 to $300,000 for a period of five years. It went on to suggest that the matter then be reviewed. In 1951 emerged the Municipal Grants Act, which attempted to regulate, on a more orderly basis than the purely *ad hoc*, the central government's financial arrangements with those municipalities like Ottawa possessing concentrations of federal property.

Although the Joint Committee was primarily concerned with financial questions, it appears to have led to other changes relating directly to the growth of the Federal District Commission. In 1945 came the delineation of the area to be known as the National Capital District. As defined at this time it encompassed approximately 900 square miles, of which 536 square miles were in Quebec and 364 in Ontario. In whole or in part, the territories of some 28 municipalities fell within the District (Perry, 20).

Several crucial changes in the powers and structure of the Federal District Commission took place the following year. The newly defined capital area was brought within the purview of the Commission. It was also given the power to co-ordinate all construction and development on Crown-owned land within the District. Further, the annual grant of the

Commission was increased to $300,000 and capital expenditures of up to $3,000,000 were authorized (Perry, 20). Two years later, in 1948, the financial powers of the Federal District Commission were again strengthened with the creation of the National Capital Fund. Twenty-five million dollars were made available through the Fund, in 10 annual grants (Eggleston, 250).

Just as important were the changes which took place in the structure of the Commission. In 1944, the Joint Parliamentary Committee had recommended "that the powers of the Federal District Commission be increased, and its personnel be enlarged to include, not only representatives of the Ottawa area, but of the people of Canada as a whole" (Eggleston, 183). Accordingly, in 1946, the membership of the Commission was expanded to 19, among whom were to be representatives of each province.

Finally, 1946 also saw the creation of a formal planning organization, the National Capital Planning Committee, whose purpose was "to draw up a master plan of the National Capital District" (Eggleston, 185). Designed to function in conjunction with the Federal District Commission, the Planning Committee counted some 23 members. The Commission appointed 12, and its chairman held membership *ex officio* (Eggleston, 185). Jacques Gréber was named consultant to the Committee.

The 1950 publication of the Master Plan for the National Capital (or Gréber Plan), coupled with the changes which took place in the preceding five years, radically expanded the functions of the Federal District Commission. The Commission outgrew its previous history as a glorified parks commission and rapidly became both the custodian and chief agent in the gradual realization of the Master Plan. Yet it was soon to undergo another transformation.

In 1956 a second Joint Parliamentary Committee of Inquiry on the capital was instituted. As an outgrowth of its deliberations the National Capital Act received assent on September 6, 1958, and was proclaimed on February 6, 1959. This legislation established a modified and financially strengthened version of the Federal District Commission, to be known as the National Capital Commission. Also, the National Capital District was officially re-christened the National Capital Region and its area enlarged from 900 to 1,800 square miles, the larger portion of which (1,050 square miles) now lay in Ontario.

The 20 commissioners of the National Capital Commission are appointed by the cabinet and hold office—during pleasure—for a period not exceeding two consecutive terms of four years. The method of selection is clearly stipulated. At least one member is to be appointed from each of the 10 provinces, two from the city of Ottawa, one from the city of Hull, one from a local municipality in Ontario other than the city of Ottawa, and one from a local municipality in Quebec other than the city of Hull. The chairman and vice-chairman of the Commission are appointed directly by the cabinet rather than elected by their fellow members.

One point is worth noting in regard to the selection of commissioners. The formal ties between the federal agency and the municipalities are less direct now than they were prior to 1959. Since the days of the Ottawa Improvement Commission the city of Ottawa had had the right to appoint a member to the Commission. In 1946 this right had been extended to the city of Hull. In practice the two mayors were appointed to represent their respective cities. However, the National Capital Act removed this power and required simply that "at least two members [shall be appointed] from the city of Ottawa" and "at least one member from the city of Hull" (National Capital Act, section 3(3)).

Purposes and Powers. The primary purpose of the National Capital Commission is the development of the federal capital. More specifically, the National Capital Act (section 10(1)) provides that: "The objects and purposes of the Commission are to prepare plans for and assist in the development, conservation and improvement of the National Capital Region in order that the nature and character of the seat of the Government of Canada may be in accordance with its national significance."

The listing of the Commission's powers under section 10(2) of the Act shows more clearly the kinds of operations in which the Commission is involved. Thus the Commission is authorized, for the purposes of the Act, to acquire, hold, administer, or develop property, and also to dispose of property. Apart from its own property, the Commission may also manage other government property at the request of the authority or minister in charge. The National Capital Commission's power to acquire and dispose of property is subject to the approval of the Governor in Council in certain instances. The Commission may construct, maintain, and operate parks, highways, bridges, buildings, and other works as well as places of public interest or accommodation such as recreation and refreshment centres. It may also administer historic sites and conduct research in connection with the planning of the National Capital Region. Finally, a general grant of power enables it to "do and authorize such things as are incidental or conducive to the attainment of the objects and purposes of the Commission and the exercise of its powers."

The National Capital Commission acts as co-ordinator in the development of public lands. Obviously if each government agency went its own way in the development of its property the result would be a capital of inharmonious aspect, to say the least. To avert this possibility the National Capital Act requires that all departmental proposals for the location, erection, alteration, or extension of a building or other work in the National Capital Region be submitted to the National Capital Commission and its approval obtained prior to the commencement of the work. Moreover, non-governmental agencies or individuals who wish to erect, alter or extend a building or other work on Crown-owned land within the National Capital Region must also obtain the National Capital Commission's permission to do so. While the Governor in Council may overrule a Commission decision not to grant approval to the plans submitted to it, federal government property in the capital is submitted to the discipline of overall planning.

However, the federal government does not own all or even most of the land within the National Capital Region. While Parliament can call upon the National Capital Commission to co-ordinate the development of government land, it has been unable to give the Commission any authoritative voice in the planning of the National Capital Region as a whole.

It should be borne in mind that, for most purposes, constitutional jurisdiction over town planning falls within the provincial domain. Although anyone or any agency may draw up a plan, it can only be realized—if it is in the public domain—through powers which find their source in the provincial, rather than the federal, grant of powers. The National Capital Plan, though accepted by the Parliament of Canada, has no official status vis-à-vis the National Capital Region. As Mr. Justice Gibson has observed:

> The adoption of the Master (Gréber) Plan by the National Capital Commission has no legal effect on lands in the National Capital Region. . . .

But, in contrast to this, such is not the case when a municipality enacts an "official plan" under *The Planning Act* [of Ontario]. For example, section 20 of that Act provides that no re-development . . . shall be approved by the Municipal Board unless it conforms with the Official Plan. It is also provided in section 15(1) that where an official plan is in effect in a municipality no public work shall be undertaken that does not conform therewith.[4]

The nub of the matter is that the National Capital Commission has no legal authority to realize its plans unless they are being executed on land owned by the agency or by the federal government. The Commission can approach the municipalities, attempt to sway them to the merits of its case, offer financial aid, even assistance in drawing up the highly technical zoning by-laws required, but unless the municipalities agree, it has no power to act on its own—unless it owns the land on which the project is to be carried out.[5]

We discussed earlier in this chapter the federal government's role as the largest single landowner in the region. We come now to a major reason for its massive holdings: under present arrangements there appears to be no other way in which the central government, insulated as it is from the local municipalites, can exercise some degree of control over land use in the National Capital Region. Because of its lack of legal authority in matters pertaining to the realization of the Master Plan, particularly in relation to zoning, the federal government, through the National Capital Commission, has resorted to the purchase of large parcels of land. This has not been an inexpensive approach to the problem.

Compared to the days when the Ottawa Improvement Commission functioned on an annual grant of $60,000, the National Capital Commission's resources are truly vast. For example, the total expenditures of the Commission for the year ending March 31, 1967, were $38.2 million.[6] During the twenty years from April 1, 1947 to March 31, 1967, the National Capital Commission and its predecessor, the Federal District Commission, have spent in total $189 million on developing and improving the National Capital Region. About 59 per cent of this amount (or $111.6 million) was used to acquire property or to pay interest charges on the loans needed to acquire property. In contrast, during the same period, Commission expenditures on "assistance to municipalities, construction projects and grants for sewers and water mains" totalled some $14.6 million (*Annual Report, 1966-67*, 19-20). For a more detailed listing of Federal District Commission-National Capital Commission expenditures, *see* Appendix H.

Clearly, much of this money was spent on projects which normally require the public purchase of private holdings, such as the acquisition of land for the Queensway—a multi-

---

[4] Gibson J., *National Capital Commission* v. *Munro* (Canada Law Reports, Exchequer Court, 1965), II, 616.

[5] The most obvious way around this bottleneck would be for the municipalities to adopt the Gréber Plan as their own official plan. As of April 1965 suggestions to this end had met with only a resounding silence: "... except for streets and certain parks, neither the Townships of Gloucester and Nepean nor the City of Ottawa has adopted an official plan under *The Planning Act,* although each of these municipalities was invited to adopt the Master (Gréber) Plan...as their respective official plan under *The Planning Act.* In the province of Quebec, also, there has been no adoption of the equivalent of any so-called 'official plan' or the Master (Gréber) Plan...in so far as the lands of the Province of Quebec within the National Capital Region under the *National Capital Act* are concerned." Gibson J., *National Capital Commission* v. *Munro,* 616-17.

[6] National Capital Commission, *Annual Report,* 1966-67, Part II, 18.

lane highway crossing Ottawa from east to west—or on lands for future government use. A significant amount, however, was spent on projects whose primary aim was, in a sense, "defensive." Many properties were bought because the maintenance of large tracts of land in a natural state, as called for by the Master Plan, could only be insured by actually buying up the land.

A glance at the two major projects of this type, the 88,000-acre Gatineau Park and the 41,000-acre Greenbelt, is revealing. From 1947 to 1967 the National Capital Commission spent approximately $41 million on the acquisition of land for these two developments. This figure highlights the manner in which the financial resources of the agency have been employed to compensate for the Commission's lack of jurisdiction over land use in the National Capital Region.

Finally, it appears that the National Capital Commission's property acquisition policy, though past its peak, will continue to exercise an important influence on its expenditures for some time to come. Of the approximately 88,000 acres in Gatineau Park, the Commission owns some 68,000. Of the remaining 20,000 acres, roughly 10,500 are owned by the province of Quebec, the rest being in private hands. Similarly, federal holdings amount to about 33,000 acres in the Greenbelt, though the latter will eventually comprise some 41,000 acres. (These figures, provided by the National Capital Commission, are for holdings as of May 1967.)

Besides the power of the purse, the National Capital Commission is also able to acquire land by way of expropriation. Section 13 of the National Capital Act provides that "the Commission may, with the approval of the Governor in Council, take or acquire lands for the purposes of this Act without the consent of the owner. . . ." The section goes on to make provision for the compensation of expropriated landowners.

The Commission has used its right to expropriate where necessary when other means of acquisition are not open but, in doing so, it appears to have paid an intangible but very real price in terms of public sympathy. On the one hand, there is appreciation for the many fine works with which the National Capital Commission has enriched life in the region; on the other, there is the feeling, justifiable or not, that the Commission operates as a law unto itself, more concerned with the monumental than the human.[7] Much of this sentiment can be traced directly to the Commission's expropriations. Indeed, the National Capital Commission has recently emerged from a major legal challenge *(Munro* v. *National Capital Commission)* as to the validity of its right to expropriate, which was carried to the Supreme Court of Canada and which may prove a decision of some importance. The judgement pronounced on June 28, 1966 upheld the Exchequer Court decision of April 28, 1965 which had found in favour of the Commission.

The courts had been called upon to determine whether it is within the powers of Parliament to authorize the establishment of a Greenbelt within the National Capital Region. Munro contended that such authorization could only be given by the provincial legislature, as under the B.N.A. Act the provinces were assigned the power to legislate on property and civil rights in the province. The Supreme Court, however, held that while the National

---

[7] As this interpretation is based primarily on newspaper articles it is quite possible that it does not completely mirror underlying attitudes of the local residents. It does, however, reflect those articulated by and in the local press.

Capital Act incidentally affected property and civil rights, its primary purpose was to develop the National Capital Region, and as such was within the legislative competence of the federal Parliament. The Court held that the grant of powers of expropriation to the National Capital Commission was a valid exercise of that legislative competence. Speaking for the Court, Mr. Justice Cartwright stated:

> I find it difficult to suggest a subject matter of legislation which more clearly goes beyond local or provincial interests and is the concern of Canada as a whole than the development, conservation and improvement of the National Capital Region in accordance with a coherent plan in order that the nature and character of the seat of the Government of Canada may be in accordance with its national significance (Cartwright J., *Munro* v. *National Capital Commission,* Canada Law Reports, Supreme Court of Canada, 1966, 671).

Although the potential implications of this decision may be very broad, the immediate result of the Supreme Court judgement appears to be simply the ratification of the Commission's right to expropriate. Yet this power, as well as that of the National Capital Commission to acquire property by other means, represents fundamentally a federal attempt to bridge the cleavages created by divided jurisdictions. At the present time, the National Capital Commission, in its efforts to realize the goal of a fitting capital for Canada, must work in areas which can only be approached indirectly by the federal Parliament.

Although a right to expropriate—subject to cabinet approval—belongs to the National Capital Commission legally, political considerations have limited this power to some extent. Historically, the Federal District Commission was considerably more reluctant to expropriate land in Quebec than in Ontario. One important reason was the view of the former province—which dates back to the days of Premier Maurice Duplessis—that the Commission's power to expropriate, though admitted for roads and buildings, did not extend to parklands. In view of this attitude and the opposition encountered,[8] the National Capital Commission's predecessor appears to have decided that discretion is the better part of valour. According to the brief submitted by the Federal District Commission to the 1956 Parliamentary Inquiry: "Expropriations are being carried out in the Province of Ontario but the Commission has not expropriated property in the Province of Quebec since 1949."[9]

Although expropriations were carried out on the Quebec side in the post-1956 period, this sensitivity appears to have persisted. Early in 1966, a member of Parliament from a local riding asked whether the National Capital Commission had been instructed to halt expropriations in Quebec. The answer, read in the House on February 2, 1966, is illustrative both of this sensitivity and of the ties which bind the National Capital Commission to the cabinet. The statement read as follows:

> On August 23, 1963, during the temporary absence of the Chairman of the National Capital Commission, an informal request was made from the Minister [of Public Works] to the Commission asking it to temporarily withhold further requests for authority to expropriate in the Province of Quebec until further instructions were given.

---

[8]Thus at one time it was believed that the late Mr. Duplessis would aid any Quebec resident who challenged in the courts the Federal District Commission's power of expropriation.

[9]Joint Committee of the Senate and House of Commons on the Federal District Commission, *Minutes of Proceedings and Evidence,* 1956, 59.

On April 16, 1964, instructions were given that the National Capital Commission could feel free again to seek authority to expropriate properties in Quebec as the need arose. (House of Commons, *Debates,* February 2, 1966, 575)

Under the present scheme of things, the power to expropriate privately-held land remains an important instrument of federal capital development. This can be illustrated statistically. In the period from February 1959 to August 1967 the National Capital Commission acquired through expropriation or purchase some 2,413 parcels of land, of which 1,538, or 64 per cent, were acquired by expropriation. It might be noted that the use of expropriation varies according to the nature of the project for which the land is required. The assembly of land for Gatineau Park and the Greenbelt was carried out to a very considerable extent by purchase; that for the new bridge approaches and for the LeBreton Flats project was done entirely by expropriation. Approximately five out of every six parcels acquired in this period were on the Ontario side, and expropriation was used proportionally more in Ontario than in Quebec (65 per cent of the Ontario parcels against 57 per cent of those in Quebec).[10]

Yet it is well to remember that expropriation is not a popular instrument, and that much of the present mistrust and unpopularity of the National Capital Commission may probably be traced to its possession and use of this power. This takes us back to the central dilemma of the federal government in the capital area: its lack of authority to carry out its policy of developing and improving the capital. The federal government can carry out this policy only on lands which it owns, and the acquisition of such lands requires a frequent resort to expropriation. The only visible alternatives to this rather unpopular system are either a federal authority which would have virtually no power at all over its own seat of government, or the establishment of some new relationship between the federal government and the capital area.

Language Usage. As the preceding paragraphs have indicated, the National Capital Commission is very actively involved in the day-to-day life of the capital area. It follows, then, that its practices in regard to language usage will create a significant impression of the capital as either a unilingual or a bilingual area, and this impression will be implanted in residents and visitors alike.

In order to see the present in perspective, a brief glance at some of the linguistic practices of the National Capital Commission's predecessor is of value. The impression which one gathers today is that the Federal District Commission was not particularly sensitive to the linguistic implications of its work in the capital. According to the testimony of the chairman of this body before the 1956 Joint Parliamentary Committee of Inquiry, the Commission was at that time just beginning to employ bilingual road signs. This policy, however, was being realized only on the Quebec side of the Capital Region as it was felt that the signs should be kept in harmony with those of the local municipalities.[11]

---

[10]Figures supplied by the National Capital Commission. A full tabulation by province and project is given in Appendix I.

[11]*Minutes of Proceedings and Evidence, see* especially 171-5. Indeed, according to one M.P. from the area, the signs had been, at least for a time, in English only throughout the Region. It should be noted, however, that the Federal District Commission was not then a completely unilingual agency. There seems to have been provision for the dissemination, in French and in English, of information on the activities of the Commission.

The general consensus of the Committee was distinctly against this policy and in favour of the same treatment being accorded both official languages throughout the Capital area. Indeed, the parliamentarians ultimately recommended in their report to Parliament that: "In keeping with the character of Canada, . . . all literature, signs and advertising of the Federal District Commission be bilingual" (*Minutes of Proceedings and Evidence,* 1054).

The Commission accepted this recommendation as policy, but it would appear that some eight years elapsed before it was implemented actively and positively with respect to signs. On September 16, 1964, the *Ottawa Journal* carried an article which read, in part: "The National Capital Commission started last week to implement a new written policy which will ultimately result in all its signs being posted in French and English."

At present,[12] the National Capital Commission seems to be distinctly more aware of the capital's linguistic needs than was its predecessor a decade ago. Incoming correspondence in either English or French is always answered in the same language. Public notices of the National Capital Commission are issued in both French and English. Of the four types of forms available in the Commission's Ottawa offices for use by the public, three are either available separately in each language or in bilingual form. Similarly, all publications of the National Capital Commission appear to be either bilingual, or available separately in both official languages.[13]

The same recognition appears to be accorded to both official languages in regard to the signs of the Commission. According to the information supplied by the Commission these appear in French and English.[14] Indeed, much of whatever visual bilingual image the Ontario portion of the National Capital Region possesses today is due to the work of the National Capital Commission.

In its direct relations with the public, the Commission is able to give service in either language, though an occasional time lag between the request and the response appears likely for French-speaking citizens, given the distribution of bilingual personnel. Of the 28 National Capital Commission employees whom it classified in 1965 as "in contact with the public," 12 spoke both official languages. No unilingual French-speaking employees in this category were reported; the remaining 16 employees spoke English only.

In the Commission's contacts with local municipalities, the predominant language appears to be English. For discussions with French-speaking municipal representatives, however, an *ad hoc* interpretation service is available. To quote from a statement given by a National Capital Commission official in the summer of 1965: "At meetings with representatives of surrounding municipalities, the secretary acts as interpreter for those participants who wish to express themselves in French and this arrangement seems to be satisfactory."

---

[12]It should be noted that much of the following analysis is based on data supplied by the National Capital Commission in the summer of 1965.

[13]Although the data supplied by the Commission would suggest that one of its publications—*Statistical Review with Explanatory Notes, National Capital Region*—was available in English only in 1965, a French-language edition existed in the autumn of 1966.

[14]This includes both traffic and parking signs on Commission roadways, as well as signs in evidence in the offices of the Commission. Personal observation suggests that some unilingual English traffic signs still exist in 1967.

It would appear that not all French-speaking citizens share the National Capital Commission's satisfaction with this type of arrangement. During the course of an interview carried out late in 1965, one prominent politician from the area criticized the fact that English had to be employed during meetings with the National Capital Commission officials.

The pattern of language usage in the internal work world of the National Capital Commission itself appears to be markedly different from that sketched above. Although French-language correspondence is answered in French, the replies are usually—though not invariably—first drafted in English and then translated. Further, French-language documents and incoming correspondence are translated into English before being filed. The same pattern holds true with regard to the internal forms of the Commission. English is clearly the dominant language. Of the 22 types of documents which were classified as internal forms (defined as "any form which must be filled in by a civil servant") only three were either bilingual or available separately in either language. The remaining 19 were available in English only. No unilingual French documents were reported.

C. Other Federal Agencies

Along with the National Capital Commission, two other agencies play major roles in the Ottawa-Hull area. These are the Department of Public Works and the Department of Finance. Clearly these two differ from the Commission in that the primary orientation of these departments as a whole is not towards the capital as such. Public Works, for instance, participates in the construction of roads, bridges, and marine works throughout Canada. While it might be involved in such operations in the Ottawa region, it is by no means performing a function peculiar to the capital. However, both departments contain within them divisions which do play a special role in the affairs of the Ottawa area.

The Department of Public Works. This Department is the agency responsible for providing the necessary physical structures of the federal administration. As much of the physical "plant" of the federal government is in the Ottawa area, this function is far from being an unimportant one. During 1966 the Department was re-organized on a geographical basis. As a result, since April 1967 one of the six new territorial divisions has been devoted to the National Capital Region affairs alone, while the other five are concerned with the Atlantic, Quebec, Ontario, Western, and Pacific regions. For the Public Works Department the National Capital Region division extends over considerably more territory than does the National Capital Region of the National Capital Commission, and includes some 11 counties or districts in Eastern Ontario and four in Western Quebec.[15] The vast bulk of the Department's operations, however, lies in Ottawa and Hull.

Perhaps the most important Public Works activity—at least in terms of its impact on the development of the capital area—is its role in the construction of public buildings. In general, it is the Department of Public Works which evolves the plans, chooses the site, and finances the construction of federal buildings. The choice of site is subject to National

---

[15] Specifically, the region comprises the electoral districts of Glengarry-Prescott, Stormont-Dundas, Leeds, Grenville-Carleton, Ottawa-Carleton, Lanark and Renfrew, Renfrew North and urban Ottawa in Ontario; Hull, Gatineau, Pontiac, and Témiscamingue in Quebec.

Capital Commission approval. The affected agency is also consulted, though in cases of disagreement it is generally the cabinet which decides.[16]

In addition to its role in the construction of government buildings, the Department of Public Works is responsible for their maintenance and operation in the post-construction period. While the National Capital Commission looks after the grounds surrounding the building, it is Public Works which must maintain the building and provide such services as are required. As an example, elevator operators in federal buildings are Public Works employees.

These two functions alone give rise to very considerable federal expenditures in the capital area. During the fiscal year 1967-68 it is estimated that the expenditures for construction, repairs, and improvements of public buildings in Ottawa and Hull alone will amount to about $26 million or 54 per cent of the total for Canada of $48 million. Similarly, departmental expenditures for the maintenance and operation of public buildings in 1967-68 are expected to amount to approximately $36 million out of a total for Canada of $85 million. This amount includes an estimate of $14.6 million for rental of leased space in the Ottawa-Hull area.

A third aspect of the Department's impact on the capital area is its contribution, along with the provincial and municipal levels of government, to joint projects not primarily concerned with the governmental aspects of this region, such as the Queensway and the Macdonald-Cartier Bridge linking Ottawa and Hull.

It should be emphasized that the National Capital Commission, as co-ordinator of federal development, and Public Works, as builder of the federal "plant," co-operate closely with each other in joint federal-provincial-municipal undertakings as well as in federal building development. While their differing roles lead to somewhat different perspectives and while the two organizations are administratively distinct, both have a common focus in being answerable to Parliament through the same minister. As a result of this combination the minister of Public Works occupies a very central position in the relations of the federal government with the land, people, and institutions of the capital area.

The Municipal Grants Division. The part played by the Municipal Grants Division of the Department of Finance in the development of the capital is more specialized than that of the Department of Public Works. Strictly speaking the Municipal Grants Division, originally organized separately, is now part of the Federal-Provincial Relations Division of the Department. It administers a programme of annual federal grants in lieu of municipal taxation on the federal government's departmental properties located in municipalities across Canada.

As noted earlier, section 125 of the B.N.A. Act exempts federal property from taxation. Commencing in 1950, however, the federal government evolved a general policy of grants in lieu of taxation to municipalities having concentrations of federal property within their boundaries. Prior to this date the only federal payments to municipal authorities with respect to departmental property were the relatively small ones to the city of Ottawa under the

---

[16]Ministers have been known to object strongly to the proposed location of their departments. A case in point was the insistence of the minister of Northern Affairs that his department retain its midtown location and not be moved out to a new building in Confederation Heights (*Ottawa Journal*, February 2, 1966). Although Public Works' plans were here overridden, this is not always the case. The Department of External Affairs, for example, will be moved to Sussex Drive despite its minister's protests to Public Works (*Ottawa Citizen*, November 16, 1965).

Ottawa Agreement Act of 1944, though the federal government had also made payments, extending back as far as 1877, for specific services provided by the city, such as water supply to federal properties.

The first general legislation, the Municipal Grants Act of 1951, was designed to alleviate the position of municipalities with large concentrations of federal property rather than of those with only a few federal buildings. Thus the Act stipulated that grants would only be paid to those municipalities where government property formed at least 4 per cent of the total taxable plus federal property in the municipality. In 1955 an amendment to the Act increased the number of municipalities eligible for a grant by providing that grants would now be paid to any municipality in which federal holdings stood in excess of 2 per cent of total taxable plus federal property. Finally, in 1957, a further amendment removed all such restrictions: every municipality containing federal property could apply for a grant.

Several points about the Municipal Grants Act are worth noting. First, although the Act authorizes the payment of grants in lieu of taxes on federal property, not all federal real property comes within the provisions of the Act. Crown corporations, commissions, boards and agencies, such as the Canadian National Railways, the Bank of Canada, Central Mortgage and Housing Corporation, the Canadian Broadcasting Corporation, the National Capital Commission and Atomic Energy of Canada, are excluded from the scope of the Act. These agencies make payments of their own directly to the municipalities, the amounts being similar to what would be paid under the formula in the Municipal Grants Act. Some Crown corporations, however, such as the Canadian National Railways and the Bank of Canada, actually pay municipal taxes, including business tax, rather than grants in lieu of tax.

Certain classes of departmental property are not eligible for grants. Parks, historical sites, monuments, museums, public libraries, and art galleries fall within this category. The Parliament Buildings are similarly exempted, although a grant "may be made to the city of Ottawa in an amount that, in the opinion of the Minister [of Finance], is a reasonable compensation for the expenses incurred by that city in furnishing services to the property" (Municipal Grants Act, section 9). However, it might be noted that, under the Act, grants are paid on certain kinds of federal property which would not be subject to municipal taxation if owned by a body other than the Crown (for example, military hospitals, schools, chapels, fire halls, and sewage treatment plants and installations).

We may also note the discretionary nature of grants made under the Municipal Grants Act. Although the Act does provide a fairly clearly defined means by which grants may be made, it explicitly precludes recognition of any claim that municipalities have a right to grants in lieu of taxes. Section 4(2) states bluntly that "no right to a grant is conferred by this Act." Further, the minister has the final word in determining both the taxable value of federal properties and the rate of tax on which the grant is to be calculated. In practice the system today appears to function with relatively little friction, though it produced some sharp disagreements in earlier years. In general grants are calculated according to the assessment base used by the municipality and the prevailing municipal tax rates. Instances of grants being withheld from a municipality, though not unprecedented,[17] have been exceedingly rare.

---
[17]For example, in 1955 one Nova Scotian municipality, which had been levying a poll tax on American military personnel in violation of a federal statute, had its grant withheld to the extent of the amount collected.

Although, as we have said, grants are now paid on federal property across Canada, the concentration of government holdings in the capital area is such that the city of Ottawa receives by far the largest grant of any municipality in the country. Table 5.1 gives the distribution of the four largest grants under the Act in recent years. It shows that the grant to the city of Ottawa, which a decade ago was roughly equal to the next three largest grants combined, is now somewhat above this figure. Understandably the municipal grant figures largely in the Ottawa budget. Depending on which categories of federal payments are included, an estimated 10 to 15 per cent of the city's income comes from this one federal source alone.[18]

Table 5.1. Payments of grants in lieu of taxes to selected municipalities, 1957-1966 (in millions of dollars)

	City of Ottawa	City of Halifax	City of Toronto	City of Montreal
1957	3.6	1.4	.8	1.4 (1957-58)*
1958	3.8	1.5	.9	1.3 (1958-59)
1959	4.3	1.5	1.0	1.5 (1959-60)
1960	4.9	1.5	1.3	1.5 (1960-61)
1961	5.4	1.5	1.5	1.6 (1961-62)
1962	5.7	1.6	1.6	1.6 (1962-63)
1963	5.9	1.6	1.7	1.6 (1963-64)
1964	6.3	1.6	1.8	1.8 (1964-65)
1965	6.7	1.6	1.9	2.0 (1965-66)
1966	7.3	1.6	2.1	2.2 (1966-67)

Source: Figures supplied by Municipal Grants Division.
* The Montreal financial year runs from May 1 to April 30.

Other channels of federal influence. While three agencies—the National Capital Commission, the Department of Public Works and the Department of Finance—have considerable impact in the capital area, several others play some part in the life of the capital and thus contribute to the overall image which the federal government presents to the resident or visitor. As examples, the Royal Canadian Mounted Police protects federal property; the Department of the Secretary of State is responsible for many of the cultural facilities of the capital; and the Department of Transport operates Ottawa International Airport and the Rideau Canal.

One further agency which merits particular attention is the Central Mortgage and Housing Corporation. Although the activities of the Corporation in the capital area do not appear to be radically different from its operations elsewhere, it is of some interest to note that the Corporation (or that part of it dealing with the region) has been used on certain occasions in the past as a vehicle for the implementation of federal policies concerned with the development of the capital.

---

[18]In addition to the grants and taxes already mentioned, the Department of Finance estimates that in 1966 a further $1.3 million was paid to the city of Ottawa as taxes on private property leased to the federal government, and recovered from the federal government through rental payments.

One case had to do with the Greenbelt. In the early 1950's, developers and individual home builders began to move into that area south of Ottawa which Jacques Gréber's Master Plan had suggested remain in an undeveloped state. Since large-scale residential development of the area would have precluded the establishment of the Greenbelt, the government in 1956 instructed the Corporation not to approve loans for construction by private owners within the designated area (Joint Committee of the Senate and House of Commons on the Federal District Commission, *Minutes of Proceedings and Evidence,* 1956, 296-7). This undoubtedly impeded the spread of housing on land designated to remain in its natural state, although not yet owned by the federal government.

The involvement of the Central Mortgage and Housing Corporation in helping to control pollution of the Ottawa River was less explicitly linked to the federal plan for the capital than its part in the development of the Greenbelt. It does, however, provide a good example of how the Corporation is being used towards the furtherance of broad federal aims within the complicated jurisdictional structure of the capital area.[19]

In the early 1960's provincial pressure was applied to the city of Ottawa—which for years had been dumping its sewage directly into the river—to construct a sewage treatment plant. When the municipal authorities proved unheeding, Ontario refused to allow the city to extend its sewer and water systems. As the city was undergoing a period of rapid expansion a great deal of pressure was generated by local developers. At the same time, the federal government, *via* the National Capital Commission, allocated a $5,000,000 grant and made available through the Central Mortgage and Housing Corporation, a low interest loan which provided for a $2 1/2 million rebate if the plant was built within a specified time. With this combination of provincial stick and federal carrot, the plant was constructed and a major source of pollution eliminated.

Apart from the agencies discussed so far, the nature of whose powers and duties is clearly defined by statute or otherwise, there are two other federal institutions that deserve consideration here. Both the cabinet and the House of Commons, whose interests are far-reaching, concern themselves with the federal capital from time to time and in various ways as they see fit.

The National Capital Region is not normally an area of interest for the cabinet as a whole but rather the cabinet's interest varies with individual cabinet posts and individual ministers. The two major cabinet posts vis-à-vis the National Capital Region seem to be those of the prime minister and the minister of Public Works. The prime minister is influential not only because of his own position within the cabinet, but also because of the historic links between the Ottawa Improvement Commission and its successor, the Federal District Commission, and the office of prime minister. It was only after the Joint Parliamentary Inquiry of 1956 that the federal planning agency ceased to report to Parliament through the prime minister.

---

[19]Three further illustrations of federal-municipal relations may be found in Appendix K. The second of these, dealing with the Lower Town East Urban Renewal issue, provides yet another example of the Corporation at work.

The cabinet may make its influence felt indirectly through Crown agencies. Examples already cited are the practices of the National Capital Commission with regard to its expropriation power and the intervention of the Central Mortgage and Housing Corporation in maintaining the Greenbelt area south of Ottawa.

The cabinet may also exercise a more direct influence on the activities of local institutions. An illustration is the project for an Ottawa civic centre. In 1965 the federal government was asked by the city authorities if financial aid for such a project might be forthcoming. Prime Minister Pearson offered such assistance, contingent on a provincial grant, and also carrying a condition that federal timetables on construction starts be met. This condition was part of the government's attempt to counter inflationary pressures in the construction industry. Differing priorities on the federal and municipal levels were subsequently resolved in an agreement that the project could proceed more quickly provided that other capital projects of equivalent value be postponed. The provincial government then furnished the required provincial grant to complete the financial foundation of the project. Thus through the participation of the federal cabinet and the Prime Minister, considerable aid was contributed to a project of great local significance.[20]

Members of Parliament have also influenced the development of the capital. Of prime importance in shaping the present context of federal-municipal relations have been the joint parliamentary committees of inquiry. The Municipal Grants Act is largely due to the 1944 Joint Parliamentary Inquiry, while the establishment of the National Capital Commission in its present form owes much to another Inquiry of 1956.

Individually, few members of Parliament outside of those elected from the local ridings show any sustained interest in the capital. Lloyd Francis, former member for Carleton has commented that, "There is not really that much interest with most MPs on what goes on in the city" (*Ottawa Citizen*, July 18, 1966). Admittedly parliamentary complaints about the state of Ottawa streets are not infrequent, but members have voiced these more in a tone of exasperation than hope of remedy. The more subtle and long-term problems of federal-municipal relations are rarely touched upon, either because members themselves feel constricted by the limited powers of intervention the federal government presently possesses, or perhaps because such an interest is not expected of them by their constituents. Some Quebec members in recent years have voiced their concern individually from time to time about the predominance of English in the capital—both in federal agencies and in the capital milieu more generally—but their interest has been rather sporadic, so that the issue has hardly been called to public attention in any sustained fashion.

D. *Language Usage of Federal Agencies*

Given the substantial role of the federal government in the life of the capital, the linguistic practices and policies of its agencies will not only contribute largely to the public image of Ottawa as a unilingual or bilingual area, but also may act as an example of language

---

[20]*Ottawa Citizen*, September 15, 16, 29, 1965; *Le Droit*, October 8, 1965. A further example of the Prime Minister's involvement in federal-municipal affairs, on the issue of municipal zoning, may be found in the first of the three case studies in Appendix K.

usage for other bodies to follow.[21] There are, to be sure, different levels of visibility concerning language usage. In some areas of governmental activity, direct contact with the public is so habitual as to form an integral part of the language usage of the region; in others the practices of government agencies may have little or no impact outside the agencies themselves.

To start with one of the most visible and symbolic areas, it is clear that the language of signs on streets, buildings, and public places is of great importance. The National Capital Commission is responsible for the signs erected on government lands and federal driveways and parkways, and its practice in this respect has been considered above. Signs on federal buildings have both a practical and symbolic importance. In 1960 a private organization, Le conseil de la vie française, carried out a survey of the relative use of French and English on government buildings in Ottawa. It found that of 76 buildings examined, bilingualism prevailed generally in 10, some use of French was made in a further 28, and all signs in the remaining 38 were in English only. No buildings using only French signs were discovered. The ministers of the non-bilingual departments were informed, and assurances were received that the situation would be improved.

Four years later the same organization revisited the 38 buildings that had displayed only English-language signs. It found that only one could be considered fully bilingual, while three others showed some degree of improvement.[22]

The responsibility for erecting signs on buildings lies with the Department of Public Works. Until recently, the Department did not itself make decisions on language usage, the matter being decided instead by the occupants. This has now been changed: it is government policy that all external signs on new federal buildings across the country be bilingual.[23] The policy is also applied when signs are replaced on buildings being renovated, but it is not applied to existing signs unless the agency concerned makes a specific request. With respect to external signs, the same policy is applied in the federal capital area as elsewhere in Canada.

As to other fields of written usage, the various government departments, in their own estimation, were extensively bilingual. Of 19 agencies (*see* Table 5.2) selected from the standpoint of their possible influence upon the milieu of the capital, all claimed that their Ottawa staff answered letters received in French or English in the language of the correspondent. The practice with regard to external forms, public notices, and publications varied from department to department, but generally rather less bilingualism was reported for these spheres than for correspondence.

To determine the extent to which oral communications with the public may be conducted in the two official languages, the agencies were asked to give the number of unilingual and bilingual employees working in frequent contact with the public in selected cities across the country. Table 5.2 shows the distribution of civil servants in the capital area offices of these

---

[21]The main source for this section is the material gathered in the summer of 1965 by J. LaRivière, mostly by means of questionnaires filled in by some 70 agencies, for his study on "La traduction dans la fonction publique" (prepared for the Royal Commission on Bilingualism and Biculturalism, 1966).

[22]Le conseil de la vie française, *Bilinguisme et biculturalisme au Canada* (Quebec. 1964), 144-5.

[23]Cf. statement by R.C. Honey, M.P., quoted in *The Globe and Mail,* October 10, 1966.

agencies who were reported to be able to perform their duties adequately in English, in French, and in both languages.

Table 5.2. Percentage distribution of Ottawa civil servants in contact with the public by ability to perform their duties in one or both of the official languages, selected agencies, 1965

Agency	Total civil servants in frequent public contact		Linguistic ability		
	N	%	English only	French only	Both
House of Commons	110	100	52	3	45
Senate	27	100	26	–	74
Civil Service Commission	9	100	22	–	78
Library of Parliament	28	100	43	–	57
C.B.C.	49	100	8	–	92
Centennial Commission	64	100	37	–	62
National Gallery	77	100	60	–	40
National Library-Archives	274	100	64	–	36
Health and Welfare	141	100	73	–	27
National Employment Service	56	100	59	–	41
National Revenue - Taxation	265	100	67	–	33
Postmaster General	349	100	54	–	46
Public Works	451	100	68	–	32
National Capital Commission	28	100	57	–	43
Royal Canadian Mounted Police	264	100	84	–	16
Transport	27	100	67	–	33
Air Canada	118	100	58	–	42
C.N.R.	271	100	50	–	50
Veterans Affairs	117	100	75	1	24

Source: Questionnaires filled out by agencies for LaRivière's study, "La traduction dans la fonction publique."

It is worth noting that the number of French-speaking civil servants capable of using only their own language is infinitesimal. In these 19 agencies, at least, the possibility of working exclusively in one's own mother tongue is open only to those whose language is English.

Of the 19 agencies, the R.C.M.P. has the smallest percentage of bilingual employees in contact with the public in the Ottawa area, even though it is an agency which comes into direct and habitual contact with the people of the capital region through its function of policing federal properties and driveways. In keeping with the figures reported to us, the Force seems to be viewed by many French-speaking residents as a predominantly "English" organization. Their complaints that the R.C.M.P. representatives who patrol the Gatineau Park in Quebec are unable to communicate in French are not denied by the Force's spokesman in Parliament (*Ottawa Citizen,* July 6 and 20, 1966). The situation was highlighted in

1965 by the case of the French-speaking member of Parliament who, after refusing to comply with an English-language warrant, was arrested and jailed by the R.C.M.P.[24] In a letter to the Commission, dated July 30, 1965, the R.C.M.P. Deputy Commissioner (Administration) stressed that the Force was not unaware of the linguistic needs of the capital, nor was it hostile to the provision of bilingual police services. The problem was simply a lack of bilingual staff to fulfil such routine functions as protecting and patrolling Crown lands.

Three occupational groups—elevator operators, commissionaires, and telephonists—bear special mention, even if the last two are not directly employed by the federal government, for all three groups are in continual contact with the public by the nature of their work. Indeed they are often the first people spoken to by a visitor or caller to a government building. They thus make an important contribution to the public image of the government's linguistic policy.

The provision of elevator operators in government-owned buildings is the responsibility of the Department of Public Works. In 1965, slightly over half of a total of 181 operators were bilingual. No set departmental policy in regard to their allocation was apparent, except that bilingual men would be provided if specifically requested. Of all government agencies at that time only the House of Commons, the National Gallery and the National Museum had made such a request. For operators in leased buildings no linguistic stipulations are made by the Department.

Again, in the case of commissionaires, federal agencies appeared to have no uniform policy with regard to their requirements for the capital area. According to the commandant of the division of the Canadian Corps of Commissionaires that serves the capital region, apart from some rather rare exceptions (such as, for example, the Printing Bureau, the National Gallery, and the National Museum), the demand for bilingual commissionaires was very slight. Such bilingual personnel as were to be found appeared to be there by chance rather than by intention.

Table 5.3 analyzes by language skills the commissionaires employed in 1965 in the capital area. It shows that some departments were completely bilingual in this respect; others not at all. While the total percentage of bilingual commissionaires stands around 30 per cent, it was reported that the recruiting of such persons presented no problem, the present supply easily meeting the demand (LaRivière study).

The Bell Telephone Company, which supplies the federal government with telephone operators, has a policy of recruiting bilingual personnel where possible. Some 45 per cent of the operators serving the government in the Ottawa-Hull area were bilingual in 1965. Moreover, there is a well defined procedure to be followed when a unilingual, English-speaking operator encounters a person wishing to place a call in French.

Finally, it should be noted that auxiliary telephone services, such as the provision of directories and instructions on the use of government telephone services, are generally available in both French and English. There is, however, one curious exception: in neither the white nor the yellow pages of the 1966 Ottawa-Hull general telephone directory does

---

24"Mounties arrest Grégoire, Govt. gets him out," *Ottawa Citizen,* February 13, 1965. In a subsequent newspaper article, Mr. Grégoire mentioned this incident among those which led to his disenchantment with the existing Canadian situation and his consequent conversion to separatism. "Why I sit in a parliament I don't believe in," *The Canadian,* April 22, 1967.

Table 5.3. Percentage distribution of commissionaires in Ottawa federal buildings by language knowledge, 1965

Agency	Total		Linguistic ability*	
	N	%	English only	English and French
Total	537	100	70	30
Defence - Ottawa	176	100	81	19
Unemployment - Ottawa	1	100	–	100
National Employment	1	100	100	–
Secretary of State	38	100	68	32
Veterans Affairs	16	100	75	25
R.C.M.P.	61	100	67	33
National Research Council	57	100	51	49
External Affairs	8	100	75	25
Defence Research	3	100	100	–
Archives	13	100	54	46
Justice	8	100	62	38
Trade and Commerce	12	100	67	33
Transport	5	100	40	60
Public Works	20	100	85	15
Industry	2	100	100	–
Revenue	12	100	67	33
Citizenship	5	100	80	20
Mines	26	100	77	23
Health	19	100	74	26
Finance	5	100	60	40
Forests	2	100	50	50
C.M.H.C.	2	100	100	–
C.B.C.	8	100	50	50
Postmaster General	6	100	67	33
Agriculture	11	100	64	36
Labour	3	100	100	–
Chief Electoral Office	2	100	–	100
Château Laurier	3	100	33	67
Defence - Hull	1	100	–	100
Printing	10	100	20	80
Unemployment - Hull	1	100	–	100

Source: LaRivière, "La traduction dans la fonction publique."
*No unilingual, French-speaking commissionaires were reported.

the federal government list itself in French. A member of the public who understood no English would thus be at a disadvantage from the start in seeking contact with a government department.

To sum up, the external image of the federal government in the capital area is that of an organization that is bilingual in patches. Many matters still seem to be left to the decision of individual agencies, with the result that some are far ahead of others in the provision of bilingual services. In short, the federal government in Ottawa has not yet demonstrated a fully co-ordinated and effective policy of equal status for the two languages. As a consequence, the example set by the federal authorities for other levels of government to follow has not been free from contradictions and ambiguities.

E. The Geographical Context of Federal Activity

Federal activities in the National Capital Region are by no means evenly distributed throughout the area. In fact, federal buildings are heavily concentrated in one municipality, Ottawa. The presence or absence of Crown property has three important consequences for any municipality. First, the location of government building projects, their nature (that is, whether they are high-rise or spread out horizontally), and how they are articulated with the existing and potential urban "landscape," are prime influences on the shape and direction of urban development in the region, and thus have an important bearing on town planning. Second, while such property is exempt from normal taxation, grants under the Municipal Grants Act can be a substantial element in the municipal budget. Third, the presence of government departments in the area means more employment opportunities for the local citizens, and permits the development of support industries to service the influx of people coming to work in the municipality: it means, in short, economic expansion.

That federal buildings have not been shared evenly among municipalities throughout the capital area in the past has brought forth complaints from Hull in particular. Before examining the basis of these complaints in detail, it is of some use to look first at the location of government buildings during the formative years of the capital.

At the time of Confederation, federal government administration was concentrated in the immediate environs of Parliament Hill. The construction of the Parliamentary Library and the enlargement of the West Block sufficed to accommodate the civil service on Parliament Hill until 1880. In that year the Geological Survey Building was moved from Montreal to a site east of the Rideau Canal on Sussex Drive. In 1883 considerations of space forced the government to take over commercial property immediately south of Parliament Hill on Wellington Street, where the Langevin Block was completed in 1885.

By the turn of the century, a great expansion of government buildings began. Development of the Experimental Farm land, over two miles south-west of Parliament Hill near what is now Dow's Lake (and outside the then city limits), had already begun in the late 19th century; in the 17 years preceding World War I, a number of laboratories, the Dominion Observatory, and a Geodetic Building were erected in this area. This construction of buildings for scientific rather than administrative use was an exception to the general attempt to concentrate federal buildings in the vicinity of Parliament Hill. The National Museum was established about one mile directly south of the Parliament Buildings, but the Public Archives, the Royal Mint, the Printing Bureau, and the Connaught Building were constructed in the area between Sussex Drive and the Ottawa River, within half a mile north-east of Parliament Hill.

The Holt Commission of 1915 urged that the expected increase in government buildings be accommodated along two axes radiating west and north-east of Parliament Hill, the former along Wellington Street and the latter along Sussex Drive. Expansion up to the outbreak of World War II generally followed this plan. The National Research Council Administration Centre and Laboratories were erected on Sussex. The Daly Building on Sussex was purchased in 1921 and the Printing Bureau was expanded. West of Parliament Hill, the Confederation, Justice, Supreme Court, and Bank of Canada buildings were erected. Further expansion of laboratories and administrative units on the Experimental Farm took place in this inter-war period, and the Mines Department laboratories spread into the adjacent Booth Street area, just north-east of the Experimental Farm.

World War II saw the erection of over a dozen "temporary" buildings, many following the Wellington-Sussex axes, but also spreading south of Laurier Avenue, to an area between Elgin Street and the Rideau Canal, and to the Experimental Farm area.

Following the war, federal expansion took two forms: extensive decentralization was matched by intensive development of the centre area, on the Wellington Street west axis. In the latter area, the twin Trade and Commerce and Veterans Affairs buildings were erected in the 1950's, and the new National Library and Archives Building has just recently been completed. Also in the downtown area the Lorne Building, housing the National Gallery, was built on Elgin Street. In recent years the government has also begun a policy of leasing extensive space in private office buildings, mostly in centre town.

Concurrent with the filling-out of the downtown area, however, was a radically new policy of decentralization. The Federal District Commission described this policy to the Joint Parliamentary Committee in 1956, in these words: "Decentralization was recommended as a means of avoiding downtown congestion and of permitting civil servants to live in residential areas near their offices, as well as for obvious civil defence reasons" (Eggleston, 269).

A great expansion in the buildings occupying the Experimental Farm-Booth Street area was accompanied by the growth of new office complexes west, south, and east of the centre-town area. Tunney's Pasture, over two miles west of centre town, near the Ottawa River, has been developed to the point where over a dozen buildings are now located there. More remote yet from the centre area is the extensive Confederation Heights complex, some four miles south-west of Parliament Hill, on the east bank of the Rideau River. Also on the same side of the Rideau are the Tri-Service Hospital in Alta Vista and the R.C.M.P. headquarters in Overbrook. On the eastern outskirts of Ottawa, about four miles from centre town, are the extensive National Research Council laboratories, and, nearby, the Central Mortgage and Housing Corporation Building and a Forest Products Laboratory. Well outside the city in the west, at Shirley's Bay on the Ottawa River, is the Defence Research Board establishment.

In summary, the overall geographical development of governmental activity in the capital region has taken two basic forms: on the one hand, an intensive development of the centre-town area along the general lines of two arms spreading west and north-east from the central area of Parliament Hill, with scattered buildings south of the Hill, and, on the other hand, an extension of activity to various complexes south, west, and east of the central area, generally within a radius of two to four miles.

Impact of Federal Government

In all this development, it has apparently been assumed that the city of Ottawa, as such, is synonymous with the "seat of government." Thus, the lines of development have tended to follow ever-increasing semi-circles radiating from Parliament Hill. It may be that political differences between Quebec and the federal government, inadequate transportation routes across the Ottawa River, and the feeling that the capital should be Ottawa alone, have generally served to block the development of federal activity north of Parliament Hill and, have largely isolated Hull from the effects of expansion. The first major government building to be erected on the Quebec side of the river was the Printing Bureau, in the early 1950's, but for a decade after the completion of the Printing Bureau (which has since been expanded) only an Animal Pathology Laboratory has been added to federally-owned buildings in Hull, although a relatively small amount of office space has been rented by the federal government.

Table 5.4 presents in detail the location of the federal government within the three cities of the area at March 31, 1967. As may be seen, Eastview contains no federally-owned property and only a small amount of leased property. If we take the owned and leased offices together, the proportion between Ottawa and Hull varies according to whether the number of buildings or the amount of floor-space is considered. In the former case, Ottawa has a 25:1 advantage, but this narrows to 10:1 if floor-space is compared. Whichever is taken, however, the great bulk of federal offices are clearly situated within the city of Ottawa. It should also be noted that Crown corporations leasing directly, and not through the Department of Public Works, accounted for some further 86,000 square feet of floor-space in Ottawa.

Table 5.4. Buildings and floor-space owned or leased by the federal government* in Ottawa, Hull and Eastview, March 31, 1967

	Total		Ottawa		Hull		Eastview	
	N	%	N	%	N	%	N	%
Total buildings	320	100	296	92.5	12	3.8	12	3.8
Buildings owned	128	100	123	96.1	5	3.9	–	–
Buildings leased	192	100	173	90.1	7	3.6	12	6.3
Total floor-space (in square feet)	14,120,000	100	12,803,000	90.8	1,228,000	8.7	89,000	0.6
Space owned	10,721,000	100	9,664,000	90.1	1,057,000	9.9	–	–
Space leased	3,399,000	100	3,139,000	92.4	171,000	5.0	89,000	2.6

Source: Figures supplied by the Department of Public Works.
*Only buildings administered by the Department of Public Works are covered by this table. Further, it does not include the new Sir John Carling Building in Ottawa which was occupied by the Department of Agriculture in April 1967.

Another method of describing the geographical distribution of federal activity is by comparing the taxes and grants paid by the federal government and Crown corporations to the various municipal authorities in the capital area. The most recent year for which relatively complete data on these payments could be obtained for all area municipalities was 1963. This information is given in Table 5.5.

The chief components of the amounts paid to Ottawa and Hull are the federal grants in lieu of real property taxes on federal buildings and associated grants for city services. In 1963 this amounted to 86 per cent of the total federal payment to Ottawa and 99.9 per cent of the total payment to Hull. Of the payment to Ottawa only 13 per cent was in direct taxes paid on properties owned by Crown corporations. The rather high per capita figure for the village of Rockcliffe Park is entirely explained by the grants in lieu of property taxes on diplomatic properties in the village: there are no federal government buildings in Rockcliffe. The bulk of Gloucester township's share is from payments on Crown corporation properties, especially those of the National Research Council and the National Capital Commission.

Table 5.5. Taxes and grants in lieu of taxes paid by the federal government and Crown corporations to municipalities in the National Capital Region, 1963 tax year

Municipality	Payment	As percentage of total	Payment per capita*
Total	$8,271,817	100	–
Ottawa	7,249,275	87.6	$27.03
Hull	433,660	5.2	7.62
Gloucester	316,284	3.8	17.28
Nepean	161,907	2.0	8.20
Rockcliffe Park	36,895	0.4	17.70
Other Quebec municipalities	50,233	0.6	–
Other Ontario municipalities	23,563	0.3	–

Source: Figures supplied by the Department of Finance.
*"Per capita" column is based on 1961 census population figures.

The most important recipients of grants among the smaller municipalities on the north shore were Lucerne ($13,765), West Hull ($12,333), and Masham ($11,339). Of the total amount paid to all Quebec municipalities other than the city of Hull, over 90 per cent was supplied by National Capital Commission payments in respect of Gatineau Park. For the other municipalities on the Ontario side, it is interesting to note that Eastview received only $79.

Figures for payments in the years following 1963 are only available in incomplete form. It would seem, however, that while payments to the city of Ottawa have increased steadily from year to year, those for Hull appear to have dropped slightly below the 1963 figures. Table 5.6 shows the post-1963 payments for these two cities to the extent that figures are available.

It is obvious from these figures that the city of Ottawa has been receiving the overwhelming bulk of government financial payments, and that this is the result of the concentration of federally-owned buildings in the city. The presence of government buildings is not, however, simply limited in its consequences to financial grants to the municipalities.

For one thing, the federal government wields an enormous influence on the scope and direction of urban growth by where it chooses to locate its "plant," by where it chooses to provide assistance to the provincial and municipal governments for public works and projects for urban development, and by how it chooses to link its building programme with existing city planning programmes.[25]

Table 5.6. Total of taxes and grants in lieu of taxes paid by the federal government and Crown corporations to the cities of Ottawa and Hull, 1963-1966 (in thousand of dollars)

	1963	1964	1965	1966
Ottawa	7249	8010	8717	9182
Hull	434	356	412	407*

Source: Figures supplied by the Department of Finance.
*Does not include payments by the National Capital Commission during 1966, for which figures are not available.

Nevertheless, it is a fact of considerable importance to the National Capital Region as a whole that apart from the Greenbelt the federal government's extensive powers have only rarely been used to promote and shape urban development in any of the Region's municipalities other than Ottawa.

The presence of the federal government also has important economic consequences for the residents of the various municipalities of the capital area. As the leading employer, landowner, and spending agency in the region, it could not be otherwise. That Hull and the other municipalities in Quebec should be relatively isolated from the major economic activity of the capital has long been a strong source of grievance.

In 1964 the Hull Chamber of Commerce prepared a brief[26] in which it stressed the disadvantaged position of the city in comparison with that of Ottawa. The brief maintained that in the ten-year period ending September 1964, the three major federal agencies active in the capital area, namely the National Capital Commission, the Department of Public Works, and the Department of Finance, had spent a total of $211.2 million in Ottawa and only $9.3 million in Hull. Of this total, Public Works contributed $122.1 million to Ottawa and $1.8 million to Hull, the Department of Finance distributed $41.5 million to Ottawa and $3.4 million to Hull, and the National Capital Commission contributed $47.6 million to Ottawa and $4.1 million to Hull (*see* Appendix L).

---

[25]This influence on city planning schemes is illustrated by the recent announcement of a federal project for downtown Ottawa which would not only provide new government office space but would also bring about the extension of the Sparks Street Mall, a centre-piece of the Ottawa planning programme for the urban core of the city (*see* Richard Jackson, "Giant Building Complex for Downtown Block," *Ottawa Journal,* June 29, 1967).

[26]*Mémoire sur la nécessité d'un regain industriel à Hull*. Présenté aux autorités municipales du Conseil de la Cité de Hull par la Chambre de Commerce de Hull, le 10 décembre, 1964.

It may be pointed out that the above figures cover a period falling immediately after the completion of the large Printing Bureau, thus weighting the Public Works figure against Hull. Nevertheless it is clear that by any calculation a considerable imbalance remains. That Hull residents feel very strongly about this point there can be no doubt (*Le Droit,* November 4, 12, and 22, 1966).

Although Hull has been most vocal in demanding more federal consideration, its argument may apply also to other municipalities in Quebec such as Lucerne, Aylmer, and Deschênes. Two municipalities on the Ontario side—Rockcliffe Park and Eastview—have no federally owned buildings but Rockcliffe Park is entirely residential by policy, and Eastview has such a high density of population that few sites for major construction would appear to be available at present.

On February 2, 1967, the Minister of Public Works indicated that the north shore of the Ottawa River is to be integrated further into the federal building programme with the announcement that the Department of Forestry and Rural Development will be given a new headquarters office building just west of the Printing Bureau and that a forest research centre of four to five large buildings will be built in Lucerne. In conjunction with these projects, the Minister also announced plans for two new bridges over the Ottawa, one at Lemieux Island, just above the Chaudière Falls, and the other at Deschênes rapids at the eastern end of Lake Deschênes (*Le Droit,* February 2, 1967; *Ottawa Journal,* February 2, 1967).

The inclusion of bridge construction projects in plans for greater development of federal buildings on the north shore perhaps indicates the end of the long-used argument that poor bridge connections over the Ottawa River have made it unpractical to locate government buildings on the Quebec side, despite the fact that the urban core of the north shore is considerably closer to Parliament Hill than the sites of such suburban complexes as Confederation Heights and the National Research Council cluster in the east end of Ottawa. Confederation Heights, it might be pointed out, was opened up only after completion of the Dunbar Bridge over the Rideau River, a project which had federal participation. In any event, the completion of the Macdonald-Cartier Bridge across the Ottawa has already provided easier access to future federal projects on the Quebec side of the river. Better bridges, however, are only a part of the problem of urban planning, in that they tend to intensify traffic congestion on the roads into which they lead. A further question of considerable importance is the improvement and construction of new arterial roads in the municipalities on the Quebec side, a project which calls for close co-operation of the different levels of government.

The pattern of government expansion outlined earlier in this section suggests that the physical seat of government has not coincided precisely in the past with the boundaries of the city of Ottawa, and may do so even less in the future. As early as the latter part of the 19th century, the Experimental Farm was being developed outside the city boundaries, in Nepean township. National Defence Department and Defence Research Board establishments exist today in Nepean and Gloucester townships. Mines and Technical Surveys installations are being constructed outside the city limits in both townships. And the proposed site of an Animal Research Division lies in Nepean township. The precedent of the Printing Bureau and the new projects for Hull and Lucerne indicate that the actual seat of the federal government today extends over a wide expanse of the metropolitan area, and even into the adjacent undeveloped countryside. Thus it is the vicinity of the federal capital as a whole, and not the city of Ottawa alone, that must increasingly be viewed as the seat of the Government of Canada.

F. Summary

The main points of this chapter may be summarized as follows:
1) The Canadian constitution gives the federal government no special grant of power with respect to the territory in which its capital is located.
2) Despite this, the federal government has played a prominent part in local affairs as the major employer, the major landowner, and the major contributor of cultural, recreational, and other facilities in the area.
3) Institutionally, three major channels of federal interest may be discerned: the National Capital Commission, the Department of Public Works, and the Municipal Grants Office of the Department of Finance. Many other federal agencies contribute to the process as well, although more sporadically or in less important ways.
4) Through the National Capital Commission and its predecessors, the federal government has acted as a planning agency for the area. Having no powers to implement its planning proposals except on Crown-owned land, the government has bought and, where necessary, expropriated large tracts of land. In doing this, the Commission has spent over $111 million since 1947.
5) Decisions as to the nature and location of new government buildings, which rest largely with the Department of Public Works, directly affect the urban development of the region. In construction and maintenance alone, the Department's estimates call for an expenditure of $62 million in the Ottawa area for the fiscal year 1967-68.
6) Most federally-owned buildings are exempt from municipal taxation. Nevertheless, the Municipal Grants Office channels around $8 million annually into the accounts of the local municipalities by way of grants in lieu of taxes in respect of departmental property. Furthermore, direct taxes or grants are paid by other Crown agencies, and taxes are also paid on buildings leased but not owned by the federal government for a further amount of about $2.8 million annually.
7) The linguistic image presented by the federal government itself in its services to the public is uneven. While, on the one hand, written usage appears to be fairly extensively bilingual, on the other, oral communications and signs on buildings are only partially so. No coordinated policy in favour of complete service in both official languages makes itself apparent.
8) The geographical extent of the capital, in terms of government buildings, does not coincide with the city of Ottawa's boundaries, but rather extends into the neighbouring Quebec and Ontario municipalities. However, on balance, federal property is still heavily concentrated within Ottawa, which means that the city receives by far the largest part of federal payments made in the capital area.
9) The Quebec sector of the Region and the city of Hull in particular feel strongly that they have been neglected by the federal authorities in the development of the urbanized sector of the capital area.

Chapter VI   **The Legal Systems**

A. Introduction

In the Western world there are two different schools of thought regarding the position of the judiciary in the structure of government. According to one, the judiciary forms an integral part of the executive function. The dispensing of justice is seen as an administrative matter, with no special importance attached to the position of the judiciary. According to the other tradition, the legal system stands alone, independent of the other branches of government, in order that it may defend the laws of the land and the individual's rights against executive or administrative encroachment. From this point of view the judiciary assumes a symbolic role of vital importance: as the protector of rights and freedoms, it becomes intimately associated in the public mind with them. A vigorously independent judiciary, in short, is taken as a prime indicator of the health of the state.

    Canada has always adhered to this latter school of thought. Consequently, the judicial systems in the capital area should not be considered simply as an aspect of administrative arrangements; they are to be described separately and with considerable care. Judicial action may involve the most serious consequences for the individual citizen, including loss of property, individual liberty, and even, in rare instances, life itself. In such circumstances, equality of every citizen before the law and in the judicial process is a matter of the highest importance.

    Federal states such as Canada contain at least two levels of law-making authority—the federal and provincial legislatures. They are consequently faced with a major difficulty, unknown to unitary states, in organizing their judicial systems. Balancing the need for uniform justice throughout the state is the need to respond to the local particularism which gave rise to the federal system in the first place. In the United States the structural problem is resolved by setting up what amounts to two separate judicial systems—one for cases involving state laws, the other for cases involving federal laws or certain matters outside the competence of the state courts.

    The Canadian judicial system is much closer in structure to a unified hierarchy than to the parallel systems of courts just described (*see* Diagrams 6.1 and 6.2). While there are no parallel judicial structures similar to those in the United States, yet the possibility of such a system is provided for in the British North America Act. Under that Act, a provincial legislature is competent to establish courts having jurisdiction within the province and to determine their powers. However, the federal authority is responsible for the selection, payment, and dismissal of the judges of the provincial courts at or above the level of the County and Superior Courts. Furthermore, the federal Parliament can, if it so chooses, establish a system of purely federal courts to administer federal laws to the exclusion of the provincial courts. This power has been exercised to a limited extent in the creation of the Exchequer Court of Canada which deals with some areas within federal legislative competence such as patents, trademarks, and admiralty law. For the most part, the central authority has chosen to empower the provincial courts to exercise jurisdiction in matters of federal law, notably in the important federal field of criminal law. As a result, almost all trials of both civil and criminal actions occur in provincial courts. Appeals thereafter may be taken up through provincial appeal courts and thence to the Supreme Court of Canada, the latter being a court established and staffed exclusively by the central authority. Thus, although the federal Supreme and Exchequer Courts are located physically within the capital area, the local resident will mostly be concerned with the Ontario and Quebec courts of first instance and appeal.

As the federal capital area straddles two provinces, it includes within its confines two provincial legal systems—those of Ontario and Quebec. The differences between the two are considerably greater than would normally be found between two contiguous judicial systems in Canada. For one thing, the right to use either French or English before any Quebec court is written into the B.N.A. Act.[1] As a result the Quebec system is constitutionally and officially bilingual, while the Ontario courts, free from such a provision, are substantially unilingual as far as official recognition of language is concerned.

A second difference is that, while both systems apply the same body of criminal law, on the non-criminal side the Quebec courts administer civil law and the Ontario courts common law. The civil law of Quebec has its roots in the law of France, while common law developed in England. Until 1792 the former obtained throughout Canada. In that year, however, the Upper Canada legislature adopted the common law system. Today Quebec is the only province using civil law. Between civil law and common law we find a considerable distance, especially in the field of domestic relations.

At the start we must stress the relationship of the two main judicial units in the capital area—the judicial district of Hull and Carleton county—with their respective provincial systems. While districts and counties, as basic units in the two judicial hierarchies, are independent of other such units at the same level, they are very much dependent on the superior levels of the Quebec and Ontario legal systems respectively. If the judicial systems of the capital area were entirely self contained, it would be a relatively easy matter to adapt their language practices to the requirements of the local population and the demands arising from the location of the capital in the region. This, however, is not the case: the practices of the units are determined by the system prevailing in each province as a whole. As will be shown below, this factor of dependence on

---

[1] Section 133 reads: "Either the English or the French Language may be used by any Person... or in any Pleading or Process in or issuing from ... all or any of the Courts of Quebec."

The Legal Systems

Diagram 6.1. Civil and Criminal Courts, Carleton county, Ontario, at January 1966 (showing appeal system)

	SUPREME COURT OF CANADA
	Civil and criminal appeals

	ONTARIO COURT OF APPEAL
	Civil and criminal appeals

CRIMINAL

General sessions	Magistrate's courts	County court judge's criminal court	Juvenile and family court
Criminal	Criminal	Criminal	Criminal and welfare
Jury	Non-jury	Non-jury	Non-jury
All of Carleton county	(1) Ottawa (2) Carleton county	All of Carleton county	All of Carleton county

CIVIL

Ontario high court of justice	County court	Division courts
Civil and criminal	Civil	Civil
Jury and non-jury	Jury and non-jury	Usually non-jury
Carleton co. on circuit	All of Carleton county	4 Divisions for county

the provincial systems is vital in the language usage of the courts in the capital area.

In this chapter, we shall be looking at both the written and spoken language usage in the legal institutions of Carleton county and the district of Hull. The data are based on interviews and research carried out from September to December 1965, and the report refers to the court systems of Ontario and Quebec as they were in January 1966.

B. The Legal System of the Ontario Sector

The legal system in the Ontario part of the capital region is similar to that for any other part of the province. Within Carleton county four Division Courts, a County Court and a Surrogate Court hear civil cases, while criminal cases may be brought before one of two Magistrate's Courts, a Juvenile and Family Court, the Court of General Sessions or the County Court Judge's Criminal Court. At the local sittings of the Ontario High Court of Justice, both civil and criminal cases are heard. Additional legal institutions serve the county as a whole. There is the local office of the Supreme Court of Ontario to handle proceedings begun in the county, the county jail, the local offices of certain provincial administrative bodies, registry offices (*see* Appendix M) and, of course, the legal profession itself.

Local trial courts. The Magistrate's Court is primarily a criminal court, hearing prosecutions under municipal by-laws, provincial statutes and regulations (for example, the Highway Traffic Act and Regulations), and under federal statutes and regulations (mainly the Criminal Code). Cases most frequently concern minor offences, such as drinking, traffic violations, and minor thefts, and are heard by the magistrate alone without the assistance of a jury. Persons accused of more serious offences receive their "preliminary inquiry" before a magistrate, and may in some instances elect to have their cases heard by the magistrate rather than await trial by the County Court Judge or by judge and jury.

There are two Magistrate's Courts in the area; one handles cases arising within the city of Ottawa, while the other has jurisdiction over the rest of Carleton county. At the time of our study the former was served by three magistrates (one of them bilingual) and a deputy magistrate. The staff of the Court, headed by a bilingual clerk of French mother tongue, included persons capable of carrying out their duties in both French and English. The various forms used by the Court (summonses, traffic tickets, warrants, committal forms, and so on) are available in English only; however, a person can carry on business with the staff in either language and can obtain oral explanations in French of the various forms. The actual hearings of the Court are conducted in English. Testimony is taken down in shorthand by the court reporter in English only.

In the event that an accused or a witness is unable to speak or to understand that language, an informal translation is provided by the police officer who acts as prosecutor in the main run of petty offences. This police officer is a sergeant or a staff sergeant of the Ottawa Police Force, known as the conducting officer or prosecuting officer. He is selected specifically for this function and it is a required qualification that he be fluently bilingual. Because the conducting officer is present throughout the sittings of the Magistrate's Court, he is available to act as an interpreter at the request of defence counsel or of the prosecuting counsel if one is being employed in the particular case.

The Magistrate's Court for Carleton county consists of one magistrate only. While there are no court offices as such, the administrative staffs of the various municipalities can be called upon to provide forms, set up hearing dockets, and so on. Thus the day-to-day language practice here is closely tied to the language abilities of municipal employees. Again the various forms are in English only, and hearings are in English, with interpretation as required.

A Juvenile and Family Court has been established for the whole of Carleton county, including Ottawa and Eastview. Under its criminal jurisdiction the court hears prosecutions brought against juveniles (young persons under the age of 16) or against adults accused of offences involving juveniles. The court also deals with family welfare matters: maintenance of parents, wives, and children, and family disputes. The purpose of the court is to deal with juvenile and domestic relations in a more informal, friendly and private atmosphere than that prevailing in an ordinary court.[2] It is, therefore, vitally important that the necessary rapport between the court and its clientele not be disturbed by linguistic or cultural incompatibility. As a result, more attention has been given in this court to bilingualism than in the Magistrate's Courts.

While the two judges of the court (at the time of the study a third position was vacant) were both of English mother tongue, one had a fair fluency in French and used this language whenever appropriate in emphasizing particular points to a French-speaking juvenile. The court staff was headed by a bilingual Clerk of the Court of French mother tongue. His subordinates included both Francophones and Anglophones and office business was carried out in French or English at the option of the person concerned.

Two types of court officers bear special mention: the two marriage counsellors and the five probation officers. One marriage counsellor spoke both French and English, the other only English. Two of the probation officers dealt with girls and three with boys. Both of the girls' officers spoke adequate French: one was Roman Catholic, the other Protestant. Girls were allocated to officers with some regard to matching religious persuasion. While none of the three boys' officers spoke French to any great extent, at the time of the interview an effort was under way to fill a fourth opening with a French-speaking officer. Boys were not allocated to officers with any special regard to religion. When boys or girls were sent to correctional institutions, or placed in foster homes, this was being done strictly on the basis of the religious affiliation of the child concerned.

The forms used in the court, corresponding roughly with those used in the Magistrate's Court, are in English only. However, a bilingual notice to parents, advising them to attend court with their child, is sent with the summons initiating Juvenile Court proceedings. The hearings too are, for the most part, conducted in English, but much of the work is accomplished outside the courtroom and here, as noted above, partial accommodation for French is available. When extensive interpretation is required for the purposes of the English-language transcript of the proceedings, it is generally provided by the Clerk of the Court himself, although persons appearing before the court can bring their own interpreter.

---

[2]Hence the Juvenile and Family Court, its offices and detention home are all geographically separate from the downtown locale of the ordinary courts, in close proximity to a large playground area and open space.

This is rarely done, except in cases involving persons who speak neither French nor English.

The two other courts with criminal jurisdiction—the General Sessions of the Peace and the County Court Judge's Criminal Court—will be dealt with below.

A Division Court exercises a civil jurisdiction only. Carleton county is today divided into four divisions, each of which has its Division Court. This is a small debts court, dealing with claims for sums of $400 or less. The usual cases concern unpaid accounts, bad cheques, promissory notes, minor traffic accident claims, and other small tort claims. Trial is always by a judge sitting alone, although litigants have the right to ask for a jury if the case involves $50 or more.

County Court judges preside over the Division Courts. Deputy judges may be appointed from the ranks of senior, practising lawyers to determine claims of $200 or less. In these cases no transcript of the proceedings is kept and no appeal is possible; otherwise, appeal lies to the Ontario Court of Appeal. At the time of our study it was reported that the staffs of the First and Seventh Division Courts, which are located in Ottawa, included bilingual persons, and office business was conducted in the language preferred by the person concerned. The other two Division Courts (at Carp and Galetta) were staffed only by a Clerk of the Court who, in both cases, spoke English only. In all four Division Courts, the hearings, the transcript—if one is kept—and the various forms of pleading, summonses, subpoenas, and executions are in English only. Interpreters, if required, have to be provided by the litigant.

Judges of the County Court preside over several tribunals. On the civil side, besides the Division Courts mentioned above, they sit in the County Court, with or without a jury, for trial of actions usually involving $3,000 or less, and in the Surrogate Court to handle matters concerning the estates of deceased persons or of infants. Their criminal jurisdiction covers the General Sessions of the Peace (trial by jury) and the County Court Judge's Criminal Court (trial by judge alone). Each judge may also act as a *persona designata* or arbitrator under a number of statutes to hear various applications and appeals. Appeals from most of the tribunals presided over by County Court judges go to the Ontario Court of Appeal at Toronto.

All procedural matters relating to these tribunals are handled by a single office headed by the Clerk of the County Court. Its staff did not include persons capable of conducting their business in French when we contacted them. The practice was to call in bilingual persons from adjacent offices or to enlist the assistance of bilingual lawyers who might happen to be in the court offices when the need arose. The various forms used are in English only, as are also the hearings before the court in both civil and criminal proceedings.

In civil cases, if an interpreter is required, he must be obtained and paid for by the litigant wishing to use the testimony in question. However the judge, in assessing the costs of the action, may transfer part of the financial burden of interpretation to the losing side. In criminal cases the practice varies according to which party—the prosecution or the accused—has employed an interpreter. When the prosecution, whose witnesses are the first ones heard in any case, has used an interpreter, the practice is to keep him available, if requested, for use by the defence. Then the interpreter will be paid out of court funds as part of the normal expenses of the case. If the accused is the first to call for an interpreter, he has to obtain and pay for his own, unless his limited financial means have necessitated his recourse to legal aid. In such a case, the interpreter, no matter which side uses him, will be paid as a court expense.

In Carleton county, only one person was employed by prosecution and defence alike with any regularity as an interpreter. His services were required a few times each week in pre-trial oral discovery proceedings and in trials. When he was not available, French-speaking law students were sometimes employed. Interpretation, which appeared to be of high quality, cost about $5 an hour.

The High Court of Justice, the trial division of the Supreme Court of Ontario, has both a civil and a criminal jurisdiction. It can deal with minor as well as important civil cases, although in practice all but the more serious cases are filtered off into the courts lower in the hierarchy. Only the more serious criminal cases come before the court, which can function either with or without a jury. Appeal is to the Court of Appeal in Toronto.

The justices of the High Court are based in Toronto, but move around the province, exercising their jurisdiction in the various "county towns." There is no apparent linguistic pattern in the selection of the justices who come to Ottawa (the county town of Carleton).

At the local offices of the court, proceedings are begun and continued up to trial, procedural determinations made, and judgements enforced. At the time of our study, the Ottawa office had a staff, headed by the Local Master, capable of carrying out its duties in both French and English. It should be noted, however, that the individual litigant rarely if ever has anything to do with this office, his business being handled almost invariably by lawyers. The language used is almost always English, even by lawyers whose mother tongue is French. All pleadings, procedures, and subpoenas are in English, as also are all hearings before the courts.[3]

Both civil and criminal jury trials in the Division, County and High Courts are now rare. However, they remain available at the option of the accused in serious prosecutions and at the option of either party in most civil actions. Only in the provinces of Quebec and Manitoba can a party to the proceedings call for the jury to be of a specific linguistic composition (see 155). Thus, an accused in Ontario cannot demand to be tried by a jury of his own mother tongue. On the other hand, the practice is not followed in Ottawa of striking French-speaking persons off the list from which jury panels are chosen. A unilingual Francophone would, however, be discovered when the panel was first assembled in court and would be excluded or challenged on that ground.[4]

---

[3]Thus at a murder trial in Ottawa in 1964 a witness who sought to testify in French was told by a justice of the Supreme Court of Ontario that French was not an official language of the province, and that court proceedings would be conducted in English. The next day, however, she was permitted to give her testimony in French through an interpreter. See *Ottawa Journal,* April 22 and 23, 1964, and *Le Droit,* April 22 and 23, 1964.

[4]This happened in November 1967 at the trial in Ottawa of Mr. Raymond Denis, a Montreal lawyer and former executive assistant to the Minister of Citizenship and Immigration, when four prospective jurors of French mother tongue were rejected for their insufficient knowledge of English. See *Ottawa Citizen,* November 14, 1967.

To sum up, in all its fundamentals the Ontario legal system is an English-language structure. Although there is some use of French in areas where a fair proportion of the population is French-speaking, for the most part this usage results from the various informal arrangements that may be devised within the rather narrow limits imposed by a basically unilingual system. That these limits are very real there can be no doubt. The factor of appeal to the unilingual Court of Appeal at Toronto, for example, requires the use of English-language transcripts of original proceedings, and this in turn has influenced the language of the trial itself. Further, the pressures towards uniformity in a province that is officially unilingual, and for large areas unilingual in practice, have led to the use of the English language alone in legal forms and documents throughout Ontario.

The occasions on which the French language is employed are of two kinds. First, the use of interpreters from time to time, though a costly and time-consuming procedure, has permitted persons with a poor command of English to play a fuller part in court proceedings. This is not a case of free choice of language, but rather of what is necessary in order that the requirements of justice be met. Second, the bilingualism of court officers and staff has enabled some use of the two languages outside the formal processes of the courtroom. While a deliberate policy of acquiring bilingual personnel is apparent for certain positions in Ottawa (such as probation officers), for the most part the presence of bilingual staff would seem to owe more to chance than to conscious decision. As a result, the French-speaking citizen is able to use his own language in communicating with the court and its staff on some occasions but not on others, depending upon the official with whom he has to deal.

C. *The Legal System of the Quebec Sector*

The structure of the legal institutions within the Quebec sector of the capital area is the same as that for any other part of the province outside Quebec City and Montreal. Some of the municipalities in the region have their own Municipal Court, while the three main courts serving the region as a whole are the Magistrate's Court, the Social Welfare Court, and the Superior Court of the judicial district of Hull. Within the district there are local administrative tribunals, local provincial tribunal offices, a land registry office, and the members of the legal profession (*avocats* and *notaires*).

In contrast to the situation in Carleton county, the district is virtually self-contained. No visiting judges come to hear cases, so that the only contact with more senior courts is by way of appeal to the Court of Queen's Bench (Appeal Side), which sits in Montreal and Quebec City. It should be noted that, in contrast to the situation in Ontario, no language difficulties are involved when a case is appealed in Quebec. The judges of the Court of Queen's Bench (Appeal side) are fully bilingual and all proceedings in that court— documentation of appeals and oral arguments—are in either language interchangeably. No translation of transcripts of testimony or of decisions is necessary, nor is it undertaken except to the extent that lawyers occasionally may have transcripts translated for their own use.

Local trial courts. Four municipalities in the Hull district—Hull, Aylmer, Gatineau, and Pointe-Gatineau—each have their own Municipal Court, presided over by a judge who is also engaged in the practice of law. The court tries prosecutions for infractions of municipal by-laws and cases relating to municipal contracts and taxes.

The Magistrate's Court has both a criminal and a civil jurisdiction, the former corresponding roughly to the combined jurisdictions of the Ontario Magistrate's Court and the County Court judges, and the latter approximating to that of the Ontario Division Courts. Thus, on the criminal side, the court hears prosecutions under provincial and federal statutes for such offences as thefts, drinking and traffic violations. The court also conducts preliminary inquiries, and may try some serious offences if the accused so elects. Under its civil jurisdiction the court hears claims in contract and delict up to $500,[5] municipal and school tax claims, church assessments, disputes between landlord and tenant, and so on.

At the time of our study, the Hull District Magistrate's Court was staffed by three judges, all of whom were of French mother tongue and bilingual. The staff of the court, headed by the *greffier,* was composed only of persons of French mother tongue. It is the policy, however, that service be provided in English as well as French. In practice most of the business of the court office is conducted in French, although English can be and is used to some extent.

Criminal actions are prosecuted by a *Procureur de la Couronne;* there is no prosecuting or conducting police officer as in the Ottawa Magistrate's Court. In civil actions it is usual for both sides to be represented by a lawyer.

A Social Welfare Court was established quite recently to serve Hull, Labelle, and Pontiac districts. It tries prosecutions against juveniles (in Quebec, persons under 18) and against adults accused of offences involving juveniles. The court admits juveniles to youth protection schools, determines adoption applications, and acts as a moderator or adviser in family disputes.

Like the Carleton County Juvenile and Family Court, the Social Welfare Court is intended to be more informal, more private, and more expeditious than the ordinary courts. It was reported that representation by lawyers is less frequent than in the other Hull courts. The forms used are available in either French or English, and are completed according to the known language of the accused person or parties. Proceedings very rarely involve Anglophones. When the accused is unable to understand the testimony given, it is informally passed on to him in his own language by the judge, the Clerk of the Court or by the Crown Prosecutor. Juveniles are addressed in either language by the judge, who is fully bilingual. At the time of the study there were six probation officers who served the same important function as those in the Carleton County Juvenile and Family Court. All six were of French mother tongue, bilingual, and Roman Catholic, so that there was no allocation of juveniles to officers according to language or religion.

---

[5]Under Quebec's revised Code of Civil Procedure, which went into effect on September 1, 1966, the Magistrate's Court was replaced by a Provincial Court with powers to hear actions for amounts up to $999.

Diagram 6.2. Courts of the judicial district of Hull, Quebec, at January 1966 (showing appeal system)

SUPREME COURT OF CANADA
Civil and criminal appeals

QUEBEC COURT OF QUEEN'S BENCH (APPEAL SIDE)
Civil and criminal appeals

MUNICIPAL COURT
Civil and criminal
Non-jury
Hull, Gatineau, Pointe-Gatineau, Aylmer

SOCIAL WELFARE COURT
Criminal and welfare
Non-jury
Hull district

SUPERIOR COURT
Civil and criminal
Jury and non-jury
Hull district

MAGISTRATE'S COURT
Civil and criminal
Non-jury
Hull district

The Superior Court hears suits that are beyond the competence of the other Quebec courts of first instance. The court itself is composed of 72 justices for the entire province, who exercise their functions in the various judicial districts to which they are appointed. Three justices, with residence in Hull, are responsible in rotation for the districts of Hull, Labelle, and Pontiac. Under its civil jurisdiction the court tries actions involving $500 or more, and is, therefore, the equivalent of the Ontario County Court and High Court of Justice. On the criminal side, the court, like the Ontario High Court of Justice, hears certain appeals from Magistrate's Court and tries those offences beyond the jurisdiction of Magistrate's Court.

A jury trial is available in both civil and criminal cases, although in practice it is only used in the latter. The linguistic composition of the jury (wholly Francophone, wholly Anglophone, or composed of equal representation from each group) is at the discretion of the accused. The proportion of wholly French to wholly English juries in Hull varies widely from year to year. Mixed juries are very rarely requested.[6]

Due to the importance of the matters involved and the technicality of the court procedure, lawyers are almost invariably employed. The Superior Court staff, headed by the Prothonotary, included at the time of the study only persons of French mother tongue, although it is policy and practice to provide service in English.

Language usage. The linguistic practices of the Carleton county courts tend to vary from court to court. In the Hull district, by contrast, they are in many respects uniform. This enables us to describe in general terms the language of forms and trials.

All forms used in criminal proceedings were reported to be available in either French or English. Formally, the complainant or prosecutor is free to select either language for the initial documents—the information, summons or warrant. However, he is expected to employ the language of the prospective accused. To some extent this criterion also applies to the summons in a non-criminal action. The pleadings in these cases can also be in either language, and it is possible for them to vary in language between the plaintiff and defendant. In the Hull district, however, only a small proportion of the pleading is done in English. Documents relating to land and personal property are accepted for registration in both French and English.

Either French or English can be used in all aspects of court proceedings. In actual trials this means that witnesses can testify in either language, and their testimony enters the transcript in the language in which it is given. Witnesses are examined and cross-examined in their own language. Oral argument can be in either language, as can also the judge's comments and decision.

The need for interpretation is met in different ways in different courts. When translation is necessary in the Social Welfare Court all requirements are met by the court officials themselves. In criminal proceedings in the Magistrate's and Superior Courts, if the accused is represented by a lawyer, it is presumed that the lawyer is bilingual and that he will interpret as required to his client. However, in the Superior Court, even when the

---

[6]The whole question of the language of juries in Canada is examined in some detail by C.-A. Sheppard, "The Law of Languages in Canada" (study prepared for the Royal Commission on Bilingualism and Biculturalism, 1966).

accused is represented, an interpreter is made available to him and paid by the court, if he insists on translation.[7] In either the Magistrate's Court or the Superior Court, if the accused is unrepresented, an interpreter may be ordered if the accused indicates that he cannot understand the language of the proceedings. This rarely happens. It is said to be a fairly common occurrence that an unrepresented accused in Magistrate's Court, rather than being provided with an interpreter, is given the gist of what witnesses have said against him by the judge. He is then called on to question the witnesses through the judge by suggesting the appropriate questions to be asked.

In civil cases, in both the Magistrate's and Superior Courts, the two sides are almost invariably represented by counsel. Both lawyers are presumed to be bilingual, and it appears to be a matter of pride in lawyers of both language groups to be able to carry on in either language as required. However, it occasionally happens that a unilingual lawyer from outside Hull comes in to take a case and indicates formally that he would prefer to plead in one language only. In these rare instances the court provides an interpreter and delays the steps in the trial to permit translation. The interpreter so provided is obtained by the court but his fee becomes an item which may, in the judge's discretion, be allowed as a taxed cost against the losing side. The general practice, however, is to presume that all lawyers are bilingual and to depend on their facility to ensure that their clients receive an adequate understanding of the proceedings and that a witness is examined in his own language.

Lawyers' oral arguments to the court may be in either language and each is heard frequently. It is reported that to some extent Anglophone lawyers try to use French in their arguments because they feel that in so doing they can convey their meaning more clearly to the court. Also, both Francophone and Anglophone lawyers have been known to use their second language in order to enable a client to follow and appreciate their argument. The position of lawyers in Hull is important, for when a person is not represented, some linguistic difficulty may arise. For example, a more detailed study of the reactions of the unrepresented accused in the Magistrate's and Social Welfare Courts might reveal some disadvantages for the unilingual person. However, in this connection, two further points should be stated. First, these lower level courts deal with matters of lesser gravity in their potential consequences to the individual; and second, those persons most in need of translation facilities—those who speak English only—in most instances make a point of securing legal representation, perhaps in specific recognition of the linguistic factor. These cases apart, it is fair to say by way of conclusion that the overall impression given by the Hull district courts is one of general and genuine bilingualism.

D. *The Legal Profession in the Ontario and Quebec Sectors*

In any legal system the lawyer acts as a buffer between the individual and the system. In the capital area, as we have seen above, he may also be required to act, quite literally,

---

[7]In Hull, two retired, highly qualified gentlemen are regularly employed as interpreters in all types of court proceedings. In Campbell's Bay the prothonotary and in Mont Laurier the court reporter act as interpreters and receive the fee as such in addition to their regular salaries.

The Legal Systems 157

as an interpreter. Furthermore, the relationship between lawyer and client demands the utmost in confidence and trust. Common language and, to a certain extent, cultural inheritance are no doubt important in this relationship, although they should not be overrated. In a large area of contact between solicitor and client concerning, for example, commercial matters and real estate, the relationship can be and is based purely on business considerations. Here the client chooses his legal adviser on the grounds of reputation, previous references and the specialization of the lawyer; a shared language and culture may be of lesser importance. Still, the ability of the legal profession to remove linguistic obstacles and explain the intricacies of a legal system unfamiliar to their clients is clearly a point worth consideration in the capital area. We turn first to the Ontario sector.

Ontario. A study of the *Canada Legal Directory,* edited by J.H. Wharton (Toronto, 1964) indicates that 289 members of the legal profession are located within Carleton county. This figure includes both government and academic lawyers. Nine of the total group are listed as qualified to practise in Quebec as well as Ontario. An analysis of names suggests that nearly four-fifths of the lawyers are of British origin. More precisely, 225 (or 77.9 per cent) appear to be of British origin, 36 (or 12.5 per cent) to be of French origin, and 28 (or 9.7 per cent) to be of other origins. It is interesting to compare these figures with those for the ethnic origin of the general population of Carleton county in 1961: at that time those of British, French, and other origins accounted for 54.9, 26.9, and 18.2 per cent of the population respectively.[8]

Table 6.1 shows the structure of legal firms in Carleton county from the standpoint of apparent ethnic origin of members of the legal profession. It will be seen that most lawyers, whatever their origin, practise in firms of two or more partners or associates. The largest firms, however, include very few persons with French names: of the 92 lawyers working in firms with six or more partners, only two seem to be of French origin. As it is generally recognized that the largest firms are best equipped to deal with the more important matters, the relative absence of lawyers of French origin from these firms may dissuade the French-speaking population from seeking the more specialized assistance offered by them.

Precise linguistic data for members of the Carleton county legal profession are not available; one can only make approximate inferences from the analysis of names and origins. However, it may be assumed that all those who speak French can also function well in English, since a lawyer speaking only French could not survive in the mainly Anglophone legal system of Ontario. Furthermore, an essential qualification for admission to practise in Ontario is the completion of the teaching portion of the bar admission course of the Law Society of Upper Canada. This is taught at Toronto in English only.

Quebec. Wharton's *Canada Legal Directory,* 1964, lists 58 lawyers within the districts of Hull, Pontiac, and Labelle. Of these, 41 are located in Hull itself. Seven individuals are noted as being qualified to practise in Ontario as well as Quebec. Roughly

---

[8]Census of Canada, 1961; Catalogue 92-545.

three-quarters of the total group appear from their names to be of French origin (43 out of 58, or 74.1 per cent). Those of British and other origins number 14 and one respectively, or 24.1 and 1.7 per cent. In contrast, the combined population of Hull, Pontiac, and Labelle counties was divided by ethnic origin in 1961 as follows: 81.3 per cent of French origin, 15.2 per cent of British origin, and 3.5 per cent of other origins.[9]

Table 6.1. Carleton county legal profession, ethnic origin and firm structure, 1964

Number in firm	Firm structure			Number of such firms	Distribution of legal profession by firm structure		
	French	British	Other		French	British	Other
22	1	20	1	1	1	20	1
11	0	6	5	1	0	6	5
10	0	10	0	1	0	10	0
9	0	9	0	1	0	9	0
8	1	7	0	1	1	7	0
	0	2	6	1	0	2	6
6	0	6	0	3	0	18	0
	0	5	1	1	0	5	1
5	0	5	0	2	0	10	0
	1	4	0	2	2	8	0
	4	0	1	1	4	0	1
	5	0	0	1	5	0	0
4	0	4	0	5	0	20	0
	1	3	0	1	1	3	0
	0	2	2	1	0	2	2
3	0	3	0	10	0	30	0
	0	2	1	1	0	2	1
	2	1	0	1	2	1	0
	0	1	2	1	0	1	2
	3	0	0	1	3	0	0
2	0	2	0	16	0	32	0
	2	0	0	3	6	0	0
	1	1	0	3	3	3	0
	0	0	2	1	0	0	2
	0	1	1	1	0	1	1
Individuals practising alone					8	35	6
Total					36	225	28

Source: Name analysis of listings in Wharton, *Canada Legal Directory*, 1964.

Table 6.2 presents an analysis of the firm structure and presumed ethnic origin of the legal profession in the Hull, Labelle, and Pontiac districts. No large firms have been established. Practice in Hull is evidently characterized by two-man and individual firms.

[9]Census of Canada, 1961; Catalogue 92-545.

The Legal Systems

Table 6.2. The legal profession in Hull, Pontiac and Labelle districts, ethnic origin and firm structure, 1964

Number in firm	Firm structure			Number of such firms	Distribution of legal profession by firm structure		
	French	British	Other		French	British	Other
4	1	3	0	1	1	3	0
2	1	1	0	1	1	1	0
	2	0	0	4	8	0	0
	0	2	0	2	0	4	0
Individuals practising alone					33	6	1
Total					43	14	1

Source: Name analysis of listings in Wharton, *Canada Legal Directory*, 1964.

There are apparently no unilingual lawyers practising in the Hull area, although there is a wide range of fluency in the two languages. It is said that a unilingual person of either language would have difficulty in surviving in practice. This would be especially true of a unilingual Anglophone, despite the fact that all non-trial work can be done in English with no disadvantage whatever.

The qualifications for admission to practise in the province of Quebec consist of university study and a bar admission examination which may be written in either French or English. So long as the McGill Law Faculty continues to grant recognized law degrees, an English-speaking person should be able to enter practice in Hull.

E. Summary

From the preceding discussion we may draw out the following main points. They refer, of course, to the situation as it existed at the time of our inquiry.

1) In the court offices situated in the Hull district, service can be obtained in both languages. In Carleton county, service is offered in English only by the offices of two of the four Division Courts and of the County Court. The remaining offices can give service in both French and English.
2) In the Hull district, legal forms are available and documents are accepted as valid by the courts in either language. In Carleton county, only English forms are used.
3) In the course of judicial proceedings in Hull—that is, in the giving of testimony by witnesses and their examination and cross-examination, in the oral arguments of the lawyers, and in the judge's comments and decisions—both languages can be used almost interchangeably. In Carleton county, French is rarely employed in the courts.
4) Interpretation is provided on occasion by both systems, but in neither is this done in a thorough-going or fully satisfactory manner.
5) The Quebec legal system attaches greater importance to the language of jurors than does that of Ontario, by permitting the determination of the linguistic composition of juries.

6) On both sides of the Ottawa River, the role played by bilingual lawyers in providing the linguistic link between the court and their clients is of great importance to the functioning of the two legal systems.
7) There are lawyers of French and British origins in both sectors of the capital area, although in each case there are proportionally more lawyers than population of British origin.
8) Factors extraneous to the immediate capital area have largely shaped the language usage of courts within it. Thus, the question of appeal to the predominantly English-speaking appeal courts in Ontario has played a major role in requiring the use of English in the courts of first instance, while, in Quebec, section 133 of the B.N.A. Act has obliged both the local and the appeal courts to be bilingual.
9) In sum, there are striking differences in linguistic practice between the two legal systems, with the Quebec courts making a far more liberal provision for the use of both official languages than do the Ontario courts.

Chapter VII   **Political Representation**

A. Introduction

Any study of the place of language groups in a community would be incomplete if the question of political representation were not examined. To describe the manner in which the needs and wants of a given group are articulated with the structure of political power and expressed through the decision-making process is to approach in some measure a description of that group's integration with or alienation from the rest of the community.

In the National Capital Region there are at present three levels of political jurisdiction—federal, provincial, and municipal—at which language groups can find representation. On the federal level, the present electoral boundaries, which have been in effect for six general elections, provide six constituencies entirely or mostly within the Region and one partially so. Under the redistribution which will be in effect at the next general election there will be seven federal constituencies mainly within the area. Provincially, five members were elected to the Ontario legislature from seats within the area at the time of our inquiry. Under the redistribution of 1966, however, there are now six area seats. Four members are elected to the Quebec legislature from constituencies which lie, wholly or in part, within the Region. On the municipal level, the number of local jurisdictions in the area is high (*see* 3), and the representational systems vary considerably in structure.

On the federal and provincial levels, the constituencies of the Region form only a small percentage of the total seats in the legislatures. Moreover, the decisions which are made by these bodies are of a national and provincial significance and only rarely of special concern to the Region *per se*. The municipal councils, however, wholly based on and involved with the Region, are another matter, and it is on these that we shall concentrate first. More precisely, the concentration will be on the three cities of the area, Ottawa, Hull, and Eastview, which together encompass the bulk of the Region's population, although some reference will also be made to the other municipalities within the Ottawa metropolitan area.

A study of the representation of language groups raises at least four distinct issues:

1) the degree to which the existing electoral systems permit the direct representation of such groups, which is to say, the degree of correlation between demographic distribution and constituency boundaries;
2) the degree to which the potential of the electoral system is utilized by members of language groups to nominate or vote for representatives drawn from within their own group;
3) the degree to which elected representatives behave and act as spokesmen and agents for constituents from a minority language group;
4) language usage within the legislative body itself.

Three of these issues—the structure of the electoral system, the candidates nominated and elected, and the language usage of legislative bodies—may be approached in direct fashion without undue difficulty. However, questions as to how candidates seek the support of the electorate and what roles they play after election in relation to their own and other language groups are far more subtle. To be answered fully they would have required a complicated research programme into the attitudes of the candidates and general public that was not possible for this study. Instead a more oblique approach was employed. While rejecting at the outset any automatic assumption that minority language groups can only be adequately represented by one of their own number, an attempt was made to discover how far in fact such direct representation was sought by the minority group and to what extent representation by members of the majority group constituted an acceptable alternative.

A variety of methods were employed in the data-gathering stage of the study. For the three cities, personal interviews with council members and observation of councils in session, together with a study of press reports, provided much of the current information. In describing their historical patterns of representation, the best criterion for classification would have been the representative's main language or his cultural identification. For much of the period, however, neither of these was available. In their place primary reliance had to be placed on the origins of council members, based for the most part on an analysis of names, and supplemented by historical records and personal recollection wherever possible. This approach naturally has certain limitations, both because it does not measure the desired linguistic and cultural criteria, and because name analysis leaves a certain margin of error or indeterminacy. Nevertheless, the technique does produce in broad outline a picture of the part played by the two main linguistic communities in the past political life of the area.

Information on the councils of the other municipalities was derived largely from answers to a questionnaire filled out by officials of the municipalities themselves, along with press reports and supplementary inquiries by telephone.

B. Representation: The Cities of Ottawa, Hull and Eastview

In order to see how the municipal electoral systems have been organized and in what manner they have been utilized by language groups, the historical and contemporary patterns of representation on the councils of the three cities of the area have been examined. One major feature that these municipalities have in common is the geographical division of each city into wards for the election of aldermen.

In the province of Ontario, the Municipal Act allows a municipality to elect its councillors either at large by general vote or from geographically divided wards (R.S.O. 1960, c. 249, s. 31). Of the five local governments on the Ontario side of the metropolitan area, only Ottawa and Eastview have adopted the latter system; the other three—Gloucester, Nepean and Rockcliffe Park—employ a general vote.

On the Quebec side of the metropolitan area, the four municipalities under the Cities and Towns Act (Hull, Aylmer, Gatineau and Pointe-Gatineau) have an option of electing their aldermen either by wards or by general vote to numbered seats (R.S.Q. 1964, c. 193, s. 30). All four in fact have ward systems. The other four municipalities in the Quebec portion of the metropolitan area (Lucerne, Deschênes, Templeton, and West Templeton) come under the Municipal Code (Municipal Code of the Province of Quebec, title II, c. II, art. 80), which requires that all council members be elected by general vote but to specific numbered seats. Under this arrangement two or more candidates may contest a given seat while other councillors may be returned by acclamation.

Important consequences stem from the nature of the electoral system. Where a linguistic minority is concentrated in one or more geographical areas within a municipality, it is likely that a ward system is better designed to ensure the direct representation of that minority than a general vote system within which a minority may easily be submerged. The impact of the electoral system is most clearly seen in Ottawa. This city is unique among the municipalities of the National Capital Region in having not only a ward system for the election of aldermen, but also a four-man board of control elected by general vote, which, together with the mayor, comprises the executive level of civic government in the city.

1. Ottawa

The office of mayor has been occupied by 48 individuals since the city's incorporation in 1855. Six appear to have been of French origin, and these held office for a total of 12 man-years in this 112-year period. The remaining 42 mayors were apparently of British origin, with one early exception whose background could not be determined.

The paucity of French-speaking mayors becomes even more striking when it is noted that four of the six mayors of French origin held office in the 19th century, and that only three of the total of 12 man-years were served in the 20th century. The most recent French-speaking mayor held office almost two decades ago. Indeed, in recent years, no French-speaking candidate for the mayoralty has been able to attract serious voter support.

Section 201 of the Ontario Municipal Act provides that any Ontario city whose population exceeds 100,000 must have a board of control consisting of the mayor and four controllers, all of whom are to be elected at large from the city as a whole. At least one exception, however, is known to exist to this provision. The city of Windsor, following a city referendum which favoured the abolition of the board of control and its replacement by a city manager, had a private Act passed in the Ontario Legislature. This

Act stated that, "notwithstanding the provisions of the Municipal Act," the council of the city of Windsor shall be composed of a mayor and ten aldermen (S.O. 1957, 5-6 Eliz. II, c. 161, s. 16(1)).

Ottawa established a board of control in 1908. Table 7.1 shows that since that date the proportion of total man-years accounted for by controllers of British origin is 69 per cent, while those of French origin have accounted for 21 per cent. The remaining 10 per cent represents controllers whose origins were apparently neither French nor British, although it should be pointed out that 18 of the 24 man-years in the latter category were filled by one man.

Table 7.1. City of Ottawa, controllers by origin in ten-year periods, 1908-1967

Year	Total		Origin					
			British		French		Others	
	N	%	N	%	N	%	N	%
Total	239	100	164	68.6	51	21.3	24	10.1
1908-17	40	100	30	75.0	10	25.0	–	–
1918-27	40	100	33	82.5	7	17.5	–	–
1928-37	40	100	25	62.5	8	20.0	7	17.5
1938-47	40	100	20	50.0	10	25.0	10	25.0
1948-57	39	100	28	71.8	10	25.6	1	2.6
1958-67	40	100	28	70.0	6	15.0	6	15.0

Sources: Name analysis, interviews, press reports.

The proportion of French-speaking controllers has dropped significantly in recent years. No French-speaking candidates have been elected to board of control since 1960. The French-speaking controller who held office in 1964 was appointed by council to fill a vacancy created by resignation, and he did not contest the position in the next election. Recent elections to board of control are discussed in more detail below (*see* 168-71), but it might be noted at this point that the city-wide nature of board of control elections makes it difficult for the 21 per cent of Ottawa's population who are French by mother tongue to elect a candidate of their language to the board without extensive support from the English-speaking majority.

Taking the case of aldermen since 1869 (the first year from which full data were available), Table 7.2 shows that those of British origin apparently account for 74 per cent of those elected, those of French origin for 23 per cent, and those whose origins are neither British nor French for less than 2 per cent. The remainder represents some early aldermen whose background could not be accurately determined.

Table 7.2. City of Ottawa, aldermen by origin in five-year periods, 1869-1967

Year	Total		Origin							
			British		French		Others		Not known	
	N	%	N	%	N	%	N	%	N	%
Total	1,926	100	1,419	73.7	451	23.4	29	1.5	27	1.4
1869-74	75	100	57	76.0	17	22.7	–	–	1	1.3
75-79	75	100	54	72.0	17	22.7	–	–	4	5.3
80-84	75	100	54	72.0	17	22.7	3	4.0	1	1.3
85-89	84	100	65	77.4	16	19.0	1	1.2	2	2.4
90-94	120	100	95	79.2	19	15.8	–	–	6	5.0
95-99	120	100	92	76.7	19	15.8	–	–	9	7.5
1900-04	120	100	87	72.5	26	21.7	3	2.5	4	3.3
05-09	104	100	71	68.3	28	26.9	5	4.8	–	–
10-14	90	100	66	73.3	24	26.7	–	–	–	–
15-19	90	100	65	72.2	25	27.8	–	–	–	–
20-24	90	100	62	68.9	27	30.0	1	1.1	–	–
25-29	90	100	56	62.2	31	34.5	3	3.3	–	–
30-34	110	100	80	72.7	30	27.3	–	–	–	–
35-39	110	100	80	72.7	30	27.3	–	–	–	–
40-44	110	100	80	72.7	30	27.3	–	–	–	–
45-49	110	100	82	74.5	28	25.5	–	–	–	–
50-54	119	100	96	80.7	23	19.3	–	–	–	–
55-59	92	100	74	80.4	15	16.3	3	3.3	–	–
60-65	100	100	71	71.0	20	20.0	9	9.0	–	–
66-67	42	100	32	77.3	9	20.4	1	2.3	–	–

Sources: Name analysis, interviews, press reports.

This balance between French- and English-speaking aldermen shows a certain consistency over time. The highest proportion of representatives of French background was reached in the 1920's and 1930's; the periods of lowest representation were at the end of the nineteenth century and in the late 1950's. A comparison of these figures with the census figures for the city as a whole (Table E, Appendix A) suggests that the population of French origin was somewhat under-represented in relation to aldermen of French origin down to about 1920, slightly over-represented during the 1920's, and under-represented in varying degrees since about 1930. All in all, however, these fluctuations are not very sharp.

If the proportion between aldermen of French and British origins has remained reasonably constant, the geographical bases from which aldermen of French origin have been elected also show a remarkable consistency over time. Until 1953 such aldermen represented primarily two wards, Ottawa and By, both of which were in the traditionally French-speaking Lower Town area. These two wards together account for 320 man-years, or almost 80 per cent of the total of 399 man-years served on city council by aldermen of French origin up to that date. The remaining 79 of these man-years were filled by aldermen from Victoria, St. George's, and Central wards.

The only significant drop in the otherwise stable proportion of French-speaking aldermen came in the early 1950's when city council was expanded to include representatives of the suburbs newly annexed from Gloucester and Nepean townships. These were largely English-speaking areas, and in the consequent redrawing of ward boundaries in 1953, two traditional French-speaking wards (Victoria and Ottawa) disappeared. Although at this time the customary geographical basis of French-speaking representation was thus narrowed, by the 1960's the proportion of French-speaking aldermen had partially returned to its previous level.

To consider the present political geography of Ottawa, a more detailed study of the past five civic elections, those from 1958 to 1966, is necessary. For this period at least, it would appear that a direct relationship exists between the mother tongue of voters and the language of the aldermanic candidates they elect.

Map 7.1* shows the 1966 ward boundaries of the city of Ottawa superimposed on a map of city census tracts which showed concentrations of French and other mother tongues in 1961. This method of relating vote to language is only a visual aid: as the census tracts do not coincide with ward boundaries, no precise quantitative data can be employed. Nevertheless the visual pattern stands out sharply. Two wards, By and St. George's, would appear to have a heavy concentration of French-speaking residents. Rideau ward has a somewhat smaller concentration, and two others, Elmdale-Victoria and Dalhousie, would appear to contain a still smaller though noticeable proportion of French-speaking citizens. One ward, Dalhousie, has a relatively strong concentration of citizens of other mother tongues. The remaining wards have heavy English mother-tongue majorities.

The distribution by ethnic origin of candidates for aldermen in all wards over the past five elections is given in Table 7.3. It is obvious that French-language candidates are elected only in those wards with strong concentrations of French-speaking residents, the sole exception occurring in the new Alta Vista ward in 1966. Even in this area there are some indications that the French-speaking population may now be proportionally greater than it was at the time of the 1961 census. On the few occasions when French-speaking candidates have presented themselves for election in the predominantly English-speaking wards, they have not only lost, but usually lost badly. Conversely, no candidates of British origin have run in By, the ward with the largest concentration of French-speaking residents. In St. George's also, English-language candidates would seem to have high odds against them.

Dalhousie ward presents an intriguing counterpoint to the other wards. Here a heavy concentration of voters of other mother tongues (mainly Italian) helped elect in 1966 an alderman of Italian background, apparently the first in the city's history.

It is not unreasonable to conclude from a study of these elections, as well as from the historical survey given above, that French-speaking voters in Ottawa have tended wherever possible to vote for French-speaking candidates. As may be seen in Table 7.4, the percentage of successful aldermanic candidates of French origin in recent elections, 19 per cent, compares quite closely with the proportion of Ottawa's population of French mother tongue at the 1961 census, that is, 21 per cent. A further comparable figure was provided

---

*Maps in Chapter VII are collected together at 174.

when the 1966 election returned five French-speaking aldermen out of a total of 22, or 23 per cent.

Present ward boundaries thus seem well designed to ensure French-language aldermanic representation in proportion to the French population in the city as a whole. While the French-speaking community in Elmdale-Victoria and Dalhousie wards is submerged by majorities of English and other mother tongues, and is no longer able to elect a French-speaking alderman as was usual in Victoria ward before the 1953 redistribution, this is balanced by the fact that By and St. George's have smaller populations than some of the heavily English-speaking suburban wards.

Table 7.3. City of Ottawa, origin of aldermanic candidates in five elections, 1958-1966

Ward	Total		Origin					
			British		French		Others	
	Successful	Unsuccessful	Successful	Unsuccessful	Successful	Unsuccessful	Successful	Unsuccessful
Total	102	114	76	86	19	17	7	11
By	10	5	–	–	10	5	–	–
Rideau	10	15	8*	10	–	4	2	1
St. George's	10	12	1	7	8	4	1	1
Wellington	10	17	10	16	–	–	–	1
Capital	10	12	10	11	–	1	–	–
Dalhousie	10	9	9	4	–	–	1	5
Elmdale-Victoria	10	10	10	8	–	2	–	–
Queensboro	10	10	10	10	–	–	–	–
Carleton	10	7	10	6	–	1	–	–
Gloucester	10	14	7	12	–	–	3	2
Alta Vista**	2	3	1	2	1	–	–	1

Sources: Name analysis, interviews, press reports.
* Includes one alderman for three terms whose background is both French and British and who is fluently bilingual.
** Alta Vista became a separate ward in 1966. Previously it was part of Gloucester ward.

Table 7.4. City of Ottawa, aldermanic candidates by origin, 1958-1966 summary

Origin	Total candidates		Successful candidates		Unsuccessful candidates	
	N	%	N	%	N	%
Total	216	100	102	100	114	100
British	162	76.4	76	77.5	86	75.4
French	36	16.7	19	18.6	17	14.9
Others	18	6.9	7	3.9	11	9.6

Sources: Name analysis, interviews, press reports.

In point of fact, By ward, the traditional centre of French-speaking Ottawa, was given careful consideration when ward boundaries were being redrawn. Although the notion of establishing wards on a basis of strict equality of population has often been suggested, there does seem to exist a substantial acceptance within the English-speaking community of the principle of retaining intact the French-speaking wards. As one English-language newspaper remarked in the course of an editorial urging redistribution on a basis of population equality: "... there should be one exception. Ottawa is ethnically a bilingual city [sic], and the predominantly French-speaking wards should be preserved as separate identities" (*Ottawa Citizen,* September 8, 1966).

In the executive branch of municipal government, however, elections to the offices of mayor and board of control are all run on a city-wide basis. Hence political boundaries do not come into consideration, and French-language residents are consequently less able to influence the result of the vote. As mentioned before, the number of French-speaking mayors in Ottawa's history is small.

Since the withdrawal of former Controller Paul Tardif from municipal politics and his entry into federal politics in 1962, board of control has been without an elected French-speaking member. The idea, however, that the French community ought to have one representative on the executive branch is widely held, not only by spokesmen of that community, but also by the English-language press and English-speaking officials. When a vacancy occurred on board of control in 1963, a French-speaking alderman was appointed by council to fill out the term, one of the main reasons for his selection being that he did represent the French-speaking citizens of Ottawa.

The failure of the last few elections to return a French-speaking controller presents something of a puzzle, in that a gap seems to exist between the general approval given by press and politicians to the inclusion of one French-language member on the board, and the voting pattern expressed by the electorate. Seven French-speaking candidates have stood for election to board of control in the past three elections (1962, 1964 and 1966). Moreover in 1964 one candidate of non-French origin (David Dehler), who was himself bilingual, ran a campaign that emphasized greater recognition of bilingualism and recognition of the rights of the French-speaking population of Ottawa. Table 7.5 shows, by ward, what percentage of the vote for board of control each of these eight candidates received. It should be noted that each elector is given *four* possible votes for board of control; thus 25 per cent of the vote in any ward to one candidate indicates maximum support if all voters use four votes, and over 25 per cent indicates that some electors did not use all their votes.

Again it is clear that a direct correlation exists between the language of voters and the language of the candidates they choose. Thus French-speaking candidates tend to run best in By, St. George's, and Rideau wards, and poorly in the heavily English-speaking wards such as Carleton, Queensboro, Capital, Wellington, and Gloucester.

One point which emerges from the above analysis, however, is that while French-speaking voters will, if given the choice, tend to vote for qualified French-speaking candidates in preference to qualified English-speaking candidates, it is nevertheless just as clear that a French name is not enough in itself to guarantee a substantial vote from French-speaking electors. French-speaking candidates who are generally believed to be

Table 7.5. City of Ottawa, percentage of vote received by selected candidates for board of control, 1962-1966

Ward	1966		1964				1962		
	L. Titley	J.L. Paradis	D. Dehler	S. Tardif	J. Villeneuve	H. Racine	S. Tardif	J.L. Paradis
Total	13.2	3.8	10.0	5.2	1.3	10.3	5.0	2.2
By	29.7	6.2	14.7	14.8	3.1	28.2	14.4	5.1
St. George's	19.0	5.0	12.9	8.4	1.9	18.1	6.1	2.9
Rideau	17.5	5.4	11.3	7.1	1.8	13.1	7.2	3.4
Wellington	10.4	3.5	8.9	4.1	1.3	8.2	4.0	1.9
Capital	10.5	3.0	9.2	3.0	1.0	8.9	2.9	1.5
Dalhousie	12.4	4.6	8.8	6.8	1.7	9.1	6.4	2.4
Elmdale-Victoria	12.1	3.6	9.2	5.2	1.3	10.8	6.9	2.2
Queensboro	9.9	3.1	7.8	3.5	0.9	9.4	4.7	2.4
Carleton	10.0	2.9	9.3	3.0	0.9	8.9	4.0	2.0
Gloucester	10.6	3.9	10.3	3.6	0.9	9.3	4.1	2.4
Alta Vista	12.5	3.4						
Rank in field	5/7	7/7	5/11	9/11	11/11	6/10	8/10	10/10

Source: Electoral records of the city of Ottawa.

unqualified or to lack widespread support, although they tend to run marginally better in predominantly French-speaking areas than in English-speaking ones, do not do well absolutely in terms of actual votes in either type of ward. In other words, language and ethnicity are not the sole criteria used by French-speaking voters, but the latter nevertheless appear to support French-speaking candidates more strongly than English-speaking voters do by a perceptible margin.

This tendency to vote for members of one's own language group, or in the case of Mr. Dehler, for bilingual candidates who are seen as sympathetic to the group's interests, finds effective expression in the votes for aldermen. But in the elections for mayor and board of control, it is frustrated by the city-wide nature of the vote. The 1966 election is particularly instructive in this regard.

In 1966 the French-speaking community in Ottawa sought to unite around a single candidate for board of control and to make a concerted effort on his behalf. The candidate himself had the support not only of the French-speaking community but of substantial sections of English opinion as well. Yet he failed to get elected. A close look at this election might be useful because of the light it sheds on language and politics in Ottawa.

A few months prior to the December 1966 civic elections, stories began to appear in the Ottawa press concerning the efforts of an association known as La ligue d'action civique, headed by Pierre Mercier, to elect a French-speaking candidate to board of control. The league proposed to put forward a single French candidate so as not to split the French-speaking vote. A convention was arranged which, it was hoped, would be made up of delegates nominated by "tous les groupements représentatifs de la collectivité canadienne-française d'Ottawa. . ." (*Le Droit,* September 28, 1966). It was also planned to carry out a fund-raising drive and to set up an efficient political organization.

These plans met with a certain amount of sympathy in the English-language press. As one newspaper stated editorially: "The French-speaking community holds a special place not only because of its size, but also because it is symbolic of French Canada's presence in Confederation. It should, therefore, be represented in the executive arm of the national capital's administration" (*Ottawa Citizen,* October 5, 1966).

At the league's convention, Louis Titley, an Ottawa businessman, was chosen as candidate. Mr. Titley proposed a platform which emphasized bilingualism and the rights of French-speaking Ottawans, but touched on many other non-linguistic policy matters as well. His defeated opponent for the nomination promised his full support, and unanimity in the French community seemed to have been thus achieved.

With much of the press, both French and English, behind the Titley candidacy, it was widely predicted that it would be successful. Instead Mr. Titley finished a poor fifth, trailing the fourth-place finisher by 9,000 votes and the leading candidate by 23,000 votes.

Mr. Mercier, president of the league, attributed the defeat to the refusal of English-speaking voters to support a French-speaking candidate.[1] The candidate himself placed

---

[1] " ... Ottawa demeure sans aucun doute la ville la plus préjugée de l'Ontario," as quoted by Marcel Desjardins, "Un faible vote franco-outaouais et un rejet de l'électeur anglais," *Le Droit,* December 6, 1966.

Table 7.6. City of Ottawa, percentage distribution of vote for board of control by wards, civic election of 1966

Ward	Total	Candidate					
		K. Fogarty*	E. Webber*	M. Heit*	E. Jones*	L. Titley	I. Greenberg	J.L. Paradis
Total	100	23.2	18.5	17.4	17.2	13.2	6.8	3.8
Alta Vista	100	22.8	18.8	19.7	16.6	12.5	6.1	3.4
By	100	20.3	14.6	11.6	12.3	29.7	5.4	6.2
Capital	100	24.2	18.5	18.6	18.4	10.5	6.7	3.0
Carleton	100	23.5	19.7	18.5	18.5	10.0	7.0	2.9
Dalhousie	100	24.2	18.5	15.3	17.8	12.4	7.1	4.6
Elmdale-Victoria	100	24.3	18.0	17.2	18.0	12.1	6.7	3.6
Gloucester	100	22.4	19.3	19.7	16.7	10.6	7.3	3.9
Queensboro	100	24.1	19.2	17.8	19.2	9.9	6.7	3.1
Rideau	100	21.6	18.4	16.0	15.1	17.5	6.4	5.0
St. George's	100	22.2	17.7	14.5	14.7	19.0	6.4	5.4
Wellington	100	23.9	18.3	17.3	17.4	10.4	9.1	3.5
Advance poll	100	23.7	18.3	17.6	16.9	14.6	6.1	2.7

Source: Electoral records of the city of Ottawa.
* Successful candidate.

much emphasis on the failure of French-speaking voters to turn out in sufficient numbers, and to give him enough of a majority to carry into the English-speaking wards (*Le Droit*, December 6, 1966). An English-language newspaper expressed its disappointment at the result, but denied that prejudice was the reason for Mr. Titley's defeat (*Ottawa Citizen*, December 6, 1966). The same newspaper in its news columns, however, viewed the results as showing a rejection of "bilingualism and racial origin" in favour of the record of the previous administration, which was returned en masse (*Ottawa Citizen*, December 6, 1966).

Table 7.6 shows that Mr. Titley ran worst in those areas where French-speaking voters are fewest. Only in the three most strongly French wards (By, St. George's, and Rideau) did he even place among the top four finishers, and only in By ward did he receive exceptional support. The heavily English-speaking suburban and centre-town wards clearly rejected him.

It may be seen from Table 7.6 that the three wards which placed Mr. Titley within the top four positions did not otherwise deviate from the general pattern of voting in the city as a whole. Successful candidates did obtain smaller percentages of the vote in the three wards than they did generally, but this is accounted for by a higher than average vote for Mr. Titley; in relative terms the standing of the other six candidates remained much the same.

One aspect of the continuing failure of French-speaking candidates to achieve election to board of control which may be investigated at greater length is the complaint sometimes heard that French-speaking voters do not turn out in sufficient numbers to support candidates from their linguistic community. This complaint has on occasion been coupled with the contention that their turnout is low because the French-speaking community tends to be indifferent to what is an almost entirely English-speaking political environment in Ottawa. This question is crucial to an understanding of the place of the French-speaking community in Ottawa, and it is one which can, in part at least, be analyzed.

Table 7.7 indicates the percentage turnout by ward for the last five civic elections. These percentages are based on a comparison of the votes for mayor with the official voters lists. The mayoralty vote would seem to be the best indicator of turnout, since it is probably a safe assumption that on incomplete ballots, the mayoralty section heading the ballot is the least likely to be left blank. Besides, the four possible votes per elector for board of control make an accurate estimation of turnout on that basis very difficult.

In support of the hypothesis that French-speaking voters turn out in lower proportions than their English-speaking counterparts, it may be noted from Table 7.7 that the turnout in the three wards with the highest concentration of French mother-tongue residents (By, St. George's, and Rideau) does tend to be somewhat below the average for the city as a whole. Moreover, Dalhousie ward's low turnout record might be interpreted as reflecting similar indifference on the part of the Italian mother-tongue community in that ward.

But Wellington ward's average turnout (the lowest in the city) cannot be explained in cultural or linguistic terms. Wellington's low figures may, however, be accounted for on economic grounds. Electoral studies elsewhere have shown a tendency for lower-income areas to be politically more apathetic than higher-income areas, and voters in such areas generally fail to participate in elections in the same numbers as those in more affluent ones.[2] While this suggestion offers a plausible explanation for Wellington ward's poor turnout, it also raises serious doubts concerning the hypothesis of alienation of the French-speaking voter in Ottawa.

Table 7.7. City of Ottawa, percentage turnout by ward in voting for mayor, 1958-1966

Ward	Average for five elections	Year				
		1958	1960	1962	1964	1966
City average	53.9	42.2	63.9	58.5	59.2	45.7
Gloucester	} 61.2	49	73	67	70	55
Alta Vista						53
Carleton	60.2	46	72	66	68	49
Capital	57.2	47	67	62	61	49
Elmdale-Victoria	55.2	45	64	60	59	48
Queensboro	55.0	42	68	60	59	46
By	53.0	51	64	56	51	43
St. George's	52.2	41	62	56	56	46
Rideau	47.4	33	57	55	53	39
Dalhousie	45.2	39	56	50	46	35
Wellington	44.4	35	56	50	49	32

Source: City of Ottawa electoral records.

Map 7.2 shows the 1966 ward boundaries of the city of Ottawa superimposed on a map of city census tracts having less than $4000 average income per year in 1961. Viewed in this way, the average turnout for By and St. George's wards would appear to be actually higher than one might otherwise expect for wards with lower than average incomes. In particular By ward seems to stand higher than might be expected on economic grounds alone. Diagram 7.1 gives By ward's turnout over the last five elections as compared to the city-wide average, to Carleton ward, which is predominantly English-speaking and of high average income, and to Wellington ward, which is predominantly English-speaking but of low average income. While it is true that By ward's turnout has dropped in relative terms since 1958 (when it was actually the highest in the city), it still has experienced higher turnouts than Wellington (or, as was seen in Table 7.7, Dalhousie), and this gap cannot be explained on the basis of differing levels of income.

---

[2] *See,* e.g., Seymour Martin Lipset, *Political Man* (New York, 1963), 188-9, 194.

DIAGRAM 7.1

**PERCENTAGE TURNOUT (vote for mayor) BY SELECTED WARDS
OTTAWA CIVIC ELECTIONS, 1958 – 1966**

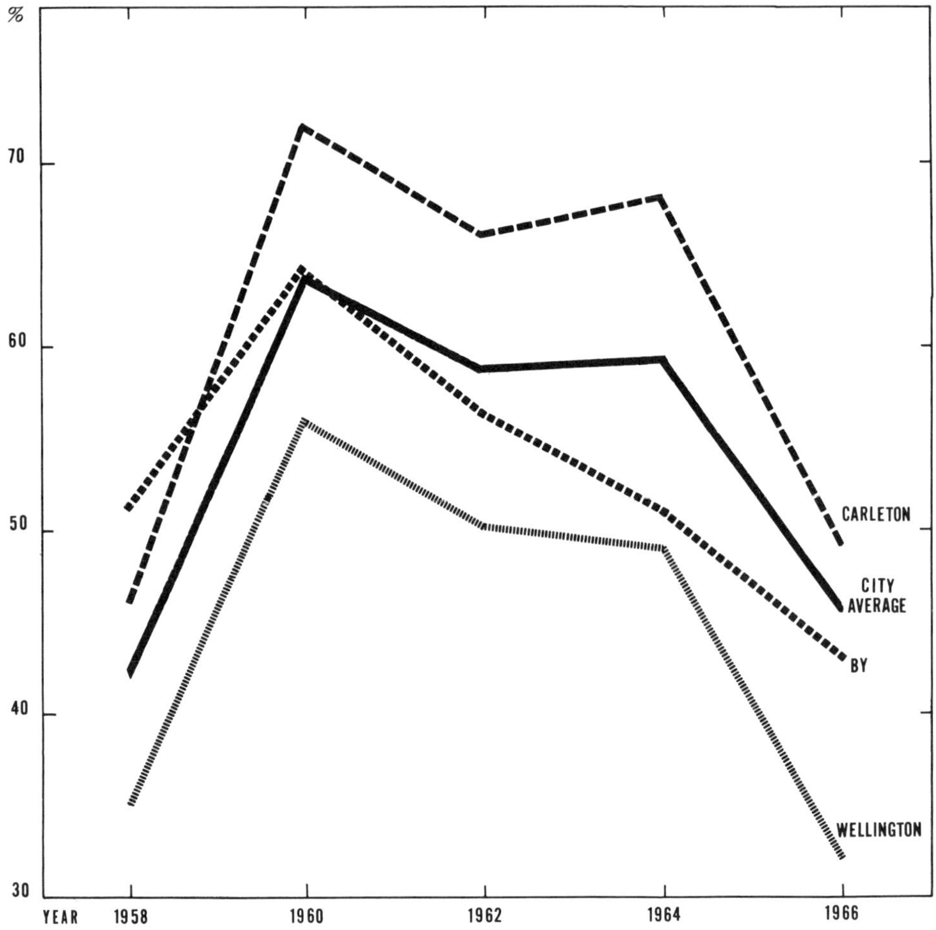

THE NATIONAL CAPITAL REGION

- — · — BOUNDARY OF THE NATIONAL CAPITAL REGION
- — — — METROPOLITAN OTTAWA BOUNDARY
- CITY OF OTTAWA AND BUILT-UP AREAS
- GREENBELT
- GATINEAU PARK

Map 1.1. THE NATIONAL CAPITAL REGION

OTTAWA METROPOLITAN AREA, 1961

Map 1.2. OTTAWA METROPOLITAN AREA, 1961

CENSUS TRACTS OF OTTAWA METROPOLITAN AREA, 1961

Map 1.3. CENSUS TRACTS,
OTTAWA METROPOLITAN AREA, 1961

LINGUISTIC CONCENTRATIONS
OTTAWA METROPOLITAN AREA, 1961

Tracts Where:

70 Percent and Over of Population is of English Mother Tongue

10 Percent and Over of Population is of Other Mother Tongue

70 Percent of Population is of English Mother Tongue and 10 Percent of Other Mother Tongue

70 Percent of Population is of French Mother Tongue

Linguistic Concentrations are Lower than the above

Map 1.4. LINGUISTIC CONCENTRATIONS, OTTAWA METROPOLITAN AREA, 1961

RICHEST and POOREST SECTORS, OTTAWA METROPOLITAN AREA, 1961

Twenty Highest Average Income Sectors

Twenty Lowest Average Income Sectors

Map 1.5. RICHEST AND POOREST SECTORS,
OTTAWA METROPOLITAN AREA, 1961

DEGREE of BILINGUALISM
OTTAWA METROPOLITAN AREA, 1961

Tracts

50 % and Over of Population Bilingual

25 to 49.9 % of Population Bilingual

Map 1.6. DEGREE OF BILINGUALISM,
OTTAWA METROPOLITAN AREA, 1961

It is even possible that the cultural and linguistic interests of the French-speaking community in Ottawa may have stimulated turnouts in the more strongly French-speaking wards which are in fact higher than one would otherwise expect on the basis of income levels, but this hypothesis cannot be proved without further study. In any event it can be fairly stated that in recent years the level of participation of voters in the three French-speaking wards in question has been below the city-wide average but apparently higher than the level for other wards with comparable income levels.

2. Hull

The shift of population in Hull from English-speaking and Protestant to French-speaking and Roman Catholic which occurred during the 19th century is reflected in the pattern of political representation. Between 1875 and 1901, six English-speaking mayors held office, but since the latter date all Hull mayors have been French-speaking. As Table 7.8 indicates, the same pattern is repeated with regard to municipal councillors.

Interestingly enough there appears to have been a distinct time lag between the decline of the English-speaking percentage of Hull's population and the decline in the number of English-speaking representatives,[3] which until 1930 were consistently more numerous than the proportion of English-speaking residents in the city as a whole. For example, in 1881, when 86 per cent of the population of Hull was of French ethnic origin and only 13 per cent of British origin, there was an English-speaking mayor and four English-speaking councillors out of a total of 10. By 1901 the proportion of the Hull population of British origin had fallen to 11 per cent; nevertheless one third of the councillors were English-speaking and an English-speaking mayor served for part of the year. In 1921, when residents of British origin accounted for only 7.6 per cent of the population, one alderman out of six was still English-speaking. While over-representation of the English-speaking population continued until about 1930, since then the situation has been reversed, with the percentage formed by the English-speaking residents in the city as a whole being consistently larger than the proportion of English-speaking councillors elected.

The changing ethnic composition of Hull Council over the years may be most effectively illustrated if Table 7.8 is condensed into 25-year periods. From 1875 to 1899, 62 per cent of all the aldermen were of French origin and 36 per cent of British origin; for the first quarter of the 20th century, the French proportion had risen to 80 per cent and the British had fallen to 19 per cent; from 1925 to 1949, the French proportion rose still further to 89 per cent and the British fell to 6 per cent; finally for the period from 1950 to 1967, the French proportion reached 97 per cent and the British proportion dropped further to 3 per cent.

---

[3] This observation parallels a similar finding with regard to the city of Montreal. *See* G. Bourassa, "Les relations ethniques dans la vie politique montréalaise" (study prepared for the Royal Commission on Bilingualism and Biculturalism, 1965).

Table 7.8. City of Hull, municipal councillors by origin in five-year periods, 1875-1967

Year	Total		Origin							
			British		French		Others		Not known	
	N	%	N	%	N	%	N	%	N	%
Total	1,128	100	172	15.2	929	82.4	4	0.4	23	2.0
1875-79	50	100	24	48.0	25	50.0	–	–	1	2.0
80-84	50	100	22	44.0	28	56.0	–	–	–	–
85-89	50	100	15	30.0	33	66.0	2	4.0	–	–
90-94	52	100	18	34.6	34	65.4	–	–	–	–
95-99	60	100	16	26.7	42	70.0	2	3.3	–	–
1900-04	60	100	16	26.7	43	71.7	–	–	1	1.7
05-09	60	100	12	20.0	47	78.3	–	–	1	1.7
10-14	60	100	10	16.7	50	83.3	–	–	–	–
15-19	50	100	6	12.0	44	88.0	–	–	–	–
20-24	36	100	6	16.7	28	77.8	–	–	2	5.6
25-29	68	100	8	11.8	52	76.5	–	–	8	11.8
30-34	70	100	3	4.3	62	88.6	–	–	5	7.1
35-39	70	100	5	7.1	65	92.9	–	–	–	–
40-44	70	100	4	5.7	63	90.0	–	–	3	4.3
45-49	70	100	–	–	68	97.1	–	–	2	2.9
50-54	70	100	–	–	70	100.0	–	–	–	–
55-59	70	100	2	2.9	68	97.1	–	–	–	–
60-64	70	100	5	7.1	65	92.9	–	–	–	–
65-67	42	100	–	–	42	100.0	–	–	–	–

Sources: Name analysis, interviews, press reports.

Of the 172 man-years attributable to councillors of British background since 1875, 96 (or 56 per cent) were accounted for by representatives of a single ward, number one, which until its disappearance with the 1954 redrawing of ward boundaries occupied much of the area now included in Wright ward in west-central Hull. Up to 1914 this ward consistently elected English-speaking candidates. After this date the number of English-speaking aldermen elected from this ward began to decline steadily, so that by the time of its disappearance it had not returned such an alderman at any of the four preceding elections.

Since 1964 there would appear to have been no representatives of British origin on the Hull Council. Indeed, in the civic elections of 1967, no English-speaking aldermanic candidates were even nominated.

3. Eastview

In 1961, the majority of Eastview residents (61 per cent) were of French mother tongue, but the English-language group comprised a substantial minority of 34 per cent. Full data on the composition of Eastview Council are available only from 1927: the study period, consequently, was taken from 1927 to 1967.

Of the eight men who have held the office of mayor in Eastview, only one was a member of the English-speaking community. He served for three years, from 1929 to 1931. There have been seven French-speaking mayors, who together have served for 36 man-years out of the total 39, that is, 92 per cent of the time.

Until 1963, when Eastview was incorporated as a city, the residents of the municipality also elected a reeve and deputy reeve to Carleton County Council. Of the 70 man-years in this period, apparently none at all were filled by an English-speaking representative, 69 being served by French-speaking representatives and one by a reeve whose background was neither French nor British.

Table 7.9 shows the distribution by origin of Eastview councillors during the study period. It will be seen that the aldermen of French origin account for the great majority of man-years served. Moreover, there has been a more or less steady increase in the proportion of aldermen of French origin since 1927, when they comprised about three-quarters of council, to the present day when all members are Francophones. Correspondingly there has been a rather uneven but nevertheless visible decline in the number of aldermen of British origin.

Table 7.9. City of Eastview, municipal councillors by origin in five-year periods, 1927-1966

| Year | Total | | Origin | | | | | |
| | | | British | | French | | Others | |
	N	%	N	%	N	%	N	%
Total	250	100	32	12.8	212	84.8	6	2.4
1927-31	30	100	2	6.7	23	76.7	5	16.7
32-36	30	100	6	20.0	23	76.7	1	3.3
37-41	30	100	6	20.0	24	80.0	–	–
42-46	30	100	6	20.0	24	80.0	–	–
47-51	30	100	6	20.0	24	80.0	–	–
52-56	30	100	2	6.7	28	93.3	–	–
57-61	30	100	4	13.3	26	86.7	–	–
62-66	40	100	–	–	40	100.0	–	–

Sources: Name analysis, interviews, press reports.

Representation of the minority language group, as in Ottawa and Hull, has been largely dependent on one or two wards. Thirty-three of Eastview's 38 councillors of British and other origins have been elected from the first and third wards. It is of some interest to note that although ward number two, in the south-east corner of the city, would appear to have either an English-speaking majority or at least some rough balance between the two language groups,[4] it has nevertheless not returned an English-speaking councillor for

---

[4] This estimate is based on 1961 census figures. As we noted before, it is not possible to relate census tracts to ward boundaries exactly, but an estimate may be made.

over three decades. Indeed, no candidate of English mother tongue has even been nominated in recent elections in this ward, or for that matter in any other of the city's wards. It would have been interesting to compare voter turnout in the second ward with that in the other wards. However, turnout figures by ward are not kept by the city.

In summary, a pronounced gap has existed between the relative size of Eastview's English-language minority and the proportion of representatives of English-speaking background. One possible conclusion is that the English-speaking population is sufficiently satisfied with representation by bilingual aldermen of French mother tongue that it does not seek the election of a candidate from within its own group.

C. Language Usage: Thirteen Municipal Councils

The pattern of language usage of municipal councils depends upon a number of factors. The provincial setting is important, whether this be expressed in the form of statutory requirements or merely of the accumulated weight of custom and expectation. The distribution of languages within the municipality and in the vicinity is also relevant as this determines the language in which items of council business originate. Not to be forgotten are the linguistic abilities of councillors themselves, which may impose limits on the ability of a council to accommodate a linguistic minority. The combination of these factors and others leads to sufficient variation among the 13 municipalities of the metropolitan area to justify an examination of each one in turn. The three cities will be treated first.

1. Ottawa

Despite the election of a significant number of French-speaking aldermen throughout Ottawa's history, there is remarkably little recognition of French in the proceedings of city council. The language employed at council meetings is almost exclusively English, as French-speaking councillors must use this language to be understood. Such oral French usage as exists appears for the most part to be limited to informal discussion between aldermen of French mother tongue. Occasionally, however, a certain symbolic place is accorded the French language, as, for example, when the city is welcoming French-speaking dignitaries.

This predominance of the English language may be illustrated by the events of the last council session of 1965, when the mayor was congratulated by council members for having played so effective a role in the administration of the city. The gratitude of the council took the form of two speeches, one delivered in English by an English-speaking alderman, the other in French by a French-speaking representative. The delivery of a French-language speech at Ottawa's City Hall was deemed sufficiently novel to warrant mention in both the capital's English-language newspapers. Indeed one of the papers organized its coverage of the event, which it termed a "breakthrough," around this theme (*Ottawa Journal* and *Ottawa Citizen,* December 21, 1965).

In the area of written usage, French is to all intents and purposes non-existent: council documents, agendas and records appear in English only. What correspondence there is between councillors and department heads was reported to be almost entirely in

English. This pattern obtains even when the alderman and the department head are both of French mother tongue. According to the statement of one French-speaking alderman, it was pointless to send a letter in French, for if the department or branch head happened to be out of the office there would not necessarily be another French-speaking person able to deal with the matter.

Even in relations between the Ottawa City Council and the general public, the French language has little place. When information is distributed through the mass media, the French-language media are normally left to make their own translation. Of the council's 25 members in 1965, only a few, so far as could be ascertained, had a policy of answering French-language letters from the public in French.

One major factor which limits the public recognition of French by Ottawa City Council is the linguistic capability of the members themselves. It would appear that the language skills of council members do not differ greatly from those of the city at large. Though the mayors of recent years have not been completely unilingual, the city has not had a chief magistrate capable of functioning fluently in English and French since the mayoralty in 1950 of G.A. Bourque who was of French mother tongue.

Of the four present controllers, none is fluently bilingual, though one is known to have a moderate knowledge of French. Of the 22 present aldermen, six are understood to be fluently bilingual (including five of French mother tongue), and two others to have a moderate knowledge of French. So far as is known, this pattern of linguistic ability is much the same as it has been during the recent past. At no period, to the best of our knowledge, has a unilingual French-speaking member been elected to the Ottawa Council.[5]

2. Hull

A resolution passed by the Hull County Council on October 1, 1856, declared "that the Council do consider that it will not be detrimental to the Inhabitants of the Municipality to publish any By-law or Resolution made passed [sic] by this Council in session in the English Language only." At this time not a single French-speaking member sat on the council, and this was to continue to be the case until the election of Hercule Gravel in 1868. Five years later there were three French-speaking councillors, and these made an unsuccessful attempt to introduce French into the County Council. It was only after Hull's incorporation as a city in 1875 that the French language came into use in municipal politics.[6]

Today all that remains of the past predominance of English are a few old by-laws in this language that have never been taken off the books. The language of debate at council meetings is now almost exclusively French, and this applies also to communications between the council and the administration. Council documents, notes, agendas, and minutes are all in French only.

---

[5] This paragraph is not intended as a comment on the linguistic capacity of members of Council in private situations: it is concerned solely with the public use of the two languages as demonstrated on official occasions.

[6] L. Brault, *Hull* (Ottawa, 1950), 42.

If Hull Council is unilingual in its internal practices, externally it presents a different picture. Public notices in Hull, as we have noted in an earlier chapter (*see* 95) are issued in bilingual form. The general policy of council members appears to be to answer letters in their original language. One exception to the use of French only in council meetings is that matters submitted to the council in English are generally dealt with without being translated. English, in short, is in a stronger position in Hull than is French in Ottawa.

One factor which contributes significantly to this stronger position is the far wider incidence of bilingualism on the Hull Council. Although all present council members are of French mother tongue, they are all reported to be at least functionally bilingual, that is, capable of handling council business in either French or English.

3. Eastview

The Eastview Council holds a bilingual centre between the English and French poles of Ottawa and Hull. Despite the fact that all the members of the present council are of French background, the position of English is strong. Given the institutional context of Eastview as an Ontario municipality, this is scarcely surprising.

The general trend appears to be for formal and written communications to be carried on in English, while informal and oral activities are conducted in French. The minutes of council meetings are kept only in English. Motions before the council may be drafted in English, debated in French, and then the final document drawn up and approved in English. This pattern holds true for communications among councillors and civic department heads as well. Correspondence received by the council is read in council and answered in the language in which it originates.

According to interviews, all members of Eastview's present council, while of French mother tongue, nevertheless have a sufficient grasp of English to be able to deal with council matters in either language. It was further reported that even council members of English mother tongue elected in the recent past have been bilingual. In fact, Eastview has not sent a unilingual member to its council for close to two decades, the last being a councillor of English mother tongue.

4. The other municipalities

It will be recalled from earlier chapters that, in addition to the three cities of Ottawa, Hull and Eastview, ten other municipalities are included within the metropolitan area. Seven of these lie on the north shore of the Ottawa River, and three on the south, or Ontario, shore.

To begin with the Ontario side, Nepean township, which contained a population almost 90 per cent English-speaking by mother tongue at the 1961 census, has a council of seven members which is entirely English-speaking in its composition and unilingual in its proceedings. Because the milieu is so predominantly English-speaking, language issues have not arisen in Nepean, and no occasion for the use of French on council could be recalled by a municipal spokesman.

Similarly, the village of Rockcliffe Park, whose population is also preponderantly English-speaking, reported that it has not found any occasion for the use of French in recent council business, although members are said to be capable of handling matters in French should the need arise. All five members of the present council are of English mother tongue.

The township of Gloucester, where some 40 per cent of the citizens are French-speaking, presents a partial contrast to Nepean and Rockcliffe Park. The present council was reported to have three bilingual members out of a total of five, one of these being of French mother tongue and two of English mother tongue. The remaining two members apparently speak English only. Council proceedings are predominantly in English, and the minutes of council meetings are kept in English only. On rare occasions French may be used to accommodate a French-speaking ratepayer appearing before council, in which case a councillor who can speak French will interpret for those who require it.

Municipalities on the Quebec side show a wide divergence of linguistic make-up, ranging from Lucerne, where the population is divided fairly evenly between those of French and English mother tongue, to Pointe-Gatineau, where the population is almost entirely French-speaking. Aylmer, where 41 per cent of the population was English-speaking at the 1961 census, accords recognition to both languages in its council proceedings, and council minutes are kept separately in both languages. The actual proportion of the two languages used would seem to vary with the linguistic abilities of the mayor who presides over council. Under the last mayor, who spoke English only, it was estimated that English was used in council discussion about 70 per cent of the time. With the present mayor, who is bilingual, and with a council made up of four French-speaking members, all of whom are bilingual, and three members of English mother tongue, one of whom is bilingual, the two languages are now reported to be used in about equal proportions.[7]

As in Aylmer, language usage in the Lucerne Council has been changing during recent years. It was reported that several years ago council proceedings were entirely in English. The place of French is apparently growing, its use now being estimated at about 25 per cent of the time. Four of the seven present councillors are of French mother tongue, all of them being bilingual, whereas the three English-speaking members are all more or less unilingual. There are French and English versions of council minutes.

Deschênes, whose population is predominantly French-speaking, uses both languages in its council meetings, but French appears to be employed more often than English. At present five out of seven councillors are of French mother tongue; one of the two English-speaking members is unilingual. Written records of council meetings are kept in French only.

Turning to the east bank of the Gatineau River, the municipalities of Gatineau and Pointe-Gatineau, both overwhelmingly French-speaking, have councils whose meetings are conducted entirely in French. In Pointe-Gatineau, at present and for the past several

---

[7] However, a recent attempt to present a brief in French only to the Aylmer Council ran into difficulty because the group presenting the brief had not provided a translation for the benefit of the two unilingual, English-speaking councillors. *See* "Le Conseil d'Aylmer approuve la vente des boissons alcooliques le dimanche," *Le Droit,* September 6, 1967. This would seem to be a case of the onus being put on the citizens to accommodate their language usage to that of their elected representatives-- an apparent reversal of what might be expected.

years, all councillors have been French-speaking. In Gatineau, six are currently French-speaking and one is of English mother tongue, but it is traditional for English-speaking members to use French in council. In both towns, however, all councillors are reported to be bilingual. The minutes of the two councils are kept only in French.

Templeton, again preponderantly French-speaking, also conducts its council meetings in French only and keeps council minutes in the original language. At present all seven councillors are of French mother tongue, and six of these are bilingual. It was further reported that, while there have been councillors of British origin in the past, they had always functioned in French at council meetings.

West Templeton, which is predominantly French-speaking but with a substantial English-speaking minority, uses both languages in its council meetings, although English was said to be employed more often than French. The seven-member council has three members of French mother tongue, including the mayor, and four of English mother tongue; all three of the Francophones and two of the Anglophones are bilingual. Council minutes are kept either in French or English according to the language of the debate.

What stands out from this survey of language usage in the 13 area municipalities is the correspondence between the linguistic usage of elected representatives and those of the general population. This is no doubt to be expected of elected representative bodies. The significant consequence is that, as was seen to be the case for the working population at large (*see* 37), the bulk of the elected representatives of French origin are functionally bilingual while most of those of British origin are not so. The presence of unilingual members on a council appears to have a very strong influence on the language practices of that body. This is particularly noticeable on some of the smaller councils where one or two unilingual members may sway the balance of language use heavily in one direction.

In comparing language usage and political representation in the municipalities of the area, the central paradox of this chapter emerges: that where there is ample recognition of minority language rights, as in Eastview or Hull, the minority group exhibits no strong tendency to seek representation by one of its own number; where the minority language is accorded little recognition, as in Ottawa, political representation of the minority is vigorously pursued. This tendency may be seen most clearly in the municipalities which elect their aldermen by wards; it may also be present in those municipalities where council members are elected at large by the whole electorate, but in these it is more difficult to assess accurately. The same tendency may be studied and described not only in terms of elected representatives but also in the nomination of unsuccessful candidates of the minority group and in the number of votes they attract. It may be that an analysis of the appeals made by each candidate to the electors (which was not possible for this study), would reveal the pattern even further.

Yet on reflection this lack of correspondence between representation of language groups and recognition of minority language rights may be less of a paradox than it appears at first sight. For where a minority group sees its language inadequately recognized, it may well deem it important to elect strong spokesmen from within its ranks to defend group interests. Where, on the other hand, the minority's language is fully recognized and free from jeopardy, its selection of candidates for public office and its patterns of voting will perhaps be influenced more strongly by other considerations.

D. Representation: Federal and Provincial

1. Federal

The National Capital Region has been represented for the last 14 years in the House of Commons by six members whose constituencies are wholly or mainly within the area.[8] Three of these are urban ridings which lie at the core of the Region (Ottawa West, Ottawa East, and Hull); the other three are mixed urban-rural ridings which form an outer ring (Carleton, Russell, and Gatineau—the latter riding having about three-fifths of its population within the Region according to the 1961 census). Table 7.10 shows the distribution of the population in the ridings by mother tongue and ethnic origin (*see* also Map 7.3). Six general elections and one by-election have been carried out under the same apportionment of seats; the 1961 census figures are particularly relevant since five of these six elections were held within four years before and after the census year.

Table 7.10. National Capital Region, population by mother tongue and ethnic origin of federal constituencies, percentages, 1961

	(a) Mother tongue				
Constituency	Total		English	French	Others
	N	%			
Carleton	130,497	100	87.4	6.1	6.4
Gatineau	58,771	100	27.5	70.4	2.2
Hull	86,563	100	9.0	89.7	1.3
Ottawa East	51,828	100	44.0	48.8	7.2
Ottawa West	67,131	100	65.1	20.1	14.8
Russell	124,368	100	54.4	40.4	5.2
	(b) Ethnic origin				
Constituency	Total		British	French	Others
	N	%			
Carleton	130,497	100	70.8	10.4	18.8
Gatineau	58,771	100	23.2	72.2	4.6
Hull	86,563	100	8.4	88.7	2.9
Ottawa East	51,828	100	33.7	51.6	14.7
Ottawa West	67,131	100	51.3	25.9	22.8
Russell	124,368	100	42.5	42.3	15.2

Source: Figures supplied by Dominion Bureau of Statistics.

---

[8] *See* Map 7.5. A seventh constituency, Pontiac-Temiskaming, impinges on the National Capital Region in the north-west, but this overlap is marginal only. By the 1961 census, it would appear that only 3 per cent of the riding's population is within the limits of the Region. The riding of Lanark also overlaps to an even more limited degree on the western edge of the Region on the Ontario side.

The figures in Table 7.10 show that two ridings (Hull and Gatineau) have a substantial majority of French-speaking residents; two (Carleton and Ottawa West) have substantial English-speaking majorities. One (Ottawa East) has slightly more French- than English-speaking voters, while in the remaining riding (Russell) there are slightly more English- than French-speaking voters.

To move to the area of actual voting behaviour, all the ridings concerned show a strikingly consistent pattern over the period considered. Four ridings have elected only French-speaking candidates, and two have elected only English-speaking candidates. This pattern relates fairly closely to the mother-tongue distribution in the ridings. Russell is an exception to this correlation, however, for in that riding an electorate which is more English- than French-speaking has consistently elected French-speaking candidates. It should be pointed out that in terms of ethnic origin the French and British groups in Russell are roughly equal.

Table 7.11. National Capital Region, candidates at federal elections by origin, 1953, 1957, 1958, 1962, 1963 and 1965

Constituency	Origin	Successful candidates	Unsuccessful candidates		
		Major parties*	Major parties*	Other parties*	Others*
Total	French	25	17	27	9
	British	12	18	32	–
	Others	–	2	2	1
Carleton	French	–	–	–	–
	British	6	6	11	–
	Others	–	–	–	–
Russell**	French	7	2	7	–
	British	–	5	5	–
	Others	–	–	–	–
Ottawa East	French	6	5	3	2
	British	–	1	6	–
	Others	–	–	1	–
Ottawa West	French	–	–	–	–
	British	6	6	9	–
	Others	–	–	1	1
Hull	French	6	6	10	5
	British	–	–	–	–
	Others	–	–	–	–
Gatineau	French	6	4	7	2
	British	–	–	1	–
	Others	–	2	–	–

Sources: Name analysis and press reports.
* Major parties: Liberals and Progressive Conservatives. Other parties: C.C.F., N.D.P., Social Credit, and Ralliement des Créditistes. Others: unaffiliated candidates and miscellaneous parties.
** Including 1959 by-election.

Table 7.11 shows the distribution by origin of the candidates for the six National Capital Region seats over the last six federal elections (1953, 1957, 1958, 1962, 1963 and 1965). A slight majority (78 out of 145) of all candidates nominated were French-speaking. This majority increases to 42 out of 74, or 57 per cent, if candidates from other than the two major parties are excluded. It is worth noting at this point that only candidates of major parties were successful in the period considered, and in only five of 37 contests did a candidate of another party or an independent finish second. Of the successful major party candidates, the proportion of French origin increases yet again to 25 out of 37, or 68 per cent. This contrasts sharply with the 41.6 per cent of the population of the six ridings which is French by mother tongue. The 6 per cent of the area population of other mother tongues has not been reflected at all among the candidates elected, while the English-speaking proportion of the population in 1961, 52.4 per cent, may be compared with that of the candidates elected, 32 per cent.

The wide variation between the linguistic proportions of the general population and those of the elected representatives may be explained in part by the unequal apportionment of voters between the six ridings. Carleton riding, 87.4 per cent of whose population was of English mother tongue in 1961, had in 1965 almost 11,000 more registered voters than the combined total of the two most heavily French-speaking ridings (Hull and Gatineau). The disparity in the proportion of the English-speaking population and elected candidates may be further accounted for by the situation in Russell which has consistently elected French-speaking candidates despite an English-speaking population of 54.4 per cent of the total.

It is possibly of interest that Russell riding in these elections included within its boundaries the city of Eastview. As we have seen in the section on municipal representation, the English-speaking population in Eastview does not seek representation by English-speaking candidates at municipal elections, but apparently is willing to choose its representatives from among French-speaking candidates. The same factor may have operated to some degree in federal elections.

Another clue to the voting behaviour of Russell riding may be found in the fact that for almost 80 years the riding has returned only Liberals to Parliament. In the seven elections studied (including the 1959 by-election) the Liberals nominated only French-speaking candidates. The Conservatives, on the other hand, nominated five English- and only two French-speaking candidates. As it would appear that the Liberal Party nomination is almost a determining factor in Russell elections, it may well be that the language of the candidate is of secondary importance.

This high degree of party fidelity may be generalized for the Region as a whole. Only one riding, Carleton, elected candidates from more than one party in the period studied, and the single instance of the election of a Liberal by a narrow majority in 1963 was a unique event in the riding's history since Confederation. The Liberal victory was reversed in 1965 with the return of the former Progressive Conservative member. No other riding in the Region has deviated from allegiance to a single party (the Liberal Party in all ridings but Carleton) since the 1920's or in some instances even earlier.

Further, the turnover of elected members is low. Three ridings (Ottawa East, Ottawa West, and Hull) elected the same candidate in all six elections. Russell elected one man three times, and the present incumbent four times if the 1959 by-election is included. Gatineau and Carleton each elected one man four times, and two others once. Three of the five instances of change in members may be attributed to the death or retirement of the incumbent, the other two being the successive contests in Carleton in 1963 and 1965.

In short, the Region has tended strongly toward traditional voting patterns, where party allegiance and loyalty to sitting members are strong influences on voting behaviour. In this context, it is scarcely surprising that on linguistic grounds as well the constituencies of the Region exhibit stable voting patterns. Indeed these three elements of stability, that is, fidelity to candidate, to party, and to language group, would seem to be interrelated and to reinforce one another.

In 1965 a nation-wide redistribution of federal seats was undertaken on the basis of the 1961 census. The electoral geography of the region has been changed considerably as a result.

On the Quebec side (*see* Map 7.6) the riding of Hull has been altered so as to exclude the municipalities east of the Gatineau River that were formerly included, and to introduce Aylmer, Lucerne, and Deschênes into the riding. This will probably increase the size of the English-speaking minority in the constituency. The eastern edge of the old Gatineau riding plus most of what was formerly Labelle make up a new Gatineau constituency, which includes the municipalities of Gatineau, Pointe-Gatineau, Buckingham, and Thurso. Much of the old Gatineau riding has been absorbed by the new Pontiac riding, which comprises mainly the eastern end of the old Pontiac-Temiskaming riding. The effect of this will likely be to introduce a substantial number of English-speaking voters into the new constituency of Pontiac. According to the 1961 census, Pontiac county was approximately 55 per cent English by mother tongue. That the provincial constituency of Pontiac over the past few elections has elected only English-speaking candidates is also significant. However, the new Pontiac riding, while including a larger part of the National Capital Region than did the old riding, will still overlap the Region only marginally.

On the Ontario side, the 1965 redistribution seems to suggest a more fundamental redrawing of the political boundaries. A third seat has been added to the city of Ottawa; the old riding of Russell has been altered, under the name of Ottawa-Carleton, so as to exclude Eastview and certain sections of Ottawa; the old riding of Carleton, now known as Grenville-Carleton, has been merged with a more southerly riding and has lost all the area it formerly held within the city of Ottawa itself, as well as much of the suburban and rural area it used to cover in the south-western portion of the National Capital Region. The latter area is now covered by the new riding of Lanark and Renfrew which extends up the Ottawa valley.

The effects of these changes may be suggested by a comparison of Maps 7.3 and 7.4. *Prima facie,* it would appear that the majority of French-speaking voters, who were previously split between Ottawa East and Russell, have now been lumped together in the new Ottawa East constituency. The new Ottawa Centre would appear to have a substantial proportion of English-speaking voters. As a result of all these changes, it now seems that only one of the five Ontario ridings has anything approaching a French-speaking majority. While it would be unwise to predict future voting behaviour on the basis of constituency boundaries alone, it does seem likely that the opportunities for French-speaking voters to back French-speaking candidates will be somewhat diminished in the Ontario sector of the capital area as a result of redistribution.

One other result of redistribution is to make the boundaries of federal constituencies coincide even less directly with the territory of the National Capital Region. The old system provided for six constituencies with populations wholly or mainly within the Region and two which overlapped only very marginally. As Map 7.6 shows, the new system has five constituencies with populations wholly or mainly within the Region, four (Pontiac, Gatineau, Grenville-Carleton, Lanark and Renfrew) whose classification as capital area ridings is somewhat doubtful, and still another (Glengarry-Prescott) which overlaps marginally the corner of the National Capital Region.

2. Ontario

For the three provincial general elections which we studied (1955, 1959 and 1963), the Ontario sector of the National Capital Region was represented in the provincial legislature by members elected from five ridings lying wholly or partly within the Region.[9] In these elections a total of 46 candidates have presented themselves. Table 7.12 analyzes them by origin.

Table 7.12. National Capital Region, Ontario sector, candidates at provincial elections by origin, 1955, 1959 and 1963

Origin	Total	Successful candidates	Unsuccessful candidates		
		Major parties*	Major parties*	Other parties*	Others*
British	29	10	9	10	–
French	13	5	4	3	1
Others	4	–	2	2	–

Sources: Name analysis and press reports.
* Major parties: Progressive Conservatives and Liberals. Other parties: C.C.F., N.D.P., and Social Credit. Others: unaffiliated candidates and miscellaneous parties.

Of all 46 candidates, 63 per cent were of British origin and 28 per cent of French origin. The two major parties nominated 30 candidates of whom 63 per cent were of British origin and 30 per cent of French origin. Among the successful candidates, for every one candidate of French origin there were two of British origin. No candidate of any other origin was elected.

---

[9] *See* Map 7.7. A sixth constituency, Lanark, very slightly overlapped the western border of the Region. The study was completed before the Ontario election of 1967.

Because provincial ridings do not coincide with the districts used by the census, no precise statistics on the distribution of their populations by mother tongue are available. However, a certain pattern does emerge from the results of the three elections. French-speaking representation seems to have centred on the Ottawa East riding where all candidates of the two major parties, both successful and unsuccessful, have been French-speaking; and to a lesser extent on Russell, where two out of the three successful candidates were French-speaking, and five out of a total of nine candidates in the three elections were of French origin. In Ottawa South, Ottawa West, and Carleton, only candidates of British and other origins were nominated.

The provincial Representation Act of 1966 changed the boundaries of the area ridings and added a new one, thus giving six Ontario seats to be found mainly within the National Capital Region. The new riding, one of four seats within the Ottawa metropolitan area, is made up of parts of the old Ottawa West and Ottawa East ridings, and is known as Ottawa Centre. The old Russell riding has become Carleton East, which is almost entirely within the boundaries of the National Capital Region, as also is the revised Carleton riding. However, two other constituencies overlap the Region to a limited extent: Prescott and Russell riding includes a fairly extensive strip on the eastern edge of the Region, while a smaller strip on the western edge forms part of Lanark riding. Maps 7.7 and 7.8 compare the old and new constituency boundaries.

Map 7.10 suggests that under the new distribution Ottawa East will continue to include the heaviest concentration of French-speaking voters. The new Ottawa Centre would appear to have a smaller concentration of French-speaking voters and also the highest concentration in the city of citizens of other mother tongues. Carleton East seems to have lost many of the French-speaking voters included within the boundaries of its predecessor, Russell.

3. Quebec

During the last five elections in the province of Quebec (1952, 1956, 1960, 1962 and 1966), the north shore of the National Capital Region has been included within the boundaries of four ridings (*see* Maps 7.7 and 7.8). Only one of these seats (Hull) is entirely within the area concerned; parts of the other three extend beyond it. Gatineau and Papineau ridings overlap sufficiently to make their consideration advisable, but Pontiac overlaps only marginally, and its voting behaviour is of only doubtful relevance to the National Capital Region.

If Pontiac is excluded from consideration, a total of 42 candidates have been nominated within the Region during the last five elections. Table 7.13 analyzes these by origin. It is immediately apparent that candidates of French origin predominate to the virtual exclusion of all others. Seemingly, it is not felt worthwhile or possible for the English-speaking minority on the Quebec side to nominate candidates from their own language group. The lone candidate of British origin was nominated in Papineau over 15 years ago and attracted only a scattering of votes. It might be noted, however, that Pontiac riding, which is not included in Table 7.13, shows a striking contrast in its voting behaviour: in the last five elections all but one of the candidates nominated were apparently of British origin.

Table 7.13. National Capital Region, Quebec sector, candidates at provincial elections by origin, 1952, 1956, 1960, 1962 and 1966

Origin	Total	Successful candidates	Unsuccessful candidates		
		Major parties*	Major parties*	Other parties*	Others*
French	41	15	15	7	4
British	1	–	–	1	–
Others	–	–	–	–	–

Sources: Name analysis and press reports.
* Major parties: Union Nationale and Liberals. Other parties: Créditistes, C.C.F., and N.D.P. Others: independents.

4. Representation and language usage

Because the language use of the senior legislatures is largely shaped by factors external to the federal capital area, there is no need to describe it in full detail here. Yet, in studying elected municipal councils, a rather unexpected relationship was noted between the pattern of representation and the recognition of the minority language: in a word, minority representation was found without language rights, and language recognition without representation. It is worth at least a brief look at language practices in the senior legislatures to see how far the same tendencies are visible there.

As we have noted, candidates in Quebec provincial ridings in the area have in recent years been almost exclusively of French-speaking background, and all successful candidates have been so. Nevertheless they sit in a legislature where the right to use either French or English is constitutionally guaranteed under section 133 of the B.N.A. Act. Further, both languages must be used in the printing of statutes, records, and journals. In the transcript of legislative debates speeches are published in the language in which they are delivered, without translation. While actual debate in Quebec City is at present overwhelmingly in French, English is nevertheless used almost on a daily basis by a few members who doubtless find it more practical to express themselves in that language.

Of course the English-speaking population on the Quebec side of the capital area is relatively small. It may well feel that to seek representation in any of the provincial seats is simply not feasible. Still, it is worth noting that no significant effort is made by the English-speaking community to seek direct representation, and that virtually no candidates of English mother tongue are put forward.

On the Ontario side of the capital area, where the French-speaking population is admittedly stronger both relatively and absolutely than the English-speaking minority on the Quebec side, approximately two out of seven candidates, and one out of three winning candidates, have been of French background in recent elections. By a comparison with population figures, it may be said that the French-speaking population has both sought and obtained representation at least proportionate to its numbers in the Ontario legislature.

On the other hand, the language usage of the Ontario legislature is based on no such constitutional guarantee as it is in Quebec. The statutes of Ontario, and the journals and records of the legislature, are published in English only. English is the sole official language of legislative debates, though in recent years practice has been changing informally so as to permit some use of French by the members, whose speeches are then reported in the published debates as spoken. However, these interventions are rather rare, and their purpose appears to be more symbolic than utilitarian.

Our findings in regard to the relationship between political recognition and recognition of language rights may be summarized as follows. At the municipal level, particularly in the three cities, there is a tendency for minority representation to be strongest where the minority language has been less than fully recognized, and for minority representation to be less strongly sought where the minority language has been fully recognized. The provincial level reveals the same tendency, although here, with larger constituencies, it becomes more doubtful if the English-speaking minorities in the Quebec ridings are of a size to have any real alternatives. The federal level, with its well-developed system for accommodating the two languages, presents a pattern involving both recognition of language rights and representation of both major groups.

E. Summary

The main conclusions that emerge from the study of political representation in the capital area are as follows:

1) In the three cities, the system of choosing aldermen according to geographical wards seems to have facilitated the election of minority representatives when the electors have wanted it. The majority of the other municipal councils, and the board of control of the city of Ottawa, are elected at large by all voters of the municipality concerned. This would appear to make minority representation more difficult.

2) In Ottawa the French-speaking minority has availed itself fully of the electoral system to elect a number of aldermen almost proportional to the size of the French-speaking population of the city. In Hull and Eastview the English-speaking minorities have shown a decreasing tendency to vote for, or even nominate, candidates drawn from their own linguistic group, even though in parts of Eastview at least the balance of numbers would appear to make this feasible.

3) Members of the Ottawa city council are not generally bilingual, and as a reflection of this the language of discussion and of record of council has been, with few exceptions, English.

4) The language of discussion and of record of the Hull council is French, but matters involving English can be handled without translation.

5) In Eastview both languages are employed extensively in council, the linguistic balance being promoted by the fact of predominantly French-speaking councillors operating within an English-speaking provincial framework.

6) The three other municipalities in the Ontario sector of the metropolitan area follow the pattern of Ottawa in using English almost exclusively in council meetings. On the

Quebec side, Gatineau, Pointe-Gatineau, and Templeton use French; while Aylmer, Lucerne, Deschênes, and West Templeton tend to use both French and English.
7) In their relations with the public, all eight municipal councils on the Quebec side appear to use both French and English, as does Eastview in Ontario. The other four Ontario councils seem on the whole to make comparatively little provision for French.
8) Neither the provincial nor the federal constituency boundaries are arranged so as to coincide closely with the capital area, no matter how the latter is defined. This is particularly noticeable with respect to the latest redistribution of federal seats in the area.
9) At the federal level, an analysis of the six area constituencies for the last six federal elections shows that roughly two-thirds of the successful candidates were of French mother tongue, a proportion well above that for the population of the constituencies concerned. This might, however, be affected in future elections by the redrawing of constituency boundaries in 1965.
10) At the provincial level, the Quebec side has elected only French-speaking representatives to a legislature where both French and English have full official status; on the Ontario side, French- and English-speaking representatives have been sent to a legislature where the use of French is unofficial and symbolic only.
11) The most striking relationship between political representation and linguistic usage that emerges is a somewhat paradoxical one: where the language of a minority group is not fully recognized, the group seeks political representation as far as the electoral system permits; where the minority language has full recognition, its speakers do not strive so actively for representation. This tendency can be discerned in pronounced fashion at the municipal level and to some degree at the provincial level as well.

Appendices

Appendix A (Chapter I) Tables A to O

Table A. Numerical distribution of population, Ontario and Quebec sides of Ottawa metropolitan area, by mother tongue, 1961

Mother tongue	M.A.	Ontario	Quebec
Total	429,750	332,899	96,851
English	239,287	225,845	13,442
French	161,980	80,084	81,896
Others	28,483	26,970	1,513

Source: Census of Canada, 1961; Catalogue 92-549.

Table B. Percentage distribution of population, Ottawa metropolitan area, by mother tongue, 1961

Mother tongue		Metropolitan area	Ottawa	Hull	Eastview	Nepean	Gloucester	Gatineau	Pte-Gatineau	Aylmer	Lucerne	Templeton	Deschênes	Rockcliffe Park	West Templeton
Total	N	429,750	268,206	56,929	24,555	19,753	18,301	13,022	8,854	6,286	5,762	2,965	2,090	2,084	943
	%	100	100	100	100	100	100	100	100	100	100	100	100	100	100
English		55.7	70.1	8.2	34.0	89.5	54.4	11.7	3.0	41.3	52.2	14.3	30.0	85.0	37.2
French		37.7	21.2	90.2	61.0	3.8	39.6	87.1	96.4	56.0	45.1	85.2	68.0	10.4	61.9
Others		6.6	8.7	1.6	5.0	6.7	6.0	1.2	0.6	2.7	2.7	0.5	2.0	4.6	0.9
German		1.4	1.7	0.2	1.3	2.3	2.3	0.2	**	**	**	**	**	**	**
Italian		1.6	2.4	0.2	0.4	0.4	0.2	0.2							
Dutch		0.6	0.6	0.1	0.5	2.0	1.2	0.0*							
Polish		0.5	0.7	0.0*	0.4	0.4	0.6	0.0*							
Yiddish		0.3	0.4	0.2	0.3	0.1	0.1	0.0*							
Scandinavian		0.2	0.2	0.0*	0.1	0.2	0.3	0.0*							
Ukrainian		0.4	0.6	0.0*	0.4	0.5	0.4	0.0*							
Others		1.6	2.1	0.6	1.5	0.8	0.7	0.7							

Source: Census of Canada, 1961; Catalogue 92-549.
* Less than 0.05%.
**Not available.

Table C. Percentage distribution of population, Ottawa metropolitan area, by ethnic origin and official language, 1961

Ethnic origin	Total		Official language			
	N	%	English only	French only	Both	Neither
Total	429,750	100	55.0	13.2	30.8	1.0
British	189,227	100	89.7	0.5	9.6	0.2
French	175,374	100	8.6	31.0	60.1	0.3
German	12,300	100	88.1	1.1	9.2	1.3
Italian	9,094	100	63.0	2.9	13.6	20.4
Dutch	5,585	100	89.3	0.3	8.5	1.9
Polish	4,243	100	84.4	0.8	12.3	2.4
Jewish	3,649	100	83.7	0.1	16.0	0.2
Scandinavian	3,318	100	90.2	0.6	8.9	0.4
Ukrainian	2,985	100	86.8	0.6	10.3	2.3
Russian	1,449	100	81.7	1.1	16.0	1.2
Other European	8,715	100	72.2	3.2	17.0	7.5
Asiatic	3,537	100	76.9	0.9	13.1	9.1
Others	10,274	100	73.7	5.3	20.5	0.5

Source: Census of Canada, 1961; Catalogue 92-561.

Table D. Percentage distribution of population, Ottawa metropolitan area and cities of Ottawa and Hull,* by ethnic origin and mother tongue, 1961

Area	Ethnic origin	Total		Mother tongue	
		N	%**	English	French
Ottawa M.A.	British	189,227	100	97.3	2.3
	French	175,374	100	11.9	87.7
City of Ottawa	British	148,129	100	98.3	1.4
	French	68,459	100	22.1	77.3
City of Hull	British	4,457	100	73.9	25.2
	French	50,908	100	1.8	97.9

Source: Census of Canada, 1961; Catalogue 92-561.
*These data are not available for Eastview.
**Percentages do not add up to 100 as those of French and British origins whose mother tongue is neither French nor English are not included in the table.

Table E. Distribution of population, city of Ottawa, by ethnic origin, 1871-1961

Ethnic origin		1871	1881	1891	1901	1911	1921	1931	1941	1951	1961
Total	N	21,545	27,412	37,269	59,928	87,062	107,843	126,872	154,951	202,045	268,206
	%	100	100	100	100	100	100	100	100	100	100
British	N	14,064	17,440	no data	37,335	52,734	68,215	78,512	94,112	121,716	148,129
	%	65.3	63.6		62.3	60.6	63.3	61.9	60.7	60.2	55.2
French	N	7,214	9,384	12,790*	19,495	26,732	30,442	37,465	48,081	57,399	68,459
	%	33.5	34.2	34.3*	32.5	30.7	28.2	29.5	31.0	28.4	25.5
Others	N	267	588	no data	3,098	7,596	9,186	10,895	12,758	22,930	51,618
	%	1.2	2.2		5.2	8.7	8.5	8.6	8.3	11.4	19.2

Sources: Censuses of Canada, 1870-71, 1880-81, 1891-1961.
*These figures are approximate. The only categories under origin in 1891 were "French Canadians" and "Others."

Table F. Distribution of population, city of Hull, by ethnic origin, 1881-1961*

Ethnic origin		1881	1891	1901	1911	1921	1931	1941	1951	1961
Total	N	6,890	11,264	13,993	18,222	24,117	29,433	32,947	43,483	56,929
	%	100	100	100	100	100	100	100	100	100
British	N	888	no data	1,532	1,577	1,830	2,403	2,106	3,982	4,457
	%	12.9		10.9	8.7	7.6	8.2	6.4	9.2	7.8
French	N	5,933	10,062**	12,330	16,416	21,918	26,507	30,541	38,849	50,908
	%	86.1	89.3	88.1	90.0	90.9	90.0	92.7	89.3	89.4
Others	N	69	no data	131	229	369	523	300	652	1,564
	%	1.0		1.0	1.3	1.5	1.8	0.9	1.5	2.8

Sources: Censuses of Canada, 1870-71, 1880-81, 1891-1961.
*The city was only incorporated in 1875.
**This figure is approximate. The only categories under origin in 1891 were "French Canadians" and "Others."

Table G. Percentage distribution of population, Ottawa metropolitan area, by ethnic origin and mother tongue, 1961

Ethnic origin	Total		Mother tongue		
	N	%*	English	French	Corresponding to ethnic group
Total	429,750	100			
British	189,227	100	97.3	2.3	–
French	175,374	100	11.9	87.7	–
German	12,300	100	57.4	3.5	38.4
Italian	9,094	100	24.5	3.6	71.3
Dutch	5,585	100	55.0	1.2	42.6
Polish	4,243	100	46.5	2.4	44.8
Jewish	3,649	100	74.8	0.1	21.0
Scandinavian	3,318	100	74.9	2.2	21.4
Ukrainian	2,935	100	50.8	2.0	44.6
Russian	1,449	100	65.2	2.1	18.6
Other European	8,715	100	33.6	7.0	20.8
Asiatic	3,537	100	34.1	2.9	25.4
Others	10,274	100	79.3	18.7	4.5

Source: Census of Canada, 1961; Catalogue 92-549.
*Figures do not add up to 100 as those whose mother tongue is other than French, English or corresponding to ethnic group are not included in the table.

Table H. Percentage distribution of male labour force, Ottawa metropolitan area, by occupation, level of education,* and ethnic origin, 1961

Occupation		Primary			Secondary (1-2 years)			Secondary (3-5 years)			University (1 or more years)		
		British	French	Others	British	French	Others	British	French	Others	British	French	Others
Total	N	8,117	18,766	5,699	9,317	9,376	2,815	18,150	8,681	5,717	10,344	4,040	3,604
	%	100	100	100	100	100	100	100	100	100	100	100	100
Managerial		7.4	5.3	9.3	10.8	7.7	13.4	19.1	13.4	20.8	23.5	18.1	19.3
Prof. and tech.		3.0	1.3	1.4	4.9	3.2	5.9	14.1	10.4	12.7	50.7	42.0	52.8
Clerical		11.7	6.2	3.5	17.6	18.2	15.0	19.3	29.0	13.6	5.6	15.7	5.4
Sales		4.9	4.3	3.3	8.1	7.2	5.3	7.8	8.7	7.9	3.9	5.9	4.4
Trans. and comm.		13.1	13.7	6.2	9.3	12.5	6.7	3.6	4.0	2.9	0.6	1.4	0.4
Serv. and rec.		18.8	13.6	16.9	18.9	11.2	15.9	18.3	10.1	16.9	10.8	7.5	9.6
Craftsmen		30.4	38.5	42.7	23.9	30.1	27.1	13.4	20.0	20.3	1.9	7.3	4.7
Labourers		5.6	13.6	13.1	3.0	7.7	4.3	1.5	1.6	1.4	1.1	0.8	1.0
Farmers		0.2	.1	0.1	0.3	.0	.0	0.1	.1	.1	.0	0.2	0.2
Other primary		2.6	1.6	1.6	0.8	0.3	2.5	0.4	0.3	1.2	0.5	0.2	0.3
Not stated		2.4	1.8	1.9	2.4	1.9	3.9	2.4	2.3	2.2	1.5	1.0	2.1

Source: Tape 3, Table 8, Parts I and II, 19-34.
* "No schooling" category omitted.

Table I. Percentage distribution of population by mother tongue, Ottawa metropolitan area census tracts, in order of average wage and salary income per tract, 1961

Census tract	Wages and salaries*	Population =100%	Mother tongue		
			English	French	Others
151 W. Temp.	$2843	943	37.2	61.9	.9
16 Ott.	2891	3,432	19.4	75.3	5.3
32 Ott.	2953	2,292	49.8	37.8	12.4
102 Hull	3006	5,596	3.7	93.8	2.5
130 Deschênes	3047	2,090	29.7	67.8	2.5
127 Temp.	3087	2,965	14.4	85.2	.4
103 Hull	3099	5,208	4.8	93.5	1.7
101 Hull	3104	7,958	3.4	95.7	0.9
30 Ott.	3182	6,255	51.4	20.5	28.0
31 Ott.	3209	7,053	50.4	26.8	22.8
100 Hull	3214	7,762	3.2	95.0	1.8
18 Ott.	3219	7,645	17.9	77.5	4.6
19 Ott.	3246	5,099	17.2	79.6	3.2
33 Ott.	3293	5,967	39.3	56.5	4.2
23 Ott.	3308	4,254	72.9	14.1	13.0
21 Ott.	3351	5,532	68.4	15.3	16.3
22 Ott.	3352	5,404	69.6	10.2	20.2
125 Pte-Gat.	3375	8,854	3.0	96.4	.6
15 Ott.	3448	2,552	32.5	59.7	7.8
17 Ott.	3450	3,577	35.7	55.8	8.5
105 Hull	3457	7,487	8.2	90.2	1.6
72 Eastv.	3501	4,353	21.6	73.9	4.5
108 Hull	3517	2,471	7.6	91.4	1.0
29 Ott.	3527	4,462	56.9	20.8	22.3
74 Eastv.	3643	4,267	24.0	72.5	3.5
131 Aylmer	3705	6,286	41.4	55.9	2.7
120 Gatineau	3804	13,022	11.7	87.1	1.2
4 Ott.	3819	2,602	37.0	57.8	5.2
34 Ott.	3851	6,154	70.9	17.4	11.7
73 Eastv.	3857	6,753	23.0	74.0	3.0
106 Hull	3890	7,277	11.1	86.9	2.0
12 Ott.	3926	2,277	80.0	17.2	2.8
20 Ott.	3926	3,257	76.7	15.4	7.9
104 Hull	3935	9,287	12.3	86.7	1.0
27 Ott.	4025	5,669	84.1	5.9	1.0
1 Ott.	4052	4,684	77.4	19.9	2.7
11 Ott.	4053	4,171	62.9	30.0	7.1
14 Ott.	4053	7,479	51.6	36.9	11.5
70 Eastv.	4078	3,926	42.4	51.0	6.6
25 Ott.	4096	3,353	76.0	12.9	11.1
50 Ott.	4180	2,483	79.0	13.2	7.8
5 Ott.	4191	5,765	58.1	34.9	7.0
41 Ott.	4258	6,129	57.6	37.8	4.6
87 Glouc.	4320	2,022	74.2	18.5	7.3
45 Ott.	4336	7,896	80.7	11.2	8.1
71 Eastv.	4345	5,256	60.4	32.7	6.9

Continued on next page

Table I. (Cont'd)

Census tract	Wages and salaries*	Population =100%	Mother tongue		
			English	French	Others
24 Ott.	4459	7,112	79.2	12.4	8.4
135 and 150 Lucerne	4496	5,762	52.3	45.1	2.6
37 Ott.	4557	7,794	80.7	11.2	8.1
13 Ott.	4571	4,824	53.1	32.7	14.2
9 Ott.	4596	4,958	88.1	4.8	7.1
44 Ott.	4718	4,089	75.2	12.1	12.7
38 Ott.	4770	9,370	86.9	6.7	6.4
84 Nepean	4778	821	79.5	8.7	11.8
3 Ott.	4928	4,049	61.4	30.5	8.1
26 Ott.	5025	4,831	83.4	7.2	9.4
86 Glouc.	5094	5,027	53.6	40.2	6.2
2 Ott.	5171	12,480	69.8	23.2	7.0
48 Ott.	5102	2,531	87.0	5.8	7.2
107 Hull	5226	3,883	23.8	73.5	2.7
82 Nepean	5253	2,143	86.3	4.2	9.5
83 Nepean	5294	1,452	90.0	4.1	5.9
49 Ott.	5329	1,959	86.6	8.0	5.4
40 Ott.	5332	5,676	87.9	6.2	5.9
36 Ott.	5423	3,144	88.6	4.2	7.2
81 Nepean	5427	5,920	92.2	3.1	4.7
28 Ott.	5618	5,044	87.3	4.7	8.0
42 Ott.	5633	6,982	78.1	17.5	4.4
7 Ott.	5678	2,528	84.6	8.9	6.5
8 Ott.	5758	2,351	94.2	2.7	3.1
80 Nepean	5815	3,813	91.3	3.9	4.8
10 Ott.	5857	5,682	83.9	10.5	5.6
46 Ott.	5868	11,711	85.7	8.3	6.0
85 Nepean	5895	2,846	88.5	3.7	7.8
43 Ott.	6211	5,077	84.4	9.5	6.1
35 Ott.	6657	4,786	88.5	4.8	6.7
47 Ott.	6678	4,752	89.8	4.7	5.5
6 Ott.	6756	12,886	85.2	10.0	4.8
39 Ott.	6865	8,147	93.1	2.9	4.0
79 Rock. Park	8326	2,084	85.0	10.4	4.6

Source: Census of Canada, 1961; Catalogue 95-528.
*Male labour force only.

Appendices

Table J. Distribution of federal public servants within the Ottawa metropolitan area, 1961

Ottawa M.A.	Total		Mother tongue					
			English		French		Others	
	N	%	N	%	N	%	N	%
	45,619	100	29,847	100	13,932	100	1,840	100
Total Ontario	38,957	85.4	28,627	95.9	8,536	61.3	1,794	97.5
Ottawa	32,620	71.5	24,570	82.3	6,529	46.9	1,521	82.7
A. East Ottawa Sectors 1-2	1,609	3.5	1,160	3.9	334	2.4	115	6.3
B. North-east Ottawa Sectors 3-4, 16-19	3,424	7.5	1,261	4.2	2,058	14.8	105	5.7
C. East-central Ottawa Sectors 11-15	2,885	6.3	1,771	5.9	985	7.1	129	7.0
D. South-east Ottawa Sectors 5-7, 41-43	4,482	9.8	3,511	11.8	734	5.3	237	12.9
E. Central Ottawa Sectors 20-25	4,786	10.5	3,958	13.3	628	4.5	200	10.9
F. West-central Ottawa Sectors 30-34	2,705	5.9	1,781	6.0	813	5.8	111	6.0
G. South-west Ottawa Sectors 8-10, 26-29, 44	4,707	10.3	4,070	13.6	399	2.9	238	12.9
H. West Ottawa Sectors 35-40, 45-50	8,022	17.6	7,058	23.6	578	4.1	386	21.0
Eastview	2,903	6.4	1,237	4.1	1,558	11.2	108	5.9
Other Ontario municipalities*	3,434	7.5	2,820	9.4	449	3.2	165	9.0
Total Quebec	6,662	14.6	1,220	4.1	5,396	38.7	46	2.5
Hull	4,525	9.9	553	1.9	3,948	28.3	24	1.3
Other Quebec municipalities**	2,137	4.7	667	2.2	1,448	10.4	22	1.2

Source: Tape 1, Table 3. For this tabulation, census sectors in Ottawa and suburban municipalities were grouped into clusters to reduce the number of categories. A breakdown by individual tracts is not available.

 * Gloucester, Nepean, and Rockcliffe Park.
 ** Aylmer, Deschênes, Gatineau, Lucerne, Pointe-Gatineau, Templeton, and West Templeton.

Table K. Distribution of federal public servants earning over $10,000, within the Ottawa metropolitan area, by mother tongue, 1961

	Total		Mother tongue					
			English		French		Others	
	N	%	N	%	N	%	N	%
Ottawa M.A.	2,017	100	1,728	100	182	100	107	100
Total Ontario	1,942	96.2	1,695	98.1	143	78.6	104	97.1
Ottawa	1,685	83.5	1,473	85.2	127	69.8	85	79.4
A. East Ottawa Sectors 1-2	118	5.9	104	6.0	7	3.8	7	6.5
B. North-east Ottawa Sectors 3-4, 16-19	53	2.6	41	2.4	12	6.6	0	–
C. East-central Ottawa Sectors 11-15	98	4.9	67	3.9	27	14.8	4	3.7
D. South-east Ottawa Sectors 5-7, 41-43	398	19.7	349	20.2	27	14.8	22	20.6
E. Central Ottawa Sectors 20-25	105	5.2	91	5.3	10	5.5	4	3.7
F. West-central Ottawa Sectors 30-34	19	0.9	16	0.9	2	1.1	1	0.9
G. South-west Ottawa Sectors 8-10, 26-29, 44	315	15.6	276	16.0	27	14.8	12	11.2
H. West Ottawa Sectors 35-40, 45-50	579	28.7	529	30.6	15	8.2	35	32.7
Eastview	15	0.7	6	0.4	5	2.8	4	3.7
Other Ontario municipalities*	242	12.0	216	12.5	11	6.0	15	14.0
Total Quebec	75	3.7	33	1.9	39	21.4	3	2.8
Hull	47	2.3	18	1.0	28	15.4	1	0.9
Other Quebec municipalities**	28	1.4	15	0.9	11	6.0	2	1.9

Source: *See* Table J.
* and ** as in Table J.

Appendices

Table L. Incidence of official bilingualism in selected Canadian municipalities (20,000 and over), 1961

Municipality	Population	Bilingual population	Bilingual population as % of total
Ottawa	268,206	66,972	25.0
Hull	56,929	27,944	49.1
Eastview	24,555	12,879	52.4
Sudbury	80,120	23,220	29.0
Sherbrooke	66,554	23,013	29.4
Moncton	43,840	14,160	32.3
Cornwall	43,639	18,996	43.5
St. Boniface	37,600	13,516	36.0
Chomedey	30,445	9,229	30.3
Timmins	29,270	11,445	39.1
Verdun	78,317	30,855	39.4
Lachine	38,630	15,309	39.6
Outremont	30,753	14,222	46.2
Westmount	25,012	10,167	40.6
Town of Mount Royal	21,182	9,016	42.6

Source: Census of Canada, 1961; Catalogue 92-549.

Table M. Percentage distribution of population, Ottawa metropolitan area census tracts, by official language spoken, 1961

Census tract	Population = 100%	Official language			
		English only	French only	Both	Neither
16 Ott.	3,432	18.2	12.8	68.8	0.2
19 Ott.	5,099	14.6	18.2	66.5	0.6
18 Ott.	7,645	16.4	17.9	65.3	0.5
72 Eastv.	4,353	19.0	16.5	62.7	1.8
74 Eastv.	4,267	21.1	16.7	60.8	1.3
33 Ott.	5,967	33.8	7.3	57.3	1.6
73 Eastv.	6,735	21.1	20.6	57.4	1.1
15 Ott.	2,552	31.0	12.1	55.6	1.3
17 Ott.	3,577	34.6	9.6	55.3	0.6
4 Ott.	2,602	33.1	11.3	55.2	0.4
130 Deschênes	2,090	25.0	20.3	54.4	0.3
100 Hull	7,762	2.1	44.2	53.0	0.7
106 Hull	7,277	8.2	39.7	51.4	0.7
107 Hull	3,883	19.4	28.4	51.4	0.8
102 Hull	5,596	2.1	46.0	50.8	1.0
104 Hull	9,287	8.3	41.3	50.4	0.1
105 Hull	7,487	5.0	44.0	50.3	0.8
70 Eastv.	3,926	40.7	9.9	48.6	0.9
131 Aylmer	6,286	34.3	17.6	47.9	0.2
103 Hull	5,208	2.8	48.8	47.7	0.8
101 Hull	7,958	1.6	55.1	43.1	0.2
14 Ott.	7,479	52.1	4.0	42.9	1.1
13 Ott.	4,824	52.8	4.0	41.5	1.7
32 Ott.	2,292	52.4	4.9	40.8	1.9
135 and 150 Lucerne	5,762	45.7	14.5	39.6	0.2
127 Templeton	2,965	9.0	51.4	39.5	0.1
120 Gatineau	13,022	8.1	52.7	39.1	0.1
125 Pte-Gatineau	8,854	1.8	59.5	38.7	0.1
41 Ott.	6,129	56.5	5.8	37.4	0.3
86 Glouc.	5,027	51.7	10.3	37.1	1.0
108 Hull	2,471	6.2	57.3	36.5	–
5 Ott.	5,765	58.0	6.2	35.1	0.7
3 Ott.	4,049	57.2	6.4	34.7	1.7
71 Eastv.	5,256	59.1	6.6	33.9	0.5
11 Ott.	4,171	62.7	5.4	31.2	0.7
79 Rock. Park	2,084	68.8	1.5	29.6	0.1
31 Ott.	7,053	58.9	4.5	29.2	7.4
151 W. Temp.	943	31.9	40.0	28.0	0.1
30 Ott.	6,255	63.1	2.6	26.6	7.8
29 Ott.	4,462	66.2	2.2	26.2	5.5
2 Ott.	12,480	68.4	4.8	26.0	0.7
20 Ott.	3,257	75.6	0.8	23.0	0.6
34 Ott.	6,154	72.7	2.2	22.8	2.3

Continued on next page

Table M. (Cont'd)

Census tract	Population = 100%	Official language			
		English only	French only	Both	Neither
1 Ott.	4,684	75.7	2.3	22.0	0.0
24 Ott.	7,112	77.1	1.0	21.5	0.4
12 Ott.	2,277	76.5	2.0	21.3	0.1
42 Ott.	6,982	75.8	3.0	21.0	0.2
23 Ott.	4,254	76.9	0.9	20.8	1.3
21 Ott.	5,532	75.5	1.8	19.8	2.9
25 Ott.	3,353	78.5	0.8	19.5	1.1
87 Glouc.	2,022	77.3	3.0	19.4	0.3
10 Ott.	5,682	80.5	1.0	18.1	0.4
44 Ott.	4,089	79.9	1.8	17.1	1.3
50 Ott.	2,483	81.2	1.7	16.5	0.6
37 Ott.	7,794	81.1	1.2	16.3	1.4
6 Ott.	12,886	82.6	1.4	15.8	0.3
45 Ott.	7,896	82.4	1.1	15.7	0.8
22 Ott.	5,404	78.3	1.1	15.3	5.3
26 Ott.	4,831	82.8	0.7	15.2	1.3
43 Ott.	5,077	83.3	1.3	14.9	0.6
7 Ott.	2,528	84.8	1.1	14.0	0.2
46 Ott.	11,711	85.1	0.8	13.7	0.4
35 Ott.	4,786	85.8	0.6	13.3	0.3
84 Nepean	821	85.6	0.9	13.3	0.2
38 Ott.	9,370	86.5	0.6	12.6	0.4
28 Ott.	5,044	85.6	0.4	12.6	1.3
48 Ott.	2,531	87.8	0.5	11.6	0.1
40 Ott.	5,676	87.1	1.1	11.5	0.3
47 Ott.	4,752	87.9	0.6	11.4	0.1
27 Ott.	5,669	87.4	0.5	10.9	1.1
9 Ott.	4,958	88.4	0.5	10.3	0.7
49 Ott.	1,959	89.1	0.6	10.3	–
85 Nepean	2,846	88.8	0.5	10.3	0.5
36 Ott.	3,144	89.9	0.3	9.7	0.2
83 Nepean	1,452	89.9	0.3	9.5	0.2
82 Nepean	2,143	91.1	0.2	8.5	0.1
80 Nepean	3,813	91.3	0.3	8.2	0.2
81 Nepean	5,920	91.4	0.3	8.2	0.1
39 Ott.	8,147	91.1	0.4	8.1	0.5
8 Ott.	2,351	91.7	0.2	7.8	0.3

Source: Census of Canada, 1961; Catalogue 95-528.

Table N. Total labour force, Ottawa metropolitan area, by ethnic origin, official language, educational level, and average annual employment income, 1961

Ethnic origin	Official language	Total labour force		No schooling		Primary		Secondary (1-2 years)		Secondary (3-5 years)		University (1 or more years)	
		N	Average income($)	N	Average income($)	N	Average income($)	N	Average income($)	N	Average income($)	N	Average income($)
Total	English	84,737	4332	142	2281	16,265	3240	17,494	3586	37,273	4175	13,563	7038
	French	6,472	2377	130	2402	4,569	2273	885	2168	701	2928	187	3760
	Both	63,526	3829	231	2169	22,844	3086	14,552	3199	17,610	3972	8,289	6700
	Neither	908	1921	99	1302	694	1915	70	2326	35	1309*	10	7250*
	Total	155,643	4033	602	2110	44,372	3041	33,001	3375	55,619	4094	22,049	6883
British	English	61,335	4511	67	2167	9,707	3422	12,990	3701	28,422	4260	10,149	7302
	French	88	3487	–	–	29	3125*	5	1400*	54	3875	–	–
	Both	8,676	4879	16	3138*	1,499	3087	1,521	3686	3,104	4434	2,536	7195
	Neither	14	4285*	5	3277*	–	–	4	3400*	–	–	5	6000*
	Total	70,113	4555	88	2407	11,235	3377	14,520	3698	31,580	4276	12,690	7280
French	English	3,503	3438	4	2700*	719	2658	1,092	3087	1,435	3713	253	5530
	French	6,125	2348	130	2402	4,364	2262	862	2175	607	2873	162	3511
	Both	50,220	3567	186	2141	20,220	3068	12,355	3145	12,934	3770	4,525	6403
	Neither	46	2048*	4	1200*	21	2067*	21	2195*	–	–	–	–
	Total	59,894	3435	324	2236	25,324	2917	14,330	3081	14,976	3728	4,940	6263
Others	English	19,899	3933	71	2365	5,839	3003	3,412	3305	7,416	3940	3,161	6310
	French	259	2659	–	–	176	2384	18	2022*	40	2424*	25	5380*
	Both	4,630	4704	29	1764*	1,125	3406	676	3100	1,572	4739	1,228	6773
	Neither	848	1874	90	1185	673	1911	45	2292*	35	1309*	5	8500*
	Total	25,636	3993	190	1740	7,813	2954	4,151	3254	9,063	4061	4,419	6436

Source: Tape 3, Table 8, Parts I and II.
* Not significant in a 20-per-cent sample such as this.

Table O. Total labour force, Ottawa metropolitan area, by ethnic origin, official language, occupational category, and average annual employment income, 1961

Ethnic Origin	Official language	Total labour force		Managerial		Professional and Technical		Clerical		Sales		Service and recreation	
		N	Average income†	N	Average income†	N	Average income†	N	Average income†	N	Average income†	N	Average income†
Total	English	84,737	4332	9,467	7615	13,759	5848	23,266	3186	5,381	3591	13,774	3781
	French	6,472	2377	133	4000	300	3384	517	2451	274	1722	1,719	1275
	Both	63,526	3829	5,573	7212	7,047	5786	15,533	3046	4,422	3297	9,373	2803
	Neither	908	1921	5	8000*	5	6000*	9	3211*	5	2000*	339	1347
	Total	155,643	4033	15,178	7435	21,111	5793	39,345	3120	10,082	3411	25,205	3222
British	English	61,335	4511	6,931	7895	10,459	6000	18,321	3239	3,957	3681	9,493	4145
	French	88	3487	4	2000*	9	6667	30	2755*	–	–	5	1125*
	Both	8,676	4879	1,193	8662	1,733	6296	2,055	3214	661	3847	1,187	4200
	Neither	14	4285*	–	–	5	6000*	4	3400*	–	–	–	–
	Total	70,113	4555	8,128	8004	12,206	6043	20,410	3236	4,168	3705	10,685	4150
French	English	3,503	3438	262	6934	383	4681	1,112	3000	260	3219	577	2713
	French	6,125	2348	112	3937	276	2990	467	2470	263	1706	1,648	1256
	Both	50,220	3567	3,602	6568	4,361	5533	12,714	3021	3,448	3110	7,500	2525
	Neither	46	2048*	–	–	–	–	5	1440*	5	2000*	20	771*
	Total	59,894	3435	3,976	6517	5,020	5333	14,298	3000	3,976	3022	9,745	2321
Others	English	19,899	3933	2,274	6821	2,917	5455	3,833	2983	1,164	3363	3,704	3003
	French	259	2659	17	4888*	15	8333*	20	1570*	11	2101*	66	1727
	Both	4,630	4704	778	7945	953	6014	784	3012	313	4209	686	3389
	Neither	848	1874	5	8000*	–	–	–	–	–	–	319	1376
	Total	25,636	3993	3,074	7099	3,885	5604	4,637	2982	1,488	3528	4,775	2941

Table O (cont'd)

Ethnic Origin	Official language	Transport and communication		Farmers		Other primary		Craftsmen		Labourers		Not stated	
		N	Average income†	N	Average income†	N	Average income†	N	Average income†	N	Average income†	N	Average income†
Total	English	3,518	3656	92	3917	596	2547	11,188	3861	1,770	2294	1,926	3664
	French	314	2735	–	–	105	3428	1,873	3035	975	2242	262	2937
	Both	4,563	3204	33	3961*	353	2606	12,684	3730	2,944	2475	981	3878
	Neither	6	3900*	–	–	5	1500*	332	1924	161	2297	41	2998*
	Total	8,401	3376	125	3929	1,059	2650	26,077	3713	5,850	2377	3,210	3662
British	English	2,652	3763	70	4419	362	2655	6,735	4068	980	2202	1,375	3749
	French	5	3000*	–	–	–	–	30	4320*	5	1200*	–	–
	Both	441	3062	–	–	67	2259	1,028	3976	179	2660	132	7315
	Neither	–	–	–	–	–	–	–	–	5	3277*	–	–
	Total	3,098	3662	70	4419	429	2592	7,793	4056	1,169	2273	1,507	4030
French	English	207	2546	17	894*	36	1743*	560	3282	50	2455	39	3348*
	French	304	2739	–	–	100	3534	1,753	3022	940	2278	262	2937
	Both	3,960	3220	22	4641*	251	2698	10,958	3716	2,635	2472	769	3200
	Neither	6	3900*	–	–	–	–	10	3050*	–	–	–	–
	Total	4,477	3157	39	3008*	387	2827	13,281	3606	3,625	2421	1,070	3140
Others	English	659	3573	5	8160*	198	2497	3,893	3585	740	2405	512	3438
	French	5	2224*	–	–	5	1300*	90	2852	30	1290*	–	–
	Both	162	3207	11	2600*	35	2624*	698	3577	130	2298	80	4888
	Neither	–	–	–	–	5	1500*	322	1889	156	2266	41	2998*
	Total	826	3493	16	4338*	243	2470	5,003	3461	1,056	2339	633	3593

Source: Tape 3, Table 8, Parts I and II.
*Not significant in a 20-per-cent sample such as this.
† In dollars.

Appendix B (Chapter I)   The Influence of Certain Factors on Inequalities in Labour Income

This appendix[1] is concerned with the influence of certain factors on inequalities in labour income between members of the male labour force of British and French origins in the Ottawa metropolitan area in 1961. Its purpose is to study the extent to which the difference in labour income for males is influenced by the following factors: education, occupational structure, industrial structure, and age. The procedure used is a method of iterative analysis.[2]

1. Method Used

It is proposed to develop a formula to measure the influence of a particular factor on the difference in labour income of males of British and French origins in the labour force.

Let J be a set of n factors ($j = 1, \ldots, n$). Each factor j can be classified according to a set I_j of m_j categories ($i = 1, \ldots, m_j$) which partitions the labour force of each ethnic group in terms of this factor.

Let—

Y^B : the average labour income of males of British origin.
Y^F : the average labour income of males of French origin.
$Y_{i,j}$: the average income of individuals belonging in category i of factor j.
$N_{i,j}$: the proportion of individuals belonging in category i of factor j.

The superscripts B and F attached to a symbol designate males of British and French origins respectively ($Y^B_{i,j}$, $Y^F_{i,j}$, $N^B_{i,j}$ and $N^F_{i,j}$). These obvious relations follow:

$$\sum_{i=1}^{m_j} N_{i,j} = 1 \qquad \text{for each factor } j$$

---

[1] Calculations were prepared by André Barsony under the general direction of Professor André Raynauld, University of Montreal.

[2] This method was employed in an analysis of the inequality of incomes among the different ethnic groups of the Montreal metropolitan district. See Raynauld et al., "La répartition des revenus selon les groupes ethniques au Canada" (study prepared for the Royal Commission on Bilingualism and Biculturalism, 1966).

$$Y^B = \sum_{i=1}^{m_j} Y_{i,j}^B \, N_{i,j}^B \quad \text{for each factor } j \cdots (1.1)$$

$$Y^F = \sum_{i=1}^{m_j} Y_{i,j}^F \, N_{i,j}^B \quad \text{for each factor } j$$

The difference in average labour income between the two ethnic groups is:

$$Y^B - Y^F = \sum_{i=1}^{m_j} Y_{i,j}^B \, N_{i,j}^B - \sum_{i=1}^{m_j} Y_{i,j}^F \, N_{i,j}^F \quad \text{for each factor } j \cdots (1.2)$$

Let us define the following relations:

$$dY_{i,j} = Y_{i,j}^B - Y_{i,j}^F$$

$$dN_{i,j} = N_{i,j}^B - N_{i,j}^F$$

It follows that formula (1.2) can be expressed as follows:[3]

$$Y^B - Y^F = \sum_{i=1}^{m_j} dY_{i,j} \, N_{i,j}^F + \sum_{i=1}^{m_j} dN_{i,j} \, Y_{i,j}^F + \sum_{i=1}^{m_j} dY_{i,j} \, dN_{i,j} \quad \text{for each factor } j \cdots (1.3)$$

The left-hand side of equation (1.3) indicates the difference between the average income of the British origin group and that of the French origin group, while the right-hand side shows the sources of this difference:

a) $\sum_{i=1}^{m_j} dY_{i,j} \, N_{i,j}^F$ is the effect ascribable to the income difference between the two ethnic groups within each category i of the factor j being considered. In other words, the income effect captures the difference in income which would exist if the British had the same labour force structure as the French, with respect to the factor being considered.

b) $\sum_{i=1}^{m_j} dN_{i,j} \, Y_{i,j}^F$ is the effect ascribable to the structural difference in the labour force

---

[3] Indeed, it is only necessary, on the one hand, to add the left-hand side and then the right-hand side of the following equations:

$$\sum_i dY_{i,j} \, N_{i,j}^F = \sum_i (Y_{i,j}^B - Y_{i,j}^F) \, N_{i,j}^F = \sum_i Y_{i,j}^B \, N_{i,j}^F - \sum_i Y_{i,j}^F \, N_{i,j}^F$$

$$\sum_i dN_{i,j} \, Y_{i,j}^F = \sum_i (N_{i,j}^B - N_{i,j}^F) \, Y_{i,j}^F = \sum_i N_{i,j}^B \, Y_{i,j}^F - \sum_i N_{i,j}^F \, Y_{i,j}^F$$

$$\sum_i dY_{i,j} \, dN_{i,j} = \sum_i (Y_{i,j}^B - Y_{i,j}^F)(N_{i,j}^B - N_{i,j}^F) = \sum_i Y_{i,j}^B \, N_{i,j}^B - \sum_i Y_{i,j}^F \, N_{i,j}^B - \sum_i Y_{i,j}^B \, N_{i,j}^F + \sum_i Y_{i,j}^F \, N_{i,j}^F$$

Appendices   214

of the two ethnic groups with respect to the factor j being considered. Put another way, the structural effect captures the income difference which would exist if the British ethnic group had the same average income as the French ethnic group in each category i of the factor j being considered.

c) $\sum_{i=1}^{m_j} dY_{i,j} \, dN_{i,j}$ is the joint influence ascribable to the difference in income and structure. The joint influence being more difficult to interpret, some assumptions must be made. If the structural effect is positive, then the $dN_{i,j}$ are positive in the upper income categories and negative in the lower ones because we have $\sum_{i=1}^{m_j} dN_{i,j} = 0$. If, furthermore, $dY_{i,j} \geqslant 0$ for all i,[4] then a joint positive influence involves more important income differences in the high income classes than in the low income classes. In these conditions, it can be said that the joint influence shows to what extent the French in these upper income classes are in an unfavourable position as opposed to the French in the low income classes when comparisons are made with British incomes.

2. Analysis of the Influence of Certain Factors on Income Inequalities

In the Ottawa metropolitan area in 1961, the average labour income was $5,504 for males of British origin and $4,008 for males of French origin. The difference of income between the two ethnic groups was $1,496 in favour of the British group.[5] The characteristics of the labour supply of the British and French differ in respect to the various factors considered. An attempt is made to evaluate successively the inequality in income due to differences in schooling, occupational structure, industrial structure, and age.

a) Influence of schooling

In using the method previously described to study the influence of schooling (i.e. in setting j = s), the following results are obtained:

$\sum_{i=1}^{m_s} dN_{i,s} \, Y_{i,s}^F$: $ 644.54   (43.04 %)

$\sum_{i=1}^{m_s} dY_{i,s} \, N_{i,s}^F$: $ 722.91   (48.28 %)

$\sum_{i=1}^{m_s} dY_{i,s} \, dN_{i,s}$: $ 129.94   (8.68 %)

Total disparity   : $ 1,497.39   (100.   %)

---

[4] This hypothesis is obviously restrictive.

[5] In the following considerations the difference varies to a very slight and unimportant degree according to the factor being considered as a result of the method of calculation.

Table A. Level of schooling and difference in labour income between males of British and French origins, Ottawa metropolitan area, 1961

Level of schooling	British origin		French origin		(5) $dY_{i,s}$	(6) $dN_{i,s}$	(7) $dY_{i,s} N^F_{i,s}$	(8) $dN_{i,s} Y^F_{i,s}$	(9) $dY_{i,s} dN_{i,s}$
	(1) Average income $Y^B_{i,s}$	(2) Percentage of labour force $N^B_{i,s}$	(3) Average income $Y^F_{i,s}$	(4) Percentage of labour force $N^F_{i,s}$					
None	2688	0.0013	2481	0.0060	207	−0.0047	1.2420	− 11.6607	− 0.9729
Elementary	3928	0.1765	3385	0.4564	543	−0.2799	247.8252	−947.4615	−151.9857
Secondary (1-2 years)	4394	0.2026	3615	0.2280	779	−0.0254	177.6120	− 91.8210	− 19.7866
Secondary (3-5 years)	5354	0.3946	4462	0.2111	892	0.1835	188.3012	818.7770	163.6820
University (1 year or more)	8023	0.2249	6925	0.0983	1098	0.1266	107.9334	876.7050	139.0068
Total	5504	0.9999	4008	0.9998		0.0001	722.9138	644.5388	129.9436

Appendices 216

Table A illustrates the method of calculation. Column 8 of the table shows that $644.54 (43.04 %) of the existing variation between the incomes of British and French is due to the poorer schooling of the French. Column 7 shows that even if the level of schooling were similar for British and French, there would still be a difference of $722.91 (48.28 %) between the incomes of the two ethnic groups. The joint influence is $129.94 (8.68%).

b) Influence of occupational structure

The occupational structure is the second factor which has been retained as an explanation of the income difference. It is proposed to evaluate that part of the variation due to the difference between the occupational structure of those of British and French origins as indicated by 11 occupational categories.
The following results are obtained:

$$\sum_{i=1}^{m_o} dN_{i,o}\ Y^F_{i,o} \quad : \quad \$\ 639.35 \quad\quad (\ 42.75\ \%\ )$$

$$\sum_{i=1}^{m_o} dY_{i,o}\ N^F_{i,o} \quad : \quad \$\ 682.20 \quad\quad (\ 45.61\ \%\ )$$

$$\sum_{i=1}^{m_o} dY_{i,o}\ dN_{i,o} \quad : \quad \$\ 173.91 \quad\quad (\ 11.63\ \%\ )$$

Total disparity   : $ 1,495.46   (100.   %)

It follows that $639.35 (42.75 %) of the difference between the incomes of British and French is ascribable to the unfavourable occupational structure of those of French origin. Even if the occupational structure of both groups were identical, there would still be an income differential of $682.20 (45.61 %) between the two.

c) Influence of schooling and occupational structure by cross-classification

Schooling and occupational structure being correlated explanatory factors, their total influence is not the sum of their individual impacts.

Cross-classification by occupational group and level of schooling permits the elimination of the problem of linear correlation among the factors. Furthermore, the partitioning of the occupational groups according to level of schooling offsets in part the relative crudeness of the occupational classification.

The method used is the same except that in this case the subscript i covers the entire cross-classification field. If it is set that $j =$ so then m_{so} will be equal to the number of occupational categories multiplied by the number of levels of schooling.
The following results are obtained:

$$\sum_{i=1}^{m_{so}} dN_{i,so}\ Y^F_{i,so} \quad : \quad \$\ 932.72 \quad\quad (\ 62.36\ \%\ )$$

$$\sum_{i=1}^{m_{so}} dY_{i,so}\ N^F_{i,so} : \$\ 470.92 \qquad (\ 31.48\ \%\ )$$

$$\sum_{i=1}^{m_{so}} dY_{i,so}\ dN_{i,so} : \$\ 92.13 \qquad (\ 6.16\ \%\ )$$

Total disparity : $ 1,495.77   (100.   %)

These results show that $932.72 (62.36 %) of the difference between the incomes of British and French is ascribable to the variation between, on the one hand, schooling and the occupational structure of the British and, on the other hand, the same factors on the French side.

In studying the effects of the two factors separately, one reaches the conclusion that the differences in schooling and occupational structure represent respectively $644.54 and $639.35 of the income difference between the British and the French. If we take schooling and occupational structure as correlated, their total influence is only $932.72 when it is evaluated by cross-classification.

On the other hand, even if schooling standards and occupational structures were the same for British and French, there would still be a difference of $470.92 (31.48 %) between the incomes of the two ethnic groups. The joint influence is $92.13 (6.16 %).

d) Influence of industrial structure

By using the same method, it is proposed to measure the influence of the industrial structure through nine industrial groups.

The following results are obtained:

$$\sum_{i=1}^{m_t} dN_{i,t}\ Y^F_{i,t} : \$\ 113.47 \qquad (\ 7.59\ \%\ )$$

$$\sum_{i=1}^{m_t} dY_{i,t}\ N^F_{i,t} : \$\ 1{,}295.08 \qquad (\ 86.61\ \%\ )$$

$$\sum_{i=1}^{m_t} dY_{i,t}\ dN_{i,t} : \$\ 86.71 \qquad (\ 5.79\ \%\ )$$

Total disparity : $ 1,495.26   (100.   %)

It follows that the difference between the industrial structures of the British and French represents only $113.47 (7.59 %) of the existing income variation between the two ethnic groups. Even if the industrial structure of the two were identical, there would still be a difference in income of $1,295.08 (86.61 %). The joint influence is $86.71 (5.79 %).

Appendices

e) Influence of occupational structure and industrial structure by cross-classification

The occupational structure and industrial structure being correlated explanatory factors, the following results are reached by cross-classification:

$$\sum_{i=1}^{m_{ot}} dN_{i,ot}\ Y^F_{i,ot} \quad : \quad \$\ 710.93 \qquad (\ 47.62\ \%\ )$$

$$\sum_{i=1}^{m_{ot}} dY_{i,ot}\ N^F_{i,ot} \quad : \quad \$\ 511.99 \qquad (\ 34.29\ \%\ )$$

$$\sum_{i=1}^{m_{ot}} dY_{i,ot}\ dN_{i,ot} \quad : \quad \$\ 270.15 \qquad (\ 18.09\ \%\ )$$

Total disparity : $ 1,493.07 (100. %)

In studying the effects of these two factors separately, one finds that the differences in the occupational structure and the industrial structure represent respectively $639.35 and $113.47 of the difference in income between British and French. Because of the correlation, their total influence is only $710.93 (47.62 %). However, the correlation appears to be relatively weak. On the other hand, even for identical occupational and industrial structures there would be a difference of $511.99 (34.29 %) between the income of the two ethnic groups. The joint influence is $270.15 (18.09 %).

f) Influence of age

According to the data available to us, income classification by age group can be made only on the basis of total income, whereas up to this point income from employment only has been used. For this reason, the income variation is significantly different from the preceding cases. However, this variation does not create a disadvantage in comparisons with the whole range of factors because adjustments will be made on the basis of percentages.

On the basis of 4 age categories, the following results are obtained:

$$\sum_{i=1}^{m_a} dN_{i,a}\ Y^F_{i,a} \quad : \quad \$\ 170.22 \qquad (\ 10.75\ \%\ )$$

$$\sum_{i=1}^{m_a} dY_{i,a}\ N^F_{i,a} \quad : \quad \$\ 1{,}268.02 \qquad (\ 80.11\ \%\ )$$

$$\sum_{i=1}^{m_a} dY_{i,a}\ dN_{i,a} \quad : \quad \$\ 144.53 \qquad (\ 9.13\ \%\ )$$

Total disparity : $ 1,582.77 (100. %)

The difference between the age structure of British and French represents $170.22 (10.75 %) of the difference in income between the two ethnic groups. Even if the age structure of the two groups were identical there would be an income difference of $1,268.02 (80.11 %). The joint influence is $144.53 (9.13 %).

g) Influence of level of employment

In addition to the factors already considered, level of employment can explain the income difference between the two ethnic groups. All other things being equal, a higher unemployment rate in one ethnic group means that that group has a lower income than the other group.

An estimate made in the Raynauld study of unemployment by level of schooling for Canada in 1960 shows that the variation between the unemployment rates of British and French is 3.3 percentage points. In the case studied, this percentage reduces the French annual income by roughly $137.00 as compared with that of the British.

h) Influence of all factors

The results are summarized in the following table:

Table B. Influence of certain factors on the inequality of incomes between males of British and French origins, Ottawa, 1961

Factor	$\Sigma dN_{i,j} Y^F_{i,j}$	$\Sigma dY_{i,j} N^F_{i,j}$	$\Sigma dY_{i,j} dN_{i,j}$
1. Schooling	$ 644.54	$ 722.91	$ 129.94
2. Occupation	639.35	682.20	173.91
3. Schooling–occupational structure	932.72	470.92	92.13
4. Industrial structure	113.47	1,295.08	86.71
5. Occupation–industrial structure	710.93	511.99	270.15
6. Age*	160.82	1,198.45	136.58
7. Level of employment	∼137.00	–	–

* Corrected values for salary and wage income as opposed to total income.

The difference in average income between the two ethnic groups is $1,496.00 in favour of the British. The differences between the British and the French with respect to schooling and occupational structure explain 62.36% ($932.72) of this difference.

The preceding estimates have shown that industrial structure is a factor having little correlation with occupational structure. While emphasizing that this is a slightly excessive estimate, we may retain 7.59% ($113.47) as representing the influence of the industrial structure.

Taking as our hypothesis the absence of linear correlation among the factors retained, we may proceed to a summation of their influence on the income variation between the two ethnic groups. Numbers 3, 4, 6 and 7 of Table B are used. The total influence of the explanatory factors that we retain on the income variation between the two ethnic groups is, then, as follows:

Schooling–occupational structure	:	$ 932.72	$ 62.36 %
Industrial structure	:	113.47	7.59
Age	:	160.82	10.75
Level of employment	:	∼ 137.00	9.16
Total	:	1,344.01	89.86

It follows that even if schooling, occupational and industrial structures, age structure, and level of employment were identical for those of British and French origins, there would still be an income difference of $151.99 (10.14%) between the two ethnic groups.

Table C compares the influence of these explanatory factors for Ottawa, Montreal, and Toronto.

Table C. Influence of selected factors on income differences between males of British and French origins, Ottawa, Montreal, and Toronto metropolitan areas

Factor	Ottawa	Montreal	Toronto
Schooling-occupational structure	62.36 %	45.1 %	44.1 %
Industrial structure	7.59	4.2	4.4
Age	10.75	5.9	16.1
Level of employment	9.16	6.3	13.0*
Total	89.86	61.5	77.6

Source: Columns 2 and 3—Raynauld et al., "La répartition des revenus."
* Estimate based on unemployment rate by level of schooling according to ethnic groups, ibid.

This comparison shows that the total influence of the factors in question is higher in Ottawa than in Montreal or Toronto—a fact which is explained by the relatively strong influence of the "schooling-occupational structure" factor on the difference in incomes between the two ethnic groups in Ottawa.

Appendix C (Chapter II)   Bilingual Traffic Signs in Ottawa

The issue of bilingual traffic signs in the city of Ottawa dates from a council resolution in 1956 calling for bilingual signs in the largely Francophone By ward. The municipal administration implemented the resolution, and the matter was not raised again until December 1962. At that time, a proposal to put up a sign bearing only the word "Yield" in By ward was called into question. This marked the start of a controversy which reached its height in the winter of 1963-64, but which has continued on and off ever since.

The opposition to the erection of bilingual signs was twofold. The first argument, which need not detain us, was procedural: namely, that no by-law had been passed in support of the 1956 resolution and therefore no action could be based upon it. The second argument held that it was beyond the competence of the city to pass a by-law, the authority for which had not been expressly granted by the province. As Mayor Whitton expressed it: "The City of Ottawa, though the Capital of the Dominion of Canada . . . is a municipality in the Province of Ontario. It is subject, as the province's creation and creature, to the provincial authority in all matters in civil and property rights" (*Ottawa Citizen*, December 10, 1963). The Mayor went on to say that nothing in the B.N.A. Act, the Ontario Municipal Act or any other legislation gave the city council the power to make Ottawa an officially bilingual city. Until such authority was granted, no bilingual signs could be legally erected. "Informal hearsay, or word, or opinion of tolerance from any member of either the federal or the provincial authority, that 'there is nothing wrong about it' or 'nothing really to stop it,'" was not such a grant of authority.

The Mayor was supported in a report prepared for council jointly by the city solicitor and the traffic director. The report stated that "there does not exist any enabling legislation or other statutory authority which would empower this or any other Ontario municipality to enact a by-law declaring as lawful the erection of bilingual signs" (*Ottawa Journal*, February 18, 1964). Only an appropriate amendment to the Highway Act or special authorization by means of a private bill could enable such signs to be legally posted in Ottawa.

The proponents of bilingual signs pointed to their use in other Ontario municipalities such as Hawkesbury, Eastview, and Sturgeon Falls.* Had these signs in fact been illegal, they argued, Queen's Park would have long since compelled their removal.

In fact, those in favour of the bilingual signs were able to cite numerous provincial authorities who had expressed themselves positively on the matter. Ontario Premier Leslie Frost did so in 1961. Two years later Premier John Robarts and the Minister of Transport, James Auld, could find nothing to prevent the use of bilingual street signs by a municipality, so long as the signs conformed to provincial requirements concerning shape, colour and size. In 1964, the Minister of Transport, Irwin Haskett, approved an Eastview by-law containing a provision for signs in the two languages. Again, the Minister of Transport told the legislature in 1966 that there would be no objections to bilingual signs.

None of these statements really answers the argument of some civic authorities that the city has no explicit statutory power to erect bilingual signs. This argument is usually countered by the statement that there is no statutory provision forbidding the city to do so. Whether the city can or cannot do so may have to be cleared up either by the Ontario legislature or by the courts.

---

*Bilingual signs have also been erected by the National Capital Commission on the federal driveway system in and around Ottawa. For further details *see* 126.

Appendix D (Chapter III)	Correspondence between the Royal Commission on Bilingualism and Biculturalism and the Cities of Ottawa, Hull and Eastview

1. OTTAWA

Co-Chairman to the Mayor

February 26, 1965.

His Worship Mayor Donald B. Reid,
Corporation of the City of Ottawa,
City Hall,
Ottawa, Canada.

Dear Sir:

You may perhaps have anticipated that since Ottawa is the capital city of Canada, The Royal Commission on Bilingualism and Biculturalism would want to carry out some research into various aspects of municipal government in the area. You are no doubt aware of the purposes of the Commission, but I am attaching, for your convenience, an extract from Order-in-Council 1106 (July 18, 1963) which states our terms of reference.

Among other studies, we are examining the capital region to determine the extent to which it reflects the dual nature of our country. One of the most important sectors of this investigation is of course the municipal government and administration of Ottawa, and we hope for your interest and aid in this part of our programme. Specifically, we would like

(1) to know something more of the past and present patterns of ethnic representation in municipal politics, and
(2) to study the patterns of ethnic representation and language usage in municipal administration.

Mr. David R. Cameron and Mr. Jean T. Fournier, under the supervision of Dr. Kenneth D. McRae, have been at work on this project for some time and they will be in contact with you in the near future. May I, therefore, earnestly request your cooperation and that of the various departments of your administration in our development of this study.

Yours sincerely,

André Laurendeau,
Co-Chairman.

Research Staff to City Clerk

March 8, 1965.

Mr. A.T. Hastey,
City Clerk,
Corporation of the City of Ottawa,
City Hall,
Ottawa, Ont.

Dear Mr. Hastey,

Following our discussion with Mayor Reid, Mr. Wilson and yourself this morning, I am happy to set down for you a brief statement of our project.

As part of its research programme the Royal Commission on Bilingualism and Biculturalism has undertaken a study of the national capital. The object is to examine the extent of cultural and linguistic dualism in the national capital, and to explore the means for its fuller attainment. One important aspect of this study will be to examine the situation of the various municipal governments in the region, particularly Ottawa, Hull and Eastview.

We enclose a brief outline of the research programme which is envisaged for the government and administration of the City of Ottawa. We trust that this information will enable you to explain the scope of our study to members of Board of Control.

Yours sincerely,

David R. Cameron.

Enclosure in above letter: Research Outline

I. *Municipal Administration*

1. *Representation.* A study of linguistic and ethnic representation in the various branches of the municipal administration (including such boards and commissions as the Ottawa Transportation Commission).
2. *Language Usage.* A study of the patterns of language usage between the various administrative agencies and the public (*the external language of communication*), and a study of the patterns of language usage *within* the various municipal agencies themselves (*the internal language of communication*).

II. *Municipal Government*

A study of past and present patterns of ethnic representation on the Ottawa City Council.

Our research methods for this study include reference to personnel material and historical sources, supplemented by interviews with heads of municipal departments and other officials as necessary. We are planning to meet the burden of compiling statistics and analysing information through the use of our own Commission staff.

Secretary, Board of Control to Research Staff

March 10, 1965.

Mr. David R. Cameron,
Royal Commission on Bilingualism
and Biculturalism,
P.O. Box 1508, Ottawa.

Dear Sir:

The Board of Control has considered your letter of March 8th addressed to the City Clerk, in which you set down for the Board of Control's consideration a brief statement of your proposed project.

The Board has authorized you to carry out your study in accordance with your submission.

Yours truly,

R.J. Gorman,
Secretary,
Board of Control.

City Clerk to Research Staff

March 11, 1965.

Mr. David R. Cameron,
Royal Commission on Bilingualism
and Biculturalism,
P.O. Box 1508, Ottawa.

Dear Sir:

I acknowledge herewith receipt of your communication of the 8th instant regarding your Commission's Research Program with respect to the Corporation of the City of Ottawa and affiliated Boards and Commissions.

I am also in receipt of a copy of a communication addressed to you and signed by Mr. R. J. Gorman, Secretary of the Board of Control, advising you of the Board's decision that it is now in order for you to carry out your study in accordance with your submission.

It should be noted however that the City of Ottawa Procedure By-law Number 5499 requires that all correspondence addressed to and received by the Head of the Council, the City Clerk or the Head of any Department in his official capacity, and having reference to the business and affairs of the Corporation, shall be laid before the Council at the first regular meeting thereof after the receipt of the same.

The City Council will meet next Monday, March 15th, 1965, at which time both your communication addressed to me and that of Mr. Andre Laurendeau addressed to His Worship the Mayor will be presented.

                                            Yours truly,

                                            A.T. Hastey,
                                            City Clerk.

Counsel, Department of the Attorney-General of Ontario to Board of Control

March 18, 1965.

Board of Control
Ottawa, Ontario
Attention: Dr. Murray A. Heit

Dear Dr. Heit:

Your letter of March 15th addressed to the Director of the Ontario Human Rights Commission has been referred to me for opinion and comment.

I point out that the B. and B. Commission is a Federal Commission and, presumably, is therefore under the jurisdiction of the Fair Employment Practices Division of the Federal Department of Labour.

I suggest that you take the matter up with the Director of the Fair Employment Practices Division, Mr. Bernard Wilson.

However, to address myself to the substance of your letter, it is my opinion that section 4 of the Code is confined to matters that are in connection with employment or prospective employment in the area of hiring and not in the area of ethnic research.

Although I concede that the inquiries that will be made by the B. and B. Commission would, literally, come within the phrase "No person shall... make any written or oral inquiry that expresses either directly or indirectly any limitation, etc. ...." nevertheless, in my view, the ambit of the section as it might be construed by a Court is not sufficiently wide to apply to the inquiries that will be made by the B. and B. Commission. Accordingly, I do not think that the inquiries of the B. and B. Commission are against the intent of the Code.

Yours very truly,

Robin Scott,
Counsel.

Appendices

Secretary, Board of Control to Research Staff

March 19, 1965.

Mr. David R. Cameron,
Royal Commission on Bilingualism
and Biculturalism,
P.O. Box 1508,
Ottawa, Ontario.

Dear Sir:

The Board of Control of the City of Ottawa, further to the request of the Royal Commission on Bilingualism and Biculturalism to conduct a Research Programme with respect to the Corporation of the City of Ottawa and affiliated Boards and Commissions, has requested that your Commission be asked to provide a completely itemized report as to who would undertake this Research Programme, the methods proposed to be employed in the Programme, and whether or not the research information and data gathered would be available to the City and its Director of Personnel for review prior to public release, so that any information considered by the City as confidential might be so retained.

Your kind attention to this request of the Board would be appreciated.

Yours truly,

R.J. Gorman,
Secretary,
Board of Control.

Director of Research to Secretary, Board of Control

March 25, 1965.

Mr. R. J. Gorman
Secretary
Board of Control
City of Ottawa

Dear Mr. Gorman:

Mr. D.R. Cameron has referred to me your letter of March 19, 1965 in which you request more information regarding our proposed study of municipal government and administration.

You will find in the enclosed research outline a list of the persons who would be responsible for carrying out the study, as well as a presentation of the research methods to be employed. We would be quite willing to make the research findings which develop from this project available to the City, and would gladly consult with the Director of Personnel or anyone else named by the City prior to releasing any of this information to the public. We can also assure you that no municipal public servants will be identified by name in our research report.

In closing, may I add that I would be delighted to meet with members of the Board of Control or its staff if any further points require discussion.

Yours sincerely,

Michael Oliver
Director of Research.

Enclosure in Above Letter: Research Outline for City of Ottawa Study

As the capital of Canada, Ottawa with its surrounding urban area has an important and unique role to play in the life of our country. Because it is the seat of the federal government, the Ottawa-Hull metropolitan area inevitably symbolizes the country as a whole both to the thousands of Canadians who travel to see it every year, and to those who visit it from abroad. Equally important, the capital region is the home of a great number of federal public servants from all parts of Canada who, in coming to the capital to work, make demands on the city and its environs quite different from those which any other Canadian municipalities must face.

The Royal Commission on Bilingualism and Biculturalism has therefore decided to undertake a thorough study of the Ottawa-Hull metropolitan area. The object of this project, which has been under way for ten months, is to determine the extent to which the capital region reflects the dual nature of our country. One important aspect of this study is to examine the situation of the various municipal governments in the region, particularly Ottawa, Hull and Eastview.

There follows an elaboration of the research design which we would like to use in examining the municipal government and administration of the City of Ottawa.

I. *Municipal Administration*

1. *Representation.* Our aim in this section of the study is to determine the role which Ottawa's major cultural groups play in the city's administration. We want to ascertain the proportion of each of these groups present in the various departments,

commissions and boards which make up the municipal administrative organization, as well as their distribution throughout the hierarchy. This objective can be attained by consultation of personnel files if they have the necessary data, or, less satisfactorily, by analysis of the names of the employees. Major attention would be devoted to the upper administrative echelons in order to find out the proportion of Canadians whose mother tongue is French who are present at this level in comparison to that of the total administration.

2. *Language Usage.* This important section of the study concerns both *external* and *internal* patterns of language usage in municipal administration. To gather material in this sphere, we envisage a series of informational interviews with heads of the various departments, top administrative and personnel officers of the large boards and commissions, and others.

The *external language of communication* refers to the patterns of language usage which exist between the various administrative agencies of the municipality and the public. We are interested in determining how the municipal administration communicates to Ottawa citizens of various mother tongues, and how it reacts to representations made to it in the various mother tongues. More specifically, we would like to know:

– to what degree languages other than English are used officially or informally in written or oral communications with the public
– what arrangements exist within the various administrative agencies to deal with written or oral citizen contacts made in a language other than English (particularly French).

The *internal language of communication* denotes the patterns of language usage within (and among) the various municipal agencies themselves. Here we are concerned with both the formal and informal situation, and with any variations in the patterns occurring in different departments and at different levels of the administrative hierarchy. Again, both written and verbal aspects of the communication flow are of interest.

II. *Municipal Government*

In the field of municipal government—that is, the elective, legislative branch of the corporation of the City of Ottawa—we are concerned with the existence, historically and currently, of elected officials who can be considered representatives of cultural groups in the urban population. This section of the study is secondary in importance to the research on administration, and must therefore be restricted to an historical examination of the cultural composition of the Ottawa council itself. We would like to discover the relationship between the numerical strength of a cultural group as well as its concentration in various parts of the city, and its apparent representation in municipal government. This research can be carried out by a comparative analysis of the cultural affiliation and, if possible, mother tongue of city council members, and that of the city population as a whole.

We plan to have the research carried out by David R. Cameron and an assistant, under the supervision of Dr. Kenneth D. McRae.

Secretary, Board of Control to City Solicitor

March 25, 1965.

Mr. D.V. Hambling,
City Solicitor,
City Hall.

Dear Sir:

Re: Royal Commission on Bilingualism and Biculturalism

You are requested to provide for Board of Control a legal opinion as to whether the request of the Royal Commission on Bilingualism and Biculturalism to conduct a research study in the City of Ottawa in the terms of their letters and attachment, forwarded herewith, is in conflict with the provisions of the Ontario Human Rights Code.

If necessary, you are authorized to communicate with the Attorney General of the Province of Ontario in this matter.

The Board is anxious to consider this matter so that it might make a recommendation to Council on April 5th, and your immediate attention to this request therefore would be appreciated.

Yours truly,

R.J. Gorman,
Secretary,
Board of Control.

City Solicitor to Secretary, Board of Control

March 26th 1965.

R.J. Gorman, Esq.,
Secretary,
Board of Control.

Dear Sir:

Re: Royal Commission on Bilingualism and Biculturalism

You have asked for my legal opinion as to whether the request of the Royal Commission on Bilingualism and Biculturalism to conduct a research study in the City of Ottawa *in the terms of their letter and attachment* as submitted to me is in conflict with the provisions of The Ontario Human Rights Code.

As the Board is well aware I had occasion to review in very great detail the provisions of The Ontario Human Rights Code on a previous occasion when a hearing was conducted before Judge J.C. Anderson at City Hall on February 15th 1964. At that time the provisions of The Ontario Human Rights Code were thoroughly discussed with respect to the complaint made against the City in requesting that applicants for employment with the City give certain information which the complainant alleged was contrary to the provisions of The Ontario Human Rights Code.

I have again carefully considered The Ontario Human Rights Code with respect to the proposed Royal Commission on Bilingualism and Biculturalism as referred to in the Board's letter to me of March 25th, and it is my considered opinion that no conflict exists between the terms of reference of the Commission and The Ontario Human Rights Code. The purport of The Ontario Human Rights Code is to prevent discrimination in job employment and to prohibit an employer from referring to the applicant's race, creed, colour, etc. when applying for a job. I am confirmed in this opinion by the Director of the Ontario Human Rights Commission, Mr. D.H. Hill, and he has stated that in his opinion there is no conflict between the proposed inquiry by the Commission and the Ontario Human Rights Code.

> Yours truly,
>
> D.V. Hambling
> City Solicitor.

Co-Chairman to the Mayor

April 5, 1965.

His Worship Mayor Donald B. Reid
City Hall
Sussex Drive
Ottawa, Ontario

Dear Sir:

In a telephone conversation on April 2nd with the Secretary of the Board of Control, the Royal Commission was informed of the Board's recommendation to City Council concerning the Commission's projected study of the City of Ottawa.

It was told that the Board is to recommend that the Royal Commission "be allowed to confer only with the City Clerk and the Director of Personnel."

If you will refer to either the original or the amplified research outline, you will see that the Commission anticipated a more extensive examination of municipal government and administration, involving interviews with a number of civic personnel in various departments and agencies, as well as reference to personnel records.

Our present interpretation of the Board's recommendation is that it gives no guarantee of access to information coming from written records, nor does it appear to permit discussion with representatives of various civic departments and agencies. If this interpretation is correct, the Commission feels that the severe restrictions now proposed by Board of Control would so seriously limit the extent of the inquiry as to make it doubtful that this part of the study would be worth undertaking.

It is my understanding that the City Solicitor, the legal counsel for the Ontario Attorney-General's Department, and our own Commission counsel have all concurred in the opinion that the Commission's research proposal as originally designed would not contravene any provincial legislation.

I should like to emphasize once again that the Commission attaches great importance to this part of its study of the capital region.

Yours truly,

A.D. Dunton
Co-Chairman.

Board of Control Recommendation to City Council

Royal Commission on Bilingualism and Biculturalism

The Board of Control recommends that the Royal Commission on Bilingualism and Biculturalism be allowed to confer only with the City Clerk and Director of Personnel on the understanding that all their findings be made public and available in all details to the City.

Correspondence relating to the request of the Commission to conduct a Research Programme with respect to the City of Ottawa is contained in the following pages.

Council, on March 15th, referred to the Board the communication from Mr. André Laurendeau, Co-Chairman, Royal Commission on Biculturalism to His Worship the Mayor requesting co-operation with respect to a study of patterns of ethnic representation in municipal politics and language usage in municipal administration.

Council, on March 15th, also referred to the Board the communication from Mr. D.R. Cameron, Royal Commission on Bilingualism and Biculturalism submitting outline of the research programme which is envisaged for the government and administration of the City of Ottawa.

Copies of the above noted correspondence are attached as noted above. [The correspondence referred to is not reprinted here.]

City Clerk to Director of Research

April 7, 1965.

Mr. M. Oliver,
Director of Research,
Royal Commission on
Bilingualism and Biculturalism,
P.O. Box 1508,
Ottawa, Ontario.

Dear Sir:

Re: Royal Commission on Bilingualism and Biculturalism

The City Council, on the 5th instant, approved of the attached recommendation of the Board of Control with respect to the above, as amended as follows:

Moved by Alderman St. Germain, seconded by Alderman O'Regan,

That the words "and any civic elected representative and civic employee" who would voluntarily agree to be interviewed be added after the words—Director of Personnel—and included in recommendation 9(3) re Royal Commission on Bilingualism and Biculturalism.

I would further advise however, that in accordance with Procedure By-law 5499, a notice of reconsideration was filed and which will be dealt with at the next regular meeting of City Council which will take place in the Council Chamber on Tuesday, April 20th next, commencing at 7:30 o'clock p.m.

Please communicate with the undersigned should you require any additional information.

Yours truly,

A.T. Hastey,
City Clerk.

The Mayor to Co-Chairman

April 7, 1965.

Dr. A.D. Dunton,
Co-Chairman,
Royal Commission on
Bilingualism and Biculturalism,
P.O. Box 1508,
Ottawa, Ontario

Dear Dr. Dunton:

I wish to advise that your letter of April 5th was presented to and considered by City Council at its meeting held on Monday, April 5th, and that the City Clerk has indicated Council's decision to Mr. Michael Oliver, your Director of Research.

Yours sincerely,

D.B. Reid,
Mayor.

Secretary, Board of Control to Research Staff

April 14, 1965.

Mr. David R. Cameron,
Royal Commission on Bilingualism
and Biculturalism,
P.O. Box 1508,
Ottawa, Ontario.

Dear Sir:

The Board of Control would be pleased to receive a copy of any proposed questionnaire which might be submitted by your Commission to Civic employees in any research programme which might be authorized by City Council.

Your kind attention to this request would be appreciated.

Yours truly,

R.J. Gorman,
Secretary,
Board of Control.

City Clerk to Director of Research

April 21, 1965.

Mr. M. Oliver,
Director of Research,
Royal Commission on Bilingualism
and Biculturalism,
P.O. Box 1508,
Ottawa, Ontario.

Dear Sir:

Re: Royal Commission on Bilingualism and Biculturalism

I advised you on April 7th, 1965, that the City Council on the 5th instant approved of a recommendation, which was appended, with respect to the above as amended to include any civic elected representative and civic employee who would voluntarily agree to the interview, but that a notice of reconsideration had been filed in accordance with the City's Procedure By-law and which would be considered at the regular meeting to be held on April 20th, 1965.

The City Council, at its regular meeting held last evening, decided not to reconsider its decision of the 5th instant which now provides for your Commission to confer with the undersigned, the Director of Personnel and any civic elected representative and civic employee who agrees to be interviewed on the understanding that all of your Commission's findings in this regard be made public and available in all details to the City.

For any additional information, please communicate with Mr. R.J. Wilson, Director of Personnel or the undersigned.

Yours truly,

A.T. Hastey,
City Clerk.

Correspondence

Director of Research to Secretary, Board of Control

May 3, 1965.

Mr. R.J. Gorman
Secretary
Board of Control
Corporation of the City of Ottawa
Ottawa.

Dear Sir:

Mr. Cameron has shown me your letter of April 14 concerning the Board's request to receive a copy of any questionnaire that we may use at City Hall. At the moment I can only say that our research plans are under discussion, particularly with Mr. Wilson, and that the desirability of using a general questionnaire has not yet been decided. However, we shall keep the Board of Control's request in mind in the event that we decide to use one.

Yours sincerely,

Michael Oliver
Director of Research.

Memorandum to All Civic Employees

May 14, 1965.

I am instructed by the Board of Control to inform you that at the regular meeting of April 20, 1965, City Council gave authorization to the Royal Commission on Bilingualism and Biculturalism "...to confer with the City Clerk, the Director of Personnel and any civic elected representative and any civic employee who agrees to be interviewed...." All employees may be guided by this directive of Council in assisting the Royal Commission to carry out its investigation.

R.J. Wilson,
Director of Personnel.

Co-Chairmen to Board of Control

April 25, 1966.

Board of Control,
Corporation of the City of Ottawa,
City Hall,
Ottawa, Canada.

Chairman and Members of Board of Control:

In order to facilitate the completion of our study of Ottawa, members of our research department, in close cooperation with Mr. R. J. Wilson, Director of Personnel, have completed the drafting of a questionnaire to be administered to civic employees. The final result of these consultations has been a survey instrument which now has the approval of the City's Director of Personnel and representatives of the employees' associations.

In accordance with the request made in your secretary's letter of April 14, 1965, we are pleased to make the questionnaire available for the information of the Board. Copies for this purpose are already in the hands of Mr. Wilson. To avoid influencing the response to the survey, we would like to stress the need for keeping the contents of the questionnaire confidential until the survey has been completed.

Will it be satisfactory if our research department works out the final details in conjunction with your Director of Personnel so as to enable us to administer the questionnaire on or about May 10? May we take this opportunity to thank you for the cooperation which has thus far been extended to our research staff.

Yours sincerely,

A. Davidson Dunton   André Laurendeau
Co-Chairmen.

Co-Chairmen to Board of Control

June 8, 1966.

Board of Control,
Corporation of the City of Ottawa,
City Hall,
Ottawa, Ontario.

Chairman and Members of Board of Control:

You will be aware that on April 25, 1966, we sent you a request concerning the administration of a questionnaire to employees of the City of Ottawa. Our letter mentioned May 10 as a target date for the administration of the questionnaire, and your acknowledgement of the request, over the signature of Mr. Gorman, Secretary of Board of Control, was dated April 29.

Since that date, we have been most disappointed to see meeting after meeting of the Board take place without action on this request. Repeated queries by telephone on the part of our research staff have been without result.

I am sure you will understand the reasons for our concern. The Commission faces the most pressing deadlines on its research program, completion of which is essential to the decisions it must make for its final report. There is the added problem of holding research personnel in readiness to analyze the survey when a date for administration is unknown.

At the present time, the research staff have waited six weeks for your authorization to complete arrangements for the survey. In the circumstances, the Commission is forced to interpret the continuing silence of Board of Control as a refusal to permit the survey. If you feel that we have misunderstood the Board's intentions on this point, we earnestly hope that you will communicate with us without delay.

Under the present circumstances, the Commission must ask its research staff to proceed with their study of the municipal administration of Ottawa by the next best means at their disposal. Among other things, they will need to fill in certain gaps in their preliminary material on the Ottawa administration through a few further personal interviews with civic employees, in accordance with City Council's authorization of April 5, 1965.

Yours faithfully,

A. Davidson Dunton   André Laurendeau
Co-Chairmen.

Secretary, Board of Control to Co-Chairmen

June 9, 1966.

Messrs. A. Davidson Dunton and
Andre Laurendeau,
Co-Chairmen,
Royal Commission on Bilingualism and Biculturalism,
P.O. Box 1508,
Ottawa, Ontario.

Dear Sirs,

The Board of Control has considered your letter of April 25, 1966, with which you enclosed a copy of the questionnaire proposed to be circulated to civic employees in conjunction with the survey being conducted by the Royal Commission on Bilingualism and Biculturalism.

I have been requested by the Board to advise you that the Board does not feel that this questionnaire, which, in the view of the Board, is beyond the scope and intention of the original proposal, should be circulated to civic employees. It is the opinion of the Board that the original intention was to have a short sample questionnaire distributed to a limited number of civic employees only.

The Board trusts that the above explanation will clarify the matter for you.

Yours truly,

R.J. Gorman,
Secretary,
Board of Control.

Letter Sent to Heads of 18 Civic Departments

June 17, 1966.

In order to document our study of the Ottawa civic administration, we would like a series of sample forms which the City uses in its daily affairs. We would appreciate having specimens of those forms which are meant for use *within* the administration as well as those which are sent to private citizens, businesses and institutions.

We are particularly interested in obtaining specimens of any forms on which languages other than English are used. Our purpose in making this request is simply to provide the study with the documentation required to illustrate our interview findings.

We earnestly solicit your co-operation in this matter. Because of our research deadlines, we would ask that samples be submitted to the Commission at the above address at your earliest convenience and in any case not later than June 30.

Permit us to thank you in advance for your kind consideration.

Yours sincerely,

Michael Oliver
Director of Research.

Co-Chairmen to Board of Control

June 29, 1966.

Board of Control
Corporation of the City of Ottawa
City Hall
Ottawa, Ontario

Chairman and Members of Board of Control:

We are in receipt of your letter of June 9th signed by Mr. R.J. Gorman which informs us of the Board's refusal to permit the Ottawa municipal administration questionnaire to be circulated to civic employees. In explanation it is suggested that the questionnaire "is beyond the scope and intention of the original proposal."

We feel that some clarification is necessary. The purpose of the study has been neither changed nor enlarged. The principal research methods envisaged in the original research plan submitted on March 8, 1965, and in the enlarged research plan of March 25, 1965, requested by City Council were consultation of personnel files and personal interviews. No mention of a questionnaire was made until April 14, 1965, when Mr. Gorman wrote that "the Board of Control would be pleased to receive a copy of any proposed questionnaire which might be submitted by your Commission to civic employees in any research program which might be authorized by City Council."

Despite this apparent willingness of Board of Control to consider a questionnaire, the Commission did not proceed immediately to develop one. The research staff soon found, however, that they had no access whatsoever to personnel files, and that the picture that emerged from interviews alone was deemed inadequate. Only then did they begin preparation of the questionnaire that was submitted to you on April 25, 1966, after it had been pretested by our research department and approved by the City's Director of Personnel and the executives of the staff associations.

We should have hoped that the Board would have consulted with us before arbitrarily refusing a questionnaire on which much time and effort had been spent. The pressure of our research deadlines, however, forces us now to explore alternative methods.

May we, therefore, arrange to have our Director of Research and other senior research personnel meet with you, or with Mayor Reid, to discuss the alternatives? As one possibility, we should be interested in obtaining a computer print-out of certain information which may be readily available in mechanical form in your Personnel Department, together with sufficient access to personnel files to apply these data to the purposes of our study. You may wish to propose other ways of obtaining the same information.

We must stress the importance to our work schedules of settling this question as soon as possible, and not later than July 15th.

It is scarcely necessary to repeat that the Commission will inevitably report on the federal capital and thus attaches considerable importance to this study. We should sincerely regret having to report on the municipal administration of Ottawa without making every effort to present the result of our inquiry in the most complete form possible.

Yours sincerely,

André Laurendeau   A. Davidson Dunton
Co-Chairmen.

Secretary, Board of Control to Co-Chairmen

July 18, 1966.

Messrs. A. Davidson Dunton and
Andre Laurendeau,
Co-Chairmen,
Royal Commission on Bilingualism and Biculturalism,
P.O. Box 1508,
Ottawa, Ontario.

Dear Sirs,

Board of Control wishes to acknowledge receipt of your letter of June 29, further to the Board's letter of June 9 with regard to a decision of the Board not to permit a proposed questionnaire to be circulated to civic employees in conjunction with the survey being conducted by the Royal Commission on Bilingualism and Biculturalism.

It would appear that the cogent question raised in your letter is that of whether or not it might be arranged to have your Director of Research and other senior research personnel meet with the Board, or with His Worship Mayor Reid, to discuss the alternatives. Until these proposed alternatives are known, however, it is difficult to reply in this regard.

With respect to a computer print-out of certain information which may be readily available in mechanical form in the Personnel Department of the City, together with sufficient access to Personnel files to apply these data to the purposes of your study, it would seem that a computer print-out, which as far as personnel are concerned would be purely in terms of names and earnings, could not have much bearing on the problem which your Commission is investigating.

The Director of Personnel, Mr. R.J. Wilson, as I am sure you will agree, has been as completely co-operative with your Commission as was possible in the matter of making information available. The Director could not personally agree to making the Personnel files available on a free basis to outsiders, since these files have a high element of confidentiality and are in this sense his responsibility and are not available even to Heads of Departments or Members of Council on an unrestricted basis. It will be readily realized that a personnel file may contain documentation with regard to health of an individual, for example, which is made available to the Director of Personnel in the course of his official duties, but which is made available because employees realize that the material is on a confidential basis. Numerous other examples could be cited.

The Board would not wish to give any impression of restricting the legitimate enquiries of your Commission through the Director of Personnel but, nevertheless, there would have to be assurances that the confidentiality which has been placed in the Director would be respected and he obviously could not allow any person outside of his Department to have free access to the files. It is the view of the Board and the Director that personnel files are as much subject to confidentiality as would be those of the Welfare Department, for example. In both cases the interests of private persons must be protected.

The Board has endeavoured in the above explanation to clarify the points raised in your letter and trusts that you will understand its position in this matter.

Yours truly,

R.J. Gorman,
Secretary,
Board of Control.

2. HULL

Co-Chairman to the Mayor (translation)

February 26, 1965.

His Worship Mayor Marcel d'Amour,
City Hall,
Hull, Quebec.

Dear Sir:

As no doubt you are aware, the Royal Commission on Bilingualism and Biculturalism is interested in the government and administration of Ottawa and other municipalities in the area. We would like to carry out some research to determine the extent to which the capital and the surrounding area reflect the dual cultural and linguistic nature of our country. For your convenience, please find enclosed an extract from Order-in-Council 1106 (July 19, 1963) which states our terms of reference.

Concerning the municipal government and administration we would like to obtain:
(1) information on present and past representation of French and English Canadians on the municipal councils;
(2) information on the representation of the various ethnic groups and on language usage in the municipal administrations.

Mr. Jean T. Fournier and Mr. David R. Cameron, under the supervision of Dr. Kenneth D. McRae, have already begun the preliminary work and will shortly be in touch with you. May I count on the co-operation of your administration in carrying out this study?

Yours sincerely,

André Laurendeau,
Co-Chairman.

The Mayor to Co-Chairman (translation)

March 17, 1965.

Mr. André Laurendeau,
Co-Chairman,
Royal Commission on Bilingualism
and Biculturalism,
P.O. Box 1508,
Ottawa, Ontario.

Dear Mr. Laurendeau:

In reply to your letter of February 26, I am pleased to inform you that you can count on the full co-operation, not only of myself but of the council members and all municipal employees.

I hope that our humble contribution will be of use to you. I wish to take this opportunity to congratulate you on the magnificent work accomplished to date.

I am looking forward to the pleasure of meeting you in the near future.

Yours sincerely,

Marcel d'Amour
Mayor.

3. EASTVIEW

Co-Chairman to the Mayor (translation)

February 26, 1965.

His Worship Mayor Gérard Grandmaître,
City Hall,
Eastview, Ontario.

Dear Sir:

As no doubt you are aware, the Royal Commission on Bilingualism and Biculturalism is interested in the government and administration of Ottawa and other municipalities in the area. We would like to carry out some research to determine the extent to which the capital and the surrounding area reflect the dual cultural and linguistic nature of our country. For your convenience, please find enclosed an extract from Order-in-Council 1106 (July 19, 1963) which states our terms of reference.

Concerning the municipal government and administration we would like to obtain:
(1) information on present and past representation of French and English Canadians on the municipal councils;
(2) information on the representation of the various ethnic groups and on language usage in the municipal administrations.

Mr. Jean T. Fournier and Mr. David R. Cameron, under the supervision of Dr. Kenneth D. McRae, have already begun the preliminary work and will shortly be in touch with you. May I count on the co-operation of your administration in carrying out this study?

Yours sincerely,

André Laurendeau,
Co-Chairman.

Extract from City Council Minute of April 21, 1965

Resolution No. 65-177

MOVED BY: Alderman Roger Crete
SEC'D BY: W. J. Champagne
WHEREAS the city Clerk has been approached by a representative of the Commission on Bilingualism and Biculturalism to carry out certain studies within the Administration of the Corporation of the City of Eastview in accordance with the terms of reference of the said Commission; AND WHEREAS the Council of the Corporation of the City of Eastview deems it desirable that said studies be made; THEREFORE the Council of the Corporation of the City of Eastview resolves the following:
1. That the Mayor be and is hereby directed to provide to Mr. Dave Cameron, a member of the Team on the Bilingualism and Biculturalism, a letter of reference introducing him to the members of the municipal staff;
2. That the Department Heads and Staff of the Corporation of the City of Eastview are hereby asked to co-operate as much as possible with Mr. Cameron in this matter.

CARRIED

The Mayor to Municipal Staff

April 22, 1965.

To Members of Municipal Staff,
Corporation of the City of Eastview.

Council has authorized by Resolution on its meeting of April 21st, 1965 that all cooperation that can be given to Mr. Dave Cameron of the Commission on Bilingualism and Biculturalism in carrying out certain studies within the Organization of the City of Eastview, in accordance with the terms of reference of the said Commission be encouraged.

You are kindly asked, therefore, to assist Mr. Cameron so that he may complete his work here in Eastview in a satisfactory manner.

I remain,

Yours truly,

G. Grandmaître,
Mayor.

Appendix E (Chapter III) Language Usage in Selected Ottawa Municipal Agencies

While each agency of the civic administration has its own role to play in providing services to the public, some are clearly more relevant than others from the standpoint of oral and written contact with the citizen. This Appendix comprises a series of brief sketches of agencies that possess service functions likely to involve an important degree of public contact.

Three agencies in particular seem to serve as important "channels" by which the resident approaches his local government: the Civic Complaints Bureau; the City Clerk's Office which, in addition to the key role it plays in the dissemination of information, is also a major access route to the municipal council; and the Office of the Secretary to Board of Control, which occupies an analogous position in relation to the executive level of local government.

The data on the Civic Complaints Bureau are less complete than they might be; its director declined to be interviewed by Commission staff. Nevertheless, from the rather limited information at hand, this bureau appears to be among the more successful civic agencies in the provision of bilingual service. During the course of the telephone survey three calls to the Bureau were made. In one call the surveyor had to request, in English, the services of a French-speaking person, which were, however, readily available. In the other two calls, although operators who could speak English only were encountered, the calls were almost immediately transferred to a French-speaking employee.

The situation in the City Clerk's Office is, in some respects, similar. In the three telephone calls made to this agency, service in French was obtained, although in two of them the French-speaking employees appear to have served simply as interpreters, presumably because the person who could give the information required was unable to express himself adequately in French. The general impression produced during the interviews was that an effort was made to provide French-language services primarily in cases where the citizen obviously could not speak English. The spokesman for this agency reported that French-language correspondence was usually answered in English.

In response to our request for sample documentation, this agency submitted several documents using French, the majority of which were promotional and tourist-oriented. One of these documents was similar to the city tourist map mentioned above: the heading was bilingual while the information contained within appeared exclusively in English. No French-language versions of the forms used by the Office were reported.

Little can be said with accuracy of the Office of the Secretary to Board of Control. An interview with a spokesman of this agency was refused, as were the checklists concerning all salaried staff. No samples of documentation could be obtained. The one call made to this agency during the telephone survey met with a complete lack of success. In the course of this call, an employee remarked, in English, that there was no one in the office capable of dealing with a request in French.

The Tourist and Convention Bureau appears to fulfil a particular kind of service function in its dissemination of specialized information about the city. Two of the four calls made to the Bureau were adequately handled, though there was some delay before the calls were transferred to a French-speaking person; in the third instance service was obtained that was qualitatively inferior to that available in English, since the employee, though co-operative, had a grasp of French inadequate to deal with the questions; in the remaining case, service in French could not be obtained at all.

The overall impression gained from the interview with the Tourist Bureau is that it is primarily an English-language agency serving an English-speaking clientele. Some attempt, however, seems to be made to provide services in French; thus during the interview it was reported that the policy was to answer French-language correspondence in French. Although this agency did not reply to our request for sample documentation, material gathered at other times by members of the research staff demonstrates that some literature, designed primarily for tourists, is available in French. The range of material in English, however, appears to be far wider.

The changes in the language of the forms employed by the Tax and Water Revenue Branch of the Treasury Department were discussed earlier. Of equal interest are the services provided orally by this agency. Two calls were made during the telephone survey. In both cases adequate service was obtained, though in one instance the employee attempted to ascertain whether or not the caller could speak English.

The interview with the Assessment Commissioner's Office gave the impression that some attempt is made to provide French-language services on the informal or unofficial level, although on the official plane little if any recognition is accorded the French language. The other available data tend to support this impression: in the one telephone call made to this agency service in French was obtained, though only after some insistence.

The sample forms submitted by this agency appear in English only. At least to some degree this "formal unilingualism" seems to be a function of the institutional context within which the agency operates; for, as the spokesman for the department pointed out during the interview, there are statutory requirements in the composition of these documents. In many cases the form itself and, therefore, the language employed on it are prescribed by law (*see* 43 and 65). It seems anomalous, however, that while the 1967 tax and water bills are in bilingual form, the assessment notices issued in 1967 for the tax year 1968, which can affect the legal rights of the citizen more directly, continue to appear in English only.

Reference was made above to the roles played by languages other than English and French in the documents of the Department of Health. In several respects the position of French, though far stronger than that of the other languages, is not qualitatively different. Analysis of the documentation submitted by this agency suggests that a considerable body of external forms and informational material exists in French. All internal forms used by the department are evidently available in English only.

During the telephone survey seven calls were made to this agency and its several subdivisions. In six of the calls some form of French-language service was obtained. Only in two calls, however, was the service as readily available as it would have been to an English-language caller. In the remaining four cases difficulties were encountered due either to the employees' attempts to handle the call in English or to their inadequate command of the French language.

According to the interview with a spokesman of the Public Welfare Department, a definite effort is made to provide services in French. Thus, French-language correspondence appears to be answered exclusively in French, though translations are made by the Department for internal use. Further, a relatively well articulated policy by which telephone calls in French are dealt with by bilingual personnel has been developed. This latter point was corroborated by the one telephone call made to this agency during the survey, which met with adequate service.

The language of written usage in this department, however, is almost completely English. Apart from one form with a French-language section which was obtained during the interview, no other documents in French were reported. All the sample forms submitted to us were in English only. Here again the institutional context appears to contribute heavily to this "official unilingualism." Many of the forms, ranging from applications for assistance under provincial law to commitment forms for the mentally ill, originate with, and are prescribed by, the province of Ontario. To quote from the letter which accompanied the submission of documentation: "You will see from examination that many of these are actually provincial welfare department forms. Their use is either prescribed or made available to us."*

Although the documentation submitted by the Recreation and Parks Department suggests that its internal forms exist only in English, a spokesman for this agency reported during the interview that almost all of their publicity and informational material destined for the public is available in both languages. Further, there is a standing policy of handling French-language correspondence completely in French.

During the telephone survey five calls were made to this department and its branches. In one of these calls service in French could not be obtained, although in three others requests in French were handled in a fully adequate manner. In the remaining case service in French was obtained, though only after insistence on the part of the caller.

---

*Letter from head of Public Welfare Department, July 4, 1966.

Appendix F (Chapter III)   **The Ottawa Police Department and
                                         Ottawa Transportation Commission**

The Ottawa Police Department*

The Ottawa Police Department operates not as a part of the civic administration, but under a Police Commission. In 1965 it had 460 men in uniform and 40 civilian employees. Of the total staff, 142 were fluently bilingual. Since all employees were salaried and since no information as to the distribution between English and French according to rank or salary was available, no comparisons with other departments are possible in these respects.

The chief estimated that the demand for French in the daily activities of the force amounted to about 10 per cent of its total business with the public. Most of this was in the form of inquiries and questions concerning traffic directions addressed to patrolmen. In addition, domestic work and accident investigation had to be conducted to a considerable degree in French. In order to increase the ability of the police force to handle these demands, the Police Department had instituted its own French-language training course, concentrating on idiomatic French of particular relevance to police work. Up to that date some 75 members of the present force had graduated from this voluntary course.

Most of the telephone operators were bilingual and if a call in French reached an English officer he would direct it to someone who could answer it in French. Written inquiries and letters in French, which came rather frequently (particularly in connection with parking tickets), were answered in French. However, a translation of both the letter and the answer was made.

The chief indicated that a person's ability to speak French was not a consideration in hiring and promotion except for a few positions where bilingual personnel were absolutely necessary (for example, telephone operators, information officers, and the staff of the licence office which sells business and other licences for the city). In spite of the fact that language was for most positions not a factor in recruitment, the chief indicated that in terms of language resources the force was well balanced, with each of the major European languages having representation.

---

* Based on an interview with the Chief of Police, 1965.

Although our original study did not examine the administrative structure of the Police Department, this question was the subject of an editorial in the *Ottawa Journal* on November 28, 1966, which noted that of the 19 officers then in the upper echelons of the Department, only two were of French mother tongue. It suggested further that "the lack of sufficient French representation is wrong." The reasons for urging special attention to this aspect of administration are worth quoting:

> The policeman is the embodiment of the law. He is often an arbiter who becomes involved in the most difficult areas of human relationships. The language of a police officer is particularly important because people dealing with the police are often under stress.
>
> The Ottawa Police Department is said to have been able to recruit some excellent young French-speaking constables. That is encouraging. But more should be done to have the force on all its levels reflect the character of the city. It is vital for the good functioning and health of the police force itself that it be a kind of extension of the citizens themselves.

The Ottawa Transportation Commission*

The O.T.C. is a public utility directed and supervised by a three-man Commission, and administered by a general manager. In 1965 it had slightly over 600 employees. Of these, 536 were wage earners, mostly bus drivers and maintenance workers. There were 77 salaried employees, including the route and shop supervisors. Table A shows the distribution according to mother tongue.

Table A. Ottawa Transportation Commission, mother tongue of wage and salaried employees, 1965

Mother tongue	Total staff		Wage earners %	Salaried employees %
	N	%		
Total	613	100	100	100
English	310	50.6	46.3	80.5
French	279	45.4	49.2	19.5
Others	24	3.9	4.5	0.0

Source: Information supplied by the general manager.

The imbalance between salaried employees of English and French mother tongues was even stronger if, as the general manager suggested, the supervisors were excluded from this group. Only six out of 43 of the Commission's clerks, secretaries, technical and professional staff were of French mother tongue.

---

* Based on an interview with the general manager, 1965.

The internal working language of the Commission was English. Even letters and inquiries directed to the Commission in French were reported to be answered in English, because no translation facilities were available. The only exception reported was that the telephone operators were bilingual and could provide information orally in both languages.

As might be expected, the bus drivers used French considerably during their work. With the exception of schedules, all promotional and informational material put out by the Commission was bilingual. The same was true of all bus markings and stop markings. The bilingual red and white stop markings, first introduced in 1964 and now distributed throughout Ottawa, stand in visible contrast to the city's unilingual traffic and street signs.

With respect to hiring and promotion, the general manager insisted that language played no role whatsoever. Since the salaries and wages of the Commission were quite competitive, there was no need to advertise for staff. Vacancies were always filled from a long list of applications; qualification and rank on the waiting list were the only criteria.

Appendix G (Chapter IV)   Tables A to E

Table A. Municipalities in the Ottawa metropolitan area, population and municipal administration, by mother tongue, percentages

Municipality	Municipal population (1961)						Municipal administration (1966)					
	Total		Mother tongue				Total		Mother tongue			
			English	French	Other				English	French	Other	Not stated
	N	%	%	%	%		N	%	%	%	%	%
Eastview	24,555	100	34	61	5		107	100	12	87	1	—
Gloucester	18,301	100	54	40	6		74	100	74	20	3	3
Nepean	19,753	100	89	4	7		165	100	85	7	2	6
Ottawa	268,206	100	70	21	9		2,676	100	66	30	4	—
Rockcliffe Park	2,084	100	85	10	5		13	100	85	15	—	—
Aylmer	6,286	100	41	56	3		34	100	12	88	—	—
Deschênes	2,090	100	30	68	2		4	100	25	50	25	—
Gatineau	13,022	100	12	87	1		77	100	—	97	—	3
Hull	56,929	100	8	90	2		147	100	3	95	1	1
Lucerne	5,762	100	52	45	3		17	100	41	59	—	—
Pte-Gatineau	8,854	100	3	96	1		43	100	2	98	—	—
Templeton	2,965	100	14	85	1		5	100	—	—	—	100
West Templeton	943	100	37	62	1		0	—	—	—	—	—
Total Ontario	332,899	100	68	24	8		3,035	100	66	30	4	—
Total Quebec	96,851	100	14	84	2		327	100	6	91	1	3
Total M.A.	429,750	100	56	38	6		3,362	100	60	36	3	1

Sources: Municipalities: Census of Canada, 1961; Catalogue 95-528.
         Administrations: Ottawa—Tape 2, Table 1, 42.
                   Others—Employee checklists, 1966.

Table B. Municipalities in the Ottawa metropolitan area, municipal servants able to give service in English or French, percentages

	Knowledge of English				Municipality	Total employees		Knowledge of French			
Fluent	Considerable	A little	None	Not stated		N	%	Fluent	Considerable	A little	None	Not stated
49	31	18	–	2	Eastview	107	100	84	7	6	1	2
86	8	3	–	3	Gloucester	74	100	19	7	27	43	4
94	1	–	–	5	Nepean	165	100	7	4	8	76	6
99			1		Ottawa*	2,676	100		38		62	
92	–	8	–	–	Rockcliffe	13	100	23	–	23	54	–
–	100	–	–	–	Aylmer	34	100	–	94	3	3	–
100	–	–	–	–	Deschênes	4	100	50	–	–	50	–
20	26	30	24	–	Gatineau	77	100	21	77	–	–	2
73	18	8	–	1	Hull	147	100	93	1	5	1	–
71	23	6	–	–	Lucerne	17	100	71	–	6	23	–
26	30	19	23	2	Pte-Gatineau	43	100	40	60	–	–	–
–	–	–	–	5	Templeton	5	100	–	–	–	–	5
–	–	–	–	–	W. Templeton	0	–	–	–	–	–	–
80	11	6	–	3	Ontario excluding Ottawa	359	100	33	5	12	46	4
	98		2		Total Ontario	3,035	100		38		62	
46	30	13	9	2	Total Quebec	327	100	82	13	2	2	–
64	20	10	4	3	M.A. excluding Ottawa	686	100	58	6	7	25	3
	96		4	1	Total M.A.	3,362	100		42		56	1

Sources: Ottawa: Tape 2, Table 1.
Other municipalities: Employee checklists, 1966.

* Ottawa percentages based on official languages as recorded by the census, e.g., a fluent or considerable knowledge of English includes those who gave English as their official language and also those who were recorded as having both French and English.

Appendices 256

Table C. Municipalities in the Ottawa metropolitan area, municipal servants by second-language knowledge, percentages

Municipality	Total employees		Knowledge of second language					Sum of "fluent" and "considerable"	Sum of "little," "none" and "not stated"
	N	%	Fluent	Considerable	A little	None	Not stated		
Eastview	107	100	43	32	22	1	2	75	25
Gloucester	74	100	11	12	30	43	4	23	77
Nepean	165	100	7	4	8	75	7	11	89
Ottawa*	2,676	100	37					37	63
Rockcliffe Park	13	100	15	–	31	54	–	15	85
Aylmer	34	100	–	94	3	3	–	94	6
Deschênes	4	100	50	–	–	50	–	50	50
Gatineau	77	100	19	26	29	23	3	45	55
Hull	147	100	73	18	8	–	2	90	10
Lucerne	17	100	41	24	12	23	–	65	35
Pte-Gatineau	43	100	23	33	19	23	2	56	44
Templeton	5	100	–	–	–	–	5	–	100
W. Templeton	0	100	–	–	–	–	–	–	–
Ontario excluding Ottawa	359	100	19	14	17	46	4	32	68
Total Ontario	3,035	100	36			63	1	36	64
Total Quebec	327	100	43	29	13	11	3	72	28
M.A. excluding Ottawa	686	100	30	21	16	29	4	51	49
Total M.A.	3,362	100	40			60	1	40	60

Sources: Ottawa: Tape 2, Table 1.
Other municipalities: Employee checklists, 1966
* For Ottawa, those who were recorded as having both English and French as their official languages at the census come under the "fluent" or "considerable" columns; those who recorded only English, only French or neither come under the remaining columns.

Tables A to E

Table D. Municipalities in the Ottawa metropolitan area, municipal servants by job classification and bilingualism (excluding protective services)

Municipality	Total employees			Wage-earner			Secretarial			Clerical			Technical			Professional			Supervisory			Not stated
	1*	2*	3*	1	2	3	1	2	3	1	2	3	1	2	3	1	2	3	1	2	3	
Eastview	50	29	58%	13	2	15%	4	4	100%	10	9	90%	13	5	39%	4	4	100%	6	5	83%	—
Gloucester	36	5	14	11	3	27	6	0	0	4	1	25	4	0	0	8	1	13	2	0	0	1
Nepean	102	12	12	55	8	15	6	1	17	10	1	10	13	0	0	3	0	0	14	2	14	1
Ottawa**	990	276	28	72	24	33	66	15	23	180	55	31	300	87	29	149	45	30	174	50	29	49
Rockcliffe Park	13	2	15	8	2	25	3	0	0	—	—	—	—	—	—	—	—	—	2	0	0	—
Aylmer	20	19	95	10	10	100	3	3	100	—	—	—	1	1	100	—	—	—	2	1	50	4
Deschênes	4	2	50	—	—	—	1	1	100	—	—	—	2	0	0	1	1	100	—	—	—	—
Gatineau	59	24	41	35	5	14	2	2	100	12	8	67	8	7	88	2	2	100	—	—	—	—
Hull	66	51	77	10	4	40	9	4	44	26	24	92	6	5	83	5	5	100	10	9	90	—
Lucerne	8	3	38	5	1	20	—	—	—	3	2	67	—	—	—	—	—	—	—	—	—	—
Pte-Gatineau	27	11	41	12	1	8	2	2	100	5	3	60	2	0	0	—	—	—	6	5	83	—
Templeton	5	—	—	—	—	—	—	—	—	—	—	—	—	—	—	—	—	—	—	—	—	5
West Templeton	0	0	0	—	—	—	—	—	—	—	—	—	—	—	—	—	—	—	—	—	—	—
Total Ontario	1,191	324	27	159	39	25	85	20	24	204	66	32	330	92	28	164	50	30	198	57	29	51
Total Quebec	189	110	58	72	21	29	17	12	71	46	37	80	19	13	68	8	8	100	18	15	83	9
Total M.A.	1,380	434	31	231	60	26	102	32	31	250	103	41	349	105	30	172	58	34	216	72	33	60

Source: Employee checklists.

* Column 1: number of employees in category; column 2: number of bilingual staff in category; column 3: number of bilingual staff expressed as percentage of total staff in category.

** Census job classifications do not correspond with those used in the checklists. In order to make comparisons, the admittedly incomplete checklists filled out by the Ottawa administration are analyzed in this table. These did not measure the degree of knowledge of English. Thus, for all the municipalities except Ottawa, the criterion of bilingualism will be a "fluent" or "considerable" knowledge of the respondents' second language. For Ottawa the criterion will be all persons of French mother tongue and those of all other mother tongues recording a "fluent" or "considerable" knowledge of French.

Table E. Municipalities in the Ottawa metropolitan area, municipal servants by degree of public contact and bilingualism (excluding protective services)

Municipality	Total employees			No public contact			Contact less than once a day			Contact more than once a day			Not stated***
	1*	2*	3*	1	2	3	1	2	3	1	2	3	
Eastview	50	29	58 %	21	3	14 %	1	0	0 %	28	26	93 %	—
Gloucester	36	5	14	—	—	—	3	0	0	32	5	16	1
Nepean	102	12	12	14	3	21	33	5	15	46	4	9	9
Ottawa**	990	276	28	122	36	30	195	52	27	599	181	30	74
Rockcliffe Park	13	2	15	—	—	—	—	—	—	12	2	17	1
Aylmer	20	19	95	10	10	100	4	4	100	5	4	80	1
Deschênes	4	2	50	—	—	—	1	0	0	3	2	67	—
Gatineau	59	24	41	27	5	19	3	1	33	29	18	62	—
Hull	66	51	77	3	0	0	8	3	38	54	48	89	1
Lucerne	8	3	38	5	1	20	—	—	—	3	2	67	—
Pte-Gatineau	27	11	41	—	—	—	15	2	13	12	9	75	—
Templeton	5	—	—	—	—	—	—	—	—	—	—	—	5
West Templeton	0	0	0	—	—	—	—	—	—	—	—	—	—
Total Ontario	1,191	324	27	157	42	27	232	57	25	717	218	30	85
Total Quebec	189	110	58	45	16	36	31	10	32	106	83	78	7
Total M.A.	1,380	434	31	202	58	29	263	67	25	823	301	37	92

Source: Employee checklists.

* Column 1: number of employees in category; column 2: number of bilingual staff in category; column 3: number of bilingual staff expressed as percentage of total staff in category.

** For the criterion used for Ottawa, see Table D, note **

*** The "not stated" column may vary between Table D and Table E on account of partial responses.

Appendix H (Chapter V)　　　　　　　　　　National Capital Commission
　　　　　　　　　　　　　　　　　　　　　　Expenditures, 1947-67*

Expenditures for development and improvement within the National Capital Region, April 1, 1947 to March 31, 1967: A. Annual Expenditures; B. Total Expenditures.

A. Annual Expenditures

Fiscal year	Expenditure	Fiscal year	Expenditure
1947-48	$ 370,638	1957-58	$ 4,533,857
1948-49	936,833	1958-59	7,740,285
1949-50	1,146,200	1959-60	13,758,703
1950-51	1,634,074	1960-61	11,862,201
1951-52	1,832,964	1961-62	11,484,739
1952-53	1,911,536	1962-63	16,933,984
1953-54	2,678,623	1963-64	21,852,600
1954-55	5,508,955	1964-65	18,582,674
1955-56	4,612,787	1965-66	25,297,115
1956-57	3,422,380	1966-67	33,352,247

*Source: Charts appended to the National Capital Commission's *Annual Report,* 1966-67, Part II.

Appendices

B. Total Expenditures

CUMULATIVE TOTAL 1947–67	$189,453,395
Interest on loans to acquire property	17,356,473
Miscellaneous maintenance	1,126,838
Assistance to municipalities, construction projects and grants for sewers and water mains.	14,579,104
Miscellaneous construction Commission properties	25,154,471
Relocation of railway facilities	35,634,719
Mackenzie King Bridge	1,351,548
Property acquisitions	94,250,242

DETAILS OF PROJECTS

Grants to Ottawa for construction of sewers and water mains in advance of need. Total 2,758,000, paid to date	2,685,971
Grant to Ottawa for construction of sewers to the sewage disposal site at Green Creek to alleviate polution of the Ottawa River paid in full	5,000,000
Share of cost of underground wiring – Downtown Ottawa	260,298
Grant to Nepean for construction of a new sewer and disposal plant paid in full	160,000
Contribution re construction of Bytown bridges and improvements to Sussex Drive	966,315
Contribution re construction of new Bronson Ave. – Canal Bridge	639,313
Contribution re construction of Riverside Drive	1,205,842
Improvements to Ottawa and Hull approaches to Chaudiere Bridge	797,603
Contribution re construction of Dunbar Bridge	190,815
Landscaping and demolition of buildings for the Queensway	456,379
Demolition of buildings for approaches to Macdonald-Cartier Bridge	200,695
Share of cost of structure at junction of Carling Ave. and proposed Western Parkway	378,956
Grants to historical societies	77,564
Miscellaneous assistance	437,671
Miscellaneous research and studies	124,114
Confederation Square changes	777,019
LeBreton Flats – studies, etc.	220,549

DETAILS OF PROJECTS

Parkways in Gatineau Park	5,918,547
Lac des Fées Parkway	507,770
Development of Hogs Back Park	523,636
Development of Hull Parks	786,394
Gatineau Park (improvement of park facilities)	1,340,554
Ottawa River Parkway	7,220,472
Improvements to LeBreton Flats	463,815
Improvements in the Greenbelt	412,188
Miscellaneous projects	6,452,786
Improvements to historic properties	348,972
Col. By Drive	1,179,337

DETAILS OF PROPERTY ACQUISITIONS

Confederation Square	3,779,281
Eastern Parkway	2,112,138
Gatineau Park	5,699,712
Greenbelt in Ontario	35,587,827
Historic Sites	3,157
Lucerne Parkway	606,564
Philemon Wright Parkway – Hull	941,604
Hull General lands	877,164
Industrial and railway sites, Twp. of Gloucester	429,989
Mackenzie King Bridge	270,962
Miscellaneous sites	2,247,338
Approaches to Macdonald-Cartier Bridge	2,015,618
Northern Entrance-Hull	631,349
New passenger railway terminal at Hurdman	819,911
Ottawa River Parkway	4,640,810
Queensway	4,541,264
Rideau River Parkway	2,694,088
LeBreton Flats	18,012,380
Station Boulevard	243,426
Sussex Drive	5,149,603
Western Parkway	1,004,151
Central Business District – Ottawa	408,626
Deschenes-Britannia Bridge	1,066,273
Col. By Drive extension	406,782
Hull-Lucerne	60,225

Appendix I (Chapter V) — Property Acquisitions by the National Capital Commission

Number of parcels expropriated and purchased by the National Capital Commission in Quebec and Ontario, by project, February 1959 to August 1967

QUEBEC

Project	Number of Parcels Exprop.	Number of Parcels Purchased	Purpose
Gatineau Park	13	156	park and parkway
Northern entrance, Route #11	27	9	highway right-of-way
Deschênes-Britannia Bridge	115	–	bridge approach and parkway
Macdonald-Cartier Bridge	50	–	bridge approach
Philemon Wright	15	–	parkway
Railway relocation	1	–	railway connection
Lucerne Parkway	–	2	parkway
Totals	221	167	

ONTARIO

Project	Number of Parcels Exprop.	Number of Parcels Purchased	Purpose
Ottawa River Parkway – West	4	8	parkway
– East	49	–	parkway
Macdonald-Cartier Bridge	118	–	bridge approach and government bldg. site
Sussex Drive	24	–	historic
Stanley-Mackay	29	–	government bldg. site and park
LeBreton Flats	283	–	government bldg. sites and parkway
Victoria Island – Richmond Landing	3	1	historic and park
Colonel By Drive	3	1	parkway
Queensway	37	80	highway right-of-way
Confederation Square	16	3	government bldg. sites
Eastern Parkway	2	3	parkway – Rideau River crossing
Western Parkway	4	3	parkway – Rideau River crossing
Rideau River	–	2	park
Railway relocation	–	1	railway connection
Miscellaneous	–	3	
Greenbelt	745	603	
Totals	1317	708	

Source: Figures supplied by the National Capital Commission.

Appendix J (Chapter V)

Payments to the City of Ottawa

Summary of tax and grant in lieu of tax payments to the city of Ottawa by the federal government for 1961-66 fiscal years of the city (thousands of dollars)

Property for which taxes or grants in lieu of taxes paid	Amount of payment*					
	1961	1962	1963	1964	1965	1966
Total payments	$6474	$7086	$7246	$8011	$8720	$9180
Departmental properties**	5484	5942	6187	6691	7247	7607
Crown corporation properties***	865	1011	917	1133	1268	1353
Diplomatic premises and residences of heads of missions	125	133	142	187	205	220

Source: Information supplied by the Department of Finance.

* Taxes included are real property tax (in respect of certain Crown corporations), local improvements, redevelopment charge, fire supply charge and sewer surcharge for water. Payments on Crown properties rented to or by the federal government are excluded. Amounts included for fire supply charge and sewer surcharge are estimates for all years. Also, the 1966 payments for other taxes of Atomic Energy of Canada, the Canadian Broadcasting Corporation and foreign governments are estimates. Payments by the National Capital Commission are estimates for all years.

** Includes payments for National Research Council properties.

*** Includes Air Canada, Atomic Energy of Canada, Bank of Canada, Canadian Broadcasting Corporation, Canadian National Railways, Central Mortgage and Housing Corporation, Eldorado Mining and Refining, and the National Capital Commission.

Appendix K (Chapter V)   Case Studies of Federal-Municipal Relations*

1. The Zoning By-law Issue

The controversy over zoning policies in the city of Ottawa highlights at least one of the qualities which have in the past characterized the relationship between the municipal administration and a major agency of the federal government, the National Capital Commission. Perhaps the element most in evidence was the deep-seated lack of co-ordination between the two bodies. Worthy of note as well, however, was the strong support which the National Capital Commission obtained from the Prime Minister when city initiatives involved him in the issue.

On September 9, 1964, the *Ottawa Citizen* carried a short report indicating that earlier in September the National Capital Commission had sought exemption from the comprehensive zoning by-law AZ-64, then being formulated by the city. The Commission was reportedly basing its request on the fact that the federal and provincial governments are exempt from municipal by-laws.

The initial reaction from City Hall appears to have been somewhat hostile. The Mayor's response was to write privately to the Prime Minister. It would appear that the National Capital Commission was approached neither formally nor informally, but was "leapfrogged" by the city in favour of the Prime Minister himself. The latter's reply was received by the municipal authorities on September 8 but was not made public.

At the municipal council meeting the following week, according to the *Ottawa Journal* of September 16, city council rejected the 13 National Capital Commission objections to the new by-law. Until that time the federal planning body had with few exceptions abided by all municipal regulations, but it now sought to have town property exempted completely from the terms of the new by-law. The Mayor was quoted as saying: "So far as we are concerned, they can come forward with individual requests for exemptions as they have been doing." The same edition of the newspaper carried a

---

* Source: Material gathered from *Le Droit, Ottawa Citizen,* and *Ottawa Journal.*

complaint by the Mayor, in another connection, that the city was not being informed of some policy changes made by the National Capital Commission: "In a recurring complaint the Mayor feels there should be closer liaison between the two bodies." Again she announced her intention of writing to the Prime Minister rather than the Commission.

In an editorial which appeared the following day, the *Ottawa Journal* commented:

> The discussion of Council might have shown greater awareness of the special status of Crown lands. The brusque treatment does no good to the relationship between Crown and town which is so vital to the progress of this city.... The city considers that it had "the right and duty to indicate publicly its opinion with respect to the use of all lands under its jurisdiction, including Federal lands." Of course it has! But this could still be done while recognizing the special position of the Federal Government's holdings.

On Monday, September 21, the *Ottawa Citizen* reported a letter from the Prime Minister to the Mayor in which he asserted the National Capital Commission's independent and extraordinary position, and its ultimate supremacy in the zoning conflict: "If the NCC and the city find themselves in a deadlocked dispute, the letter says, the will of the NCC will prevail. But the NCC will continue to follow city zoning bylaws whenever possible—because it chooses to do so; not because it has to."

The National Capital Commission's request for blanket exemption from the city's by-laws was to clarify on official documents the powers already held by the Commission, the Prime Minister was reported to have said.

In an editorial entitled "The City and the NCC," printed the following day, the *Ottawa Citizen* summed up the issue:

> The debate between civic and federal authorities ... once again points up the need for closer liaison between the two levels of government.... As long as the city and the NCC keep at arms length—a situation due largely to the unco-operative attitude shown by Mayor Whitton—there will always be obstacles in the way of orderly development of the national capital.

2. The Lower Town East Urban Renewal Issue

Early in November 1965, press reports began to appear that urban renewal for Lower Town East, a predominantly French-language neighbourhood within the city of Ottawa, was in the planning stages. According to an article in *Le Droit* of November 9, municipal staff members had met with representatives of the Central Mortgage and Housing Corporation to discuss the project. The article went on to suggest that, although initial reaction to the plan by the people affected was favourable, there were some reservations. There appears to have been some anxiety that the residents of the area would be dispersed; worry that the renovation would decrease representation of French-speaking Canadians on the municipal council; and concern that the secondary school planned for the area be bilingual.

Although more details of the project were publicized the following month, its full scope did not become apparent until the latter part of March 1966, when a detailed plan was submitted to the city council. Covering some 186 acres and affecting 9,400 people, according to the report submitted to council, the project was expected to cost some $15,000,000. Although some aspects of the plan had been public knowledge for approximately four months, the project as a whole appears to have had relatively clear sailing up to this point. The particular qualities of the neighbourhood had been recognized and the city authorities had made a major effort, to the point of distributing a bilingual pamphlet outlining their plans, to keep their lines of communication open with the residents of the area.

In an editorial dated March 23, 1966, the *Ottawa Citizen* wrote:

The city rightly plans to give those displaced by the Lower Town scheme the first opportunity to use the new facilities that will be located in the area. More than 700 public housing units will be built.... One of the reasons that Lower Town people are not raising a fuss over the city's plans is that they have been kept fully in the picture.... Civic officials have learned the hard way that good public relations can be a major factor in ensuring the success of an urban renewal scheme.

A commentator writing in the same day's edition of *Le Droit* expressed a similar view:

Le Droit recently approved the urban renewal project for Ottawa's Lower Town, on condition *sine qua non* that the social character of the area be fully respected. Now, as the report has taken into account this basic factor, we congratulate the civic officials for having already approved in principle this vast program, and hope that it may be completely realized. (Translation)

Some five days later, however, in its edition of March 28, *Le Droit* carried several articles suggesting that although the project had the general support of the Lower Town residents, objections were being raised concerning the relative lack of self-contained dwellings. Fears were also expressed as to the maintenance of the neighbourhood's French-Canadian character.

The issue hung fire for the next two months while the municipal authorities sought to obtain provincial authority to proceed and at the same time discussed federal support of the project with the Central Mortgage and Housing Corporation. In June, however, it flared to life again. On June 15, the *Ottawa Citizen* reported the opinions of a group representing the residents, the Lower Town East Ratepayers Association. The complaints centred on the lack of self-contained dwellings, which was encouraging many people to leave and thus threatening the character of the neighbourhood, and confusion over the language of instruction in the proposed new school. *Le Droit*'s coverage of the event also contained an accusation by the president of the Association of duplicity on the part of the municipality. He maintained, according to the article, that city officials were trying to convince provincial authorities and Central Mortgage and Housing Corporation officials that the project had encountered little opposition in spite of the fact that, early in June, the city had received a petition of objection with some 500 signatures.

The following day, June 16, members of the Association met with the Mayor and other civic officials to discuss the issue. According to the *Ottawa Citizen,* the same two complaints were stressed: the residents' objections to new housing and confusion over the language of instruction in the projected school.

Shortly thereafter the Central Mortgage and Housing Corporation stepped in. In its edition of June 24 the *Ottawa Citizen* carried an article stating that the previous day the federal agency had requested the city to call in special urban design consultants: "CMHC wants the consultants to study all details of land use."

The following week, according to the *Ottawa Journal* of June 28, the Ottawa Board of Control reluctantly agreed to a four-month study by outside consultants. Few other options were open to them as the approval of the Central Mortgage and Housing Corporation was required before authorization by the Ontario Municipal Board could be obtained. In an editorial appearing the same day the *Ottawa Journal* voiced qualified approval of the position taken by the Corporation, as did the *Ottawa Citizen* two days later.

On July 5, according to an article which appeared the following day in the *Ottawa Citizen,* the Collegiate Institute Board announced its intention of approaching the provincial Minister of Education to seek permission to open a high school in which French would be the primary language of instruction. This seems to have been something of an effort to win over the residents of Lower Town—an impression reinforced by the second of a series of articles on the issue written some nine weeks later by an *Ottawa Citizen* staff writer.

> To overcome some of this opposition the CIB said it would operate its proposed school as a bilingual school. . . . Apart from French language courses, the department of education only allows for social studies and Latin to be taught in French. Other subjects can be taught in French by special permission. But the CIB hasn't applied for this special permission yet nor indicated how many subjects it would attempt to teach in French.

By September 1966, little further progress had been made, the consultants' report not being due until late October or early November. In the meantime, however, a new factor had been added to the overall confusion. A number of Lower Town residents, attempting to relocate elsewhere had signed agreements to buy new homes, relying for down payments on the money they were to receive from the expropriation of their former residences. The delay in the project, however, meant that expropriation proceedings were not begun on schedule and thus the money was not available. Yet these people had made commitments to buy and several were reportedly facing legal action. According to an *Ottawa Citizen* article dated September 29, the city and the province were willing to go ahead in advance of full approval of the plan. However, the article quoted the Mayor as saying that the Central Mortgage and Housing Corporation "cannot legally advance money for a project not fully approved." According to the same source: "The Mayor has approached the Cabinet asking for an immediate payment from the federal government to be deducted from the CMHC contribution later. 'This seems the only way around the problem,' the Mayor said. 'I have discussed it with Public Works Minister McIlraith and I am very optimistic we will get the results we want.' "

There the matter rested at the end of September 1966. Although a year later the issue is still unresolved, the early stages of the project outlined above do provide an example of the interaction that takes place between the different levels of government.

3. Enforcement of Safety Regulations

One event which illustrates some of the human costs of the many overlapping jurisdictions in the capital area occurred in the spring of 1966. On April 8, while employed on a project in downtown Ottawa, Maurice Cardinal, a demolition worker, fell from a height of six storeys to his death.

At the inquest which followed it became apparent that safety regulations on the job had been largely ignored. One of the reasons appears to have been a language barrier: the French-speaking president of the demolition firm was quoted in the *Ottawa Citizen,* June 7, 1966, as testifying that he "had some trouble understanding the city inspector because he spoke fast."

In view of the legal powers which can be applied when such breaches occur, the failure of the firm to abide by the safety regulations does not explain why work was allowed to continue. According to the newspaper reports covering the inquest, the city of Ottawa inspectors were fully aware of the lack of attention which had been paid to the provincial Safety Act, but felt they could not act because the demolition was taking place on federal property and they were uncertain of their jurisdiction. On the other hand, the staff of the Department of Public Works, which had issued the contract for the job, were under the impression that the city was responsible for safety inspection. The result was that the safety regulations were enforced by neither the city of Ottawa nor the federal government.

Unfortunately the Cardinal case is not unique. After another accident which killed two workers at the new Ottawa station on August 5, 1966, a coroner's jury ruled that one of the main factors responsible was an absence of a clearly established jurisdiction over safety inspection on projects carried out on federal property (see *Ottawa Citizen,* January 31, February 1, 2, 3, 1967).

Following the accident at the station the question of responsibility was raised in the courts and an Ottawa magistrate ruled that provincial safety inspectors have no jurisdiction over contractors working on federal projects on federally-owned land. The case was then carried to the Ontario Court of Appeal, but the Ontario government withdrew from proceedings before the case was heard. As a result provincial law could not be enforced on federal projects and equivalent federal legislation was lacking (see *Ottawa Journal,* October 14 and editorial of October 17, 1967).

Appendix L (Chapter V)　　　　　　　　Comparative Federal Expenditures

Federal expenditures in the cities of Ottawa and Hull in the ten-year period, 1954-64

	OTTAWA	HULL	HULL COMPARED TO OTTAWA
POPULATION (Census of Canada, 1961)	268,206	56,929	21.23%
EXPENDITURES:			
1. Department of Public Works:			
a) Number of buildings (including additions)	80	1	1.25
b) Total cost of buildings	$114,930,000	$ 735,624	0.64
c) Special grants (Queensway, bridges, sewers, etc.)	6,043,571	----	0.00
d) Interprovincial projects (Macdonald-Cartier Bridge, maintenance of Chaudière Bridge)	1,105,218	1,105,218	100.00
Total	$122,078,789	$1,840,842	1.51
2. Department of Finance:			
Municipal taxes (including those paid to the Hull School Board)	$ 41,472,497	$3,430,354	8.27
3. National Capital Commission:			
a) Special contributions (sewers, demolitions, etc.)	$ 10,858,206	$ 563,672	5.19
b) Construction (parks)	12,803,092	1,446,296	11.30
c) Purchase/expropriation of land	23,670,357	2,045,423	8.64
d) Municipal taxes	327,109	----	0.00
Total	$ 47,658,764	$4,055,391	8.51
4. Summary:			
a) Department of Public Works	$122,078,789	$1,840,842	1.51
b) Department of Finance	41,472,497	3,430,354	8.27
c) National Capital Commission	47,658,764	4,055,391	8.51
Total	$211,210,050	$9,326,587	4.42

Source: *Mémoire sur la nécessité d'un regain industriel à Hull.* Présenté aux autorités municipales du Conseil de la Cité de Hull par la Chambre de Commerce de Hull, le 10 décembre, 1964, Annexe D, 41.

Appendix M (Chapter VI)   **Registration of Documents in Carleton County**

1. Real Property

Two systems of land registration are employed in Carleton county. Parts of the county are under the "Land Titles" system and parts under the "Registry Office" system. The former is administered by the staff of the Supreme Court of Ontario office, which includes persons capable of carrying out their duties in both English and French. The "Registry Office" system is administered in two other offices, one for land inside the city of Ottawa and the other for land outside. Both of these offices employ persons who can conduct business in French. However, under either system, it is usually not the general public but lawyers who have to deal with an office, and their communications are almost invariably in English.

At present the forms used by the two systems are in English only. As evidence, in part, of title to particular parcels of land, these documents may have to be referred to by persons of either language in the future. They are used by lawyers almost exclusively and, as indicated earlier, it is at present impossible for a lawyer to qualify for the bar in Ontario without being able to read English with some fluency.

2. Personal Property

The office of the County Court—which at the date of our inquiry had no French-speaking staff—handles the registration of bills of sale, conditional sale agreements, and chattel mortgages. These documents may be in French, but the staff make a practice of asking for a brief written explanation of the document in English to be filed at the time of registration. This facilitates the searching of title to personal property and transfers of registrations between counties. If it becomes necessary to enforce these various contracts, translations must be filed for the use of the court.

The terminology of these documents is highly technical and is probably incomprehensible to most laymen. Even when the document is in the language of the person most closely affected (the conditional purchaser or the chattel mortgagor) the only safe course is to obtain a full explanation of the purport of the document from a lawyer.

Security on personal property involves problems similar to those surrounding real estate transactions. The immediate parties may be, for example, the conditional vendor and purchaser, or the chattel mortgagor and mortgagee. Nevertheless third parties may be seriously affected to their detriment, as when the conditional purchaser or mortgagor in possession attempts to sell the chattel as though he had complete title to it. The second purchaser must be protected, as must the conditional vendor or mortgagee. This is the main reason for requiring registration of the document evidencing the transaction. The protection to third parties may require that they have as much knowledge of the purport of the document as the conditional purchaser or mortgagor and hence *their* language must be considered.

Registration of the documents is done in the county where the purchaser or mortgagor resides or where the property is located. Hence, provisions for transfer of the registration to other counties are essential and the language of the staff of the County Court office of the receiving county must also be taken into account.